# The Folklore and Folklife of New Jersey

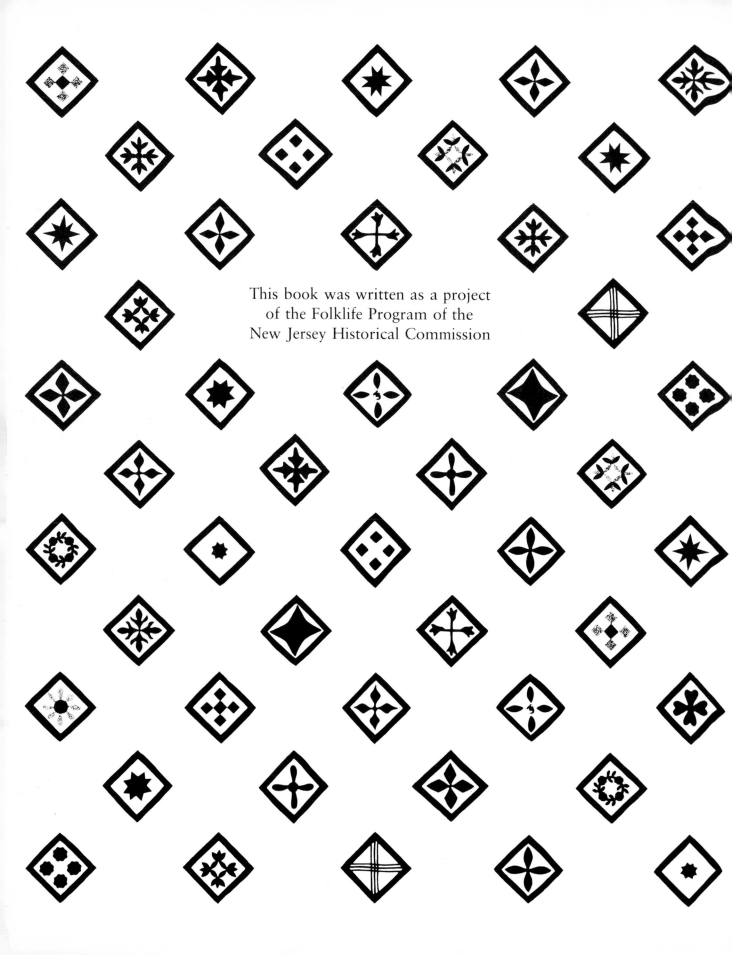

This book was written as a project
of the Folklife Program of the
New Jersey Historical Commission

DAVID STEVEN COHEN

# The Folklore and Folklife of New Jersey

RUTGERS UNIVERSITY PRESS

New Brunswick, New Jersey

Second Printing, 1984

Library of Congress Cataloging in Publication Data

Cohen, David Steven, 1943–
  The folklore and folklife of New Jersey.

  Bibliography: p.
  1. Folklore—New Jersey. 2. New Jersey—Social
life and customs.  I. Title.
GR110.N5C64       398'.09749       82-5203
ISBN 0-8135-0964-5               AACR2
ISBN 0-8135-0989-0 (pbk.)

For Linda Prentice Cohen

# Contents

Contents

Contents

# ✳ Illustrations

# Illustrations

# Foreword

WHEN I agreed to write a foreword to this book, I had seen in manuscript David Cohen's impressive bibliography, *Folklife in New Jersey: An Annotated Bibliography* (Trenton: New Jersey Historical Commission, 1982). I assumed that this volume would be primarily an anthology, giving sample texts from the wide variety of published sources he had discovered. The book before you, however, is far more ambitious. It not only presents its New Jersey examples, it also contains a laudable attempt to discuss the principles underlying selected categories of the oral tradition (folklore) and of arts, crafts, and customs (folklife). Although a few important American folklore students have preferred to use the historically older and rather more comprehensive term *Volkskunde* ("folk culture"), it is the bipartite terminology (folklore, folklife) that has had most acceptance in the United States. The introduction gives us a full listing of the subjects included under the two terms.

This book is all the more to be welcomed since until quite lately folklore research had neither academic standing nor popular support in New Jersey. There is no folklore graduate program in the state, and less than a handful of New Jersey colleges offer even undergraduate folklore courses, most of them introduced comparatively recently. So far as I know there is not one significant folklore archive. No university press in the state has developed a scholarly folklore publishing program. The small folklore periodical, *New Jersey Folklore*, which appears just once a year, did not begin publication until 1976. The reconstituted New Jersey Folklore Society (an earlier attempt never got off the ground) only started in 1979–1980.

Contrast this with the situation outside the state. Although for over half a century academic course work in folklore was offered at only a few universities and colleges in the United States, this changed dramatically after World War II. Today folklore studies are well established at many of the major state and private universities and at innumerable smaller colleges. There are more than half a dozen extensive doctoral programs; at least a dozen university presses regularly publish scholarly folklore books and monographs; and a number of extensive folklore archives have wide support, some at universities, others at libraries, historical societies, and museums.

Equally important is the existence of over a dozen high-caliber regional and state folklore journals in the United States, most of them at least twenty to forty years old, each publishing the folklore collectanea of its own area. The journals have the support of active state folklore societies that involve a broad spectrum of the population. This grass-roots base is especially evident in the varied programs of their annual meetings, normally held in different parts of the state each year. At these sessions academic folklorists are usually outnumbered by schoolteachers, local historians, craft enthusiasts, college and high school students, and interested citizens.

Since New Jersey has not had a history of active support for folklore, there is, unsurprisingly, a paucity of folklore-oriented research. Of necessity, the subject areas chosen for this book had to be primarily those in which sufficient work had already been published, often by scholars in related fields. Where such published materials are available, the author has made effective use of them. Unlike most American regional folklorists who leave American Indian folk traditions to the anthropologists, he includes some Indian lore in many chapters and by this means achieves a useful time depth. The chapters on names and folk speech give us a further sense of past history by referring not only to the Indians, but also to the earliest groups of New Jersey settlers: the Dutch, Swedes, English Quakers, Scots, and Germans. Another kind of historical information is presented in these chapters and that on traditional boats by his attention to several of the traditional occupations: canal boating, oyster dredging, glassblowing, charcoal burning, log rafting, and so on.

Happily in the area of material folk culture, especially the arts and crafts, a host of workers from other disciplines and organizations shares the folklorist's interests. For example, Cohen mentions the work of the Newark Museum, whose pioneering exhibitions in the early 1930s did much to promote the current interest in the folk arts throughout the United States. In these chapters Cohen not only assembles a rich body of material whose variety will fascinate the reader, but also interprets each category succinctly, using modern American folklore theory.

As a folklorist I find much to admire in the book. I have already stressed how well the author achieves historical perspective by his careful selection of material in two of the opening chapters. Let me add that throughout the book

# Foreword

Cohen has done an excellent job in adapting current American folklore theories to interpret the New Jersey data.

In some of the earlier chapters, Cohen refers to the contributions of some of the ethnic groups that were among the later settlers in New Jersey, but the major representation of the folkways of these peoples is found in the last three chapters. In these chapters the author relies heavily on the reports of student fieldwork projects, most of them made under his direction, and these contributions add unexpected color and variety to his depiction of the folklife of New Jersey. Despite the comparative paucity of adequate fieldwork material in accessible archives or in published form, Cohen presents an interesting and imaginative sampling of both English and ethnic folklore and folklife, demonstrating that the state's folk traditions are rich and have only been awaiting the attention of folklorists.

*Herbert Halpert*
*Memorial University of Newfoundland*
*St. John's, Newfoundland, Canada*

# Acknowledgments

THERE ARE many people who should be thanked for their contributions to this book. They include students at the Newark College of Arts and Sciences and Douglass College of Rutgers University, who did folklore-collecting projects, including: Thomas K. Daly, Kevin Guta, Christopher Hoare, Marilyn Legato, Nan Mutnick, Valerie Ruscitto, Sharon Schuessler, Barbara Schulz, Cynthia Joy Skibo, Patricia Slattery, Audrey Spelker, and Zoriana Tkacz. Thanks also to their informants: Lillian Dieter, Amelia Ferrari, Sam Hunt, Anastasia Kysilewska, Thomas MacFarlane, Modestino Magliacane, Alice Nirmaier, Earle A. Nirmaier, Mary Rozman, Billie Schuessler, Nona Schuessler, Patricia Schuessler, Theresa Schuessler, Mark A. Spelker, Andrew Szproch, and Anna Vaccaro. There were also informants from whom I collected folklore: James De Groat, Jerry Mahony, Robert Milligan, Ed Morgan, John Morgan, Madge Morgan, Wally Morgan, Harry V. Shourds, and Lewis West. Also thanks to the local history and folklore experts who helped me, including: Jim Albertson, Charles L. Aquilina, Robert Baron, Robert Fridlington, Charles T. Gehring, Angus K. Gillespie, Peter J. Guthorn, Herbert Halpert, Field Horn, Mary Hufford, Herbert C. Kraft, James Lee, Rebecca Mullen, Michael Aaron Rockland, Anne H. Sidwa, Don C. Skemer, and Peter O. Wacker. The following librarians guided me to new materials and retrieved old materials: Bette M. Barker, Ronald Becker, Rebecca B. Colesar, Charles F. Cummings, Barbara S. Irwin, Robert E. Lupp, Donald A. Sinclair, Edward Skipworth, and Miriam V. Studley.

Help in obtaining visual material came from Suzanne Corlette, Ulysses G. Dietz, Bert Denker, Jon Frank, Alan D. Frazer, Mary Ison, Terence Karschner, Arthur B. Nichols, John T. Schofield, Arlene Palmer Schwind, Kathy Stocking, Robert L. White, and Lorraine Williams. Joseph Crilley did drawings and special photographs.

My thanks also to the members of the staff of the New Jersey Historical Commission: Antoinette Raider, Nancy H. Dallaire, Ronald J. Grele, Patricia

# Acknowledgments

Thomas, and Lee R. Parks. Most important, I thank Bernard Bush, the executive director of the commission, who probed, questioned, and insisted so that a project that started as a pamphlet ended as a book.

This project was made possible by a grant from the Folk Arts Program of the National Endowment for the Arts.

Heavy with fruit, in particular, was the whole spreading bough that rustled above me during an afternoon, a very wonderful afternoon, that I spent in being ever so wisely driven, driven further and further, into the large lucidity of—well, of what else shall I call it but a New Jersey condition? . . . It might have threatened, for twenty minutes, to be almost complicating, but the truth was recorded: it was an adventure, unmistakably, to have a revelation made so convenient—to be learning at last, in the maturity of one's powers, what New Jersey might "connote."

Henry James
*The American Scene* (1904)

# The Folklore and Folklife of New Jersey

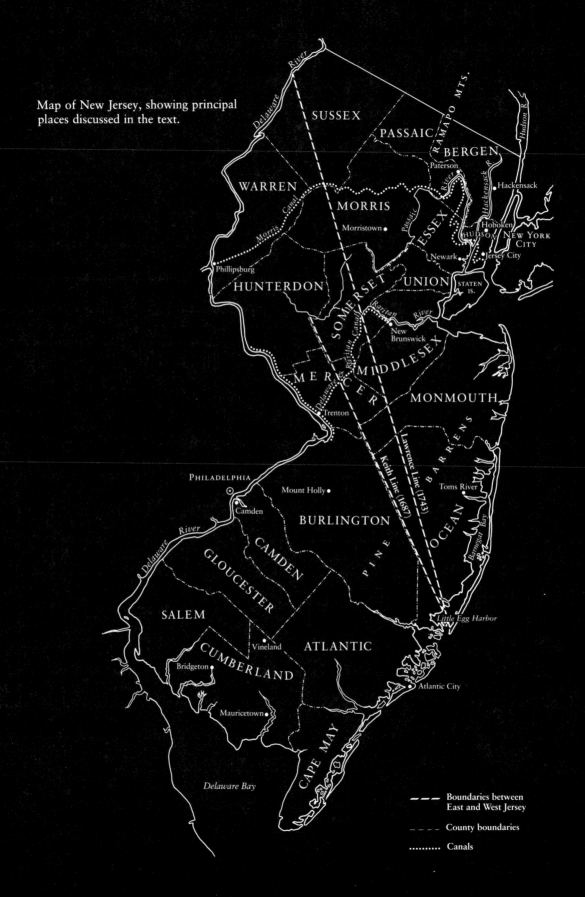

Map of New Jersey, showing principal places discussed in the text.

SUSSEX
PASSAIC
RAMAPO MTS.
BERGEN
Paterson
Hackensack
WARREN
MORRIS
Hoboken
Morristown
HUDSON
NEW YORK CITY
ESSEX
Newark
Jersey City
Phillipsburg
HUNTERDON
SOMERSET
UNION
STATEN IS.
New Brunswick
MIDDLESEX
MERCER
MONMOUTH
Trenton
BARRENS
Keith Line (1687)
Lawrence Line (1743)
PHILADELPHIA
Mount Holly
Toms River
Camden
BURLINGTON
OCEAN
PINE
Barnegat Bay
GLOUCESTER
CAMDEN
SALEM
Little Egg Harbor
Vineland
ATLANTIC
CUMBERLAND
Bridgeton
Atlantic City
Mauricetown
CAPE MAY
Delaware Bay

Delaware River
Hudson R.
Hackensack R.
Passaic River
Canal
Morris Canal
Raritan Canal
Delaware & Raritan Canal
Raritan River

– – – Boundaries between East and West Jersey
– – – County boundaries
......... Canals

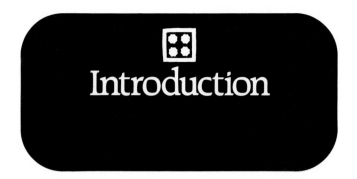

# Introduction

I T HAS become a cliché that New Jersey has an identity problem. The state, it is said, has a split personality. The northern part is oriented to New York and the southern part to Philadelphia. This divided orientation is not a recent development. From 1664 to 1702 New Jersey was actually two colonies, East Jersey and West Jersey. In fact, the old political boundary between East and West Jersey—a diagonal line running from a point on the upper Delaware River to Little Egg Harbor on the Atlantic coast—more accurately reflects some of the cultural boundaries than do the present political boundaries.

At the same time, New Jersey is viewed in terms of the derogatory stereotype of decaying cities, polluting industries, and sprawling suburbs. While there may be a kernel of truth in this image, like all stereotypes it is an oversimplification. It is an outsider's view, formed by those who only know New Jersey by traveling through on the New Jersey Turnpike. It is a stereotype held by those who live outside New Jersey or who have only recently moved here. And it is the basis for one genre of New Jersey folklore—the Jersey joke. A more complete survey of the folklore and folklife of New Jersey reveals a more complex and more interesting image. This book purports to use folklore to fight folklore. It attempts to refute the derogatory stereotype and correct the identity problem by showing the richness and diversity of New Jersey's folk heritage.

Many people think that folklore means misinformation. This is not how folklorists define the term. Some folklore may be true, some not. Several years ago I wrote a book about a racially mixed people living in the Ramapo Mountains of northeastern New Jersey and southeastern New York State. In it I studied a folk legend about their origins. I discovered that while the legend contained some accurate historical information, it was not the true account of the origins of the Ramapo Mountain People.[1] On the other hand, Gary B. Mills, a historian, studied a similar racially mixed people known as the Cane River Creoles, who live in northwestern Louisiana, and he found that the legend about their origins was substantially true.[2] Thus, whether or not it is true is not the defining characteristic of folklore.

Folklore may be defined simply as oral tradition. For a story or song to be "folk" it must have been communicated by word of mouth. Perhaps the best definition of a folktale is Nathaniel Hawthorne's term, a "twice-told tale." Folklorists use the term "traditional" as a synonym of "folk." Purists argue that to be traditional the story or song must be communicated from one person to another without the intervention of the mass media. Thus, a folktale is told, rather than read; spoken, rather than written. And a folk song is learned from another person, rather than from sheet music, a record, or the radio.

Of course, there is little that is pure oral tradition. Most traditions are a mixture of folk and popular—a song published originally on a broadside goes into oral tradition or a story that originates in oral tradition is then written down. Yet there is a difference between folklore and popular culture in form, style, esthetic, and values. For example, folklore tends to appear in numerous versions, much like the game of "telephone" in which the message is changed slightly as it is whispered from person to person. A folktale is the sum total of all its versions. In popular culture, on the other hand, there is a standard, often copyrighted, version that is duplicated or mass-produced. A song that may have originated as a folk song will be sung in a different style when it is performed by a popular singer. The difference is not between a good singer and a bad singer, but between two different esthetics.

In order to reproduce the form, style, and content of an oral tradition accurately, professional folklorists normally use tape recorders, rather than rewriting the material in their own words. The very language in which a folktale is told is itself a form of folklore, that is, folk speech. Many of the texts in this book are transcripts of tape-recorded interviews. The reader should realize that these transcripts were meant to be heard, rather than read. You might try reading them aloud.

Other folklore texts come from published sources. This is especially true of historic folklore. The tape recorder is a recent invention, so if you want to collect the folklore of the past, you must use written sources. In all the folklore appearing here, however, there was some evidence, either implicit or explicit, that the material was in the oral tradition before or after it was written down. These written versions of folklore must be understood for what they are. The language is generally more formal, and they often contain literary references that would not be found in oral traditions. In some cases there is a romanticized, nostalgic, and even condescending tone. Quite often they contain the biases and prejudices of the writer, whether in the form of a disapproving description of a folk belief as "superstitious" or of a derogatory stereotype of a group of people. These texts are quoted verbatim because they reflect the attitudes and values of the times.

Some material commonly thought to be part of the folklore of New Jersey has been purposely omitted from this book. Heroic legends about Tempe Wick, Molly Pitcher, and Sam Patch are not included, because I found no evidence they were ever in oral tradition. What we know about these people seems to come exclusively from written sources. They should properly be considered as part of the popular culture of New Jersey, rather than as folk heroes and heroines.

Other material not commonly thought to be New Jersey folklore is included. For example, some scholars think that the study of American Indians does not pertain to folklore, but to anthropology. Folk culture, they argue, is an exlusively oral subculture of a predominantly literate culture, and the entire culture of the American Indians was predominantly, if not exclusively, an oral tradition. However, from the time of the Lenape Indians' first contact with Europeans until their departure from New Jersey in the eighteenth century, they constituted an oral subculture within a predominantly literate culture. Not only that, but many of the leaders of the American Folklore Society, such as Franz Boas, A. L. Kroeber, and Ruth Benedict, were anthropologists. The early issues of the *Journal of American Folklore* contain many articles on American Indian myths. Following this precedent, I consider the culture of the Lenape Indians as part of the folklore of New Jersey.

Others argue that the lore of recent immigrants is not part of New Jersey folklore, because this folklore has not had time to adapt to the cultural environment of New Jersey. I would argue, however, that if it was collected from people living in New Jersey or is about New Jersey, it qualifies as New Jersey folklore. To do otherwise is to make invidious distinctions as to who the "real" New Jerseyans are.

Folklorists also use the term "the folk" to refer to the group of people who bear the folk tradition. There is some disagreement about who the folk are and whether they constitute a single group or a class. To some only rural people qualify, but recent research has shown that folklore can be found in the city, in the factory, and even in the suburbs. To others the folk represents a single class. However, as one archeologist told me, "You don't have to be poor to be traditional." The middle class and the upper class also have their folklore. To still others the folk represents the early settlers, but not recent immigrants. Fortunately, this notion is no longer widespread, and the field of immigrant and ethnic folklore is thriving. Other subgroups in society have their own folklore, and there is a growing interest in women's folklore and children's folklore. In my view the folk is not a single, monolithic group. On the contrary, the folklore and folklife of New Jersey reflect the regional, occupational, and ethnic diversity of the state.

Not all folk traditions are spoken or sung. They can include a traditional way of doing or making something. Folklorists use the term "folklife" to refer to these nonspoken folk traditions. The term encompasses gestures, customs, art, tools, utensils, crafts, foodways, costume, rituals, festivals, and architecture.

It is useful to distinguish between fine art, vernacular art, and folk art. Fine art is the elite tradition of art judged to be "fine" by a select group of art critics, art historians, and art dealers. What is considered "fine" often depends on an arbitrary and subjective judgment. Vernacular art, as defined by John Kouwenhoven, refers to machine-made objects that are mass-produced in factories or that are themselves the machines, factories, bridges, and office buildings of an industrial civilization.[3] They are the material manifestations of popular culture. They too have an esthetic. Folk art refers to the products of a preindustrial craft tradition that in some cases have been replaced by and in other cases exist alongside the fine and the vernacular arts.

According to the folklorist Henry Glassie, "a folk thing is traditional and nonpopular; material folk culture is composed of objects produced out of a nonpopular tradition in proximity to popular culture."[4] He explains that to be traditional the object must be old and acceptable to the individual or group that produced it. But not all traditions are folk. Excluded are what Glassie terms the "academic" (fine, elite) and the "popular" (vernacular, mass) traditions. As Kenneth Ames puts it, "Folk is tradition from the bottom up."[5]

There are several common fallacies about folk art that should be dispelled. First, folk art is not "primitive," "naive," "innocent," or "childlike"; it is simply unschooled. Folk artists are either self-taught or learn their craft through an apprenticeship. Second, folk art is not the product of poor craftsmanship. It is based on a different, often simpler, esthetic. Third, not all folk art is anonymous. Folk artists are generally not as famous as fine artists, but often their identities are known or can be determined. Fourth, not all craftsmen and craftswomen are folk artists. There are many people who learn a craft in adult education classes or from a commercial craft kit. And many contemporary craftsmen use totally original, rather than traditional designs. Fifth, not all folk art is handmade. Some folk artists use machines, like the chairmaker who uses a lathe to make his turnings. Sixth, not all folk art is utilitarian. Some types of folk art, such as folk painting, function solely as art.

4

While this book contains much about folk art, I have used a material culture, rather than a decorative arts approach. I have tried to avoid subjective esthetic judgments. Instead I have tried to place objects in their cultural context. This approach is especially useful for interpreting material folk culture, because much folk art is also artifact. "The artifact is a social document," wrote E. McClung Fleming, the art historian, "but the historian has tended to ignore this primary source in his preoccupation with printed and manuscript materials. He has consulted only one half of our memory of the past."[6] And as Henry Glassie has stated, "In order to understand the vast majority of people who left behind no literate legacy, it is necessary to learn how to obtain information from the artifacts they did make, although these artifacts—potsherds, old houses, and the like—carry no information on their surfaces. This presents a difficulty because a subtle code must be cracked."[7] This book suggests some of the things we might learn about local history from material folk culture.

Most of the folklore of New Jersey remains uncollected, and what has been collected is not representative of all groups and all regions. For example, we have precious few examples of Afro-American folklore, not because it doesn't exist, but because it hasn't been collected. I have had to rely on what has been collected by myself, my students, and a few other folklorists and their students. Any imbalances in this book reflect the fragmentary nature of folklore collection in New Jersey. This book provides only a sampling. We need many more people collecting folklore in the state before a more comprehensive study can be done. I hope this book inspires others to collect and document the rich folk heritage of New Jersey.

# Part I
# New Jersey
# Folklore

# The Jersey Joke

IN NOVEMBER 1979 Lane Kirkland, the president of the AFL-CIO, made news when he said, "Everything outside the AFL-CIO is really Hoboken."[1] Despite the protestations of the mayor of Hoboken, this is the way much of the nation views New Jersey. In April 1979 the magazine *New Jersey Monthly* published an article titled "What's So Funny About New Jersey?" in which the author, Michael Aaron Rockland, the chairman of the Douglass College American Studies Department, recited a litany of New Jersey jokes gleaned from such sources as television comedy shows, movies, short stories, nightclub comedy acts, and T-shirts. Rockland saw the New Jersey joke as a symptom of the state's "identity problem."[2]

Actually, jokes about New Jersey are not new. An article in *Picturesque America* in 1872 stated: "Although New Jersey, ever since her admission into the Union, has been the butt for the sarcasm and wit of those who live outside her borders, the gallant little State has much to be proud of."[3] In his book *American Myths and Legends* published in 1903, Charles M. Skinner recounted a Jersey joke about a nonexistent place: Lonetown, New Jersey.

> Lonetown had been stirred to its foundations by the arrival of a stranger at the tavern. Any stranger was a refreshment and an excitement, but this one was a marvel, because he was evidently going to stay. Week after week went by; still he set foot in no other township. Nobody knew his business, and not to know what everybody was doing in Lonetown was anguish. Why, the fellow did not so much as say that he had any business. He did not even give his name. Rustic curiosity could not endure this sort of thing. A committee of citizens was finally selected, at an informal meeting held in the store, and they went to the tavern to see what information could be squeezed out of the stranger. He received them with dignity, listened without surprise to their remonstrances against his seclusion and their request for knowledge, and said: "I am obliged to you, gentlemen, for this proof of interest in my

affairs, and I will say, plainly, that I am not a man with whom you are likely to associate. A jury says I am a criminal. The judge gave me the choice of being hanged or of spending six months in Lonetown. Oh, but I am sorry I chose Lonetown! Good-night."[4]

As a postscript, Skinner added:

As there isn't any Lonetown—now that you have read the story—it is evident that any one of several localities may be hidden under that name. Several towns have contended for the right to it; but, after sifting the evidence, it is said by the best authorities that the scene of the incident was either Jersey City or Camden.[5]

A modern version of this same joke was mentioned by Rockland. For his Watergate involvement, Richard Nixon was threatened with being sentenced either to life in prison or living in New Jersey. He replied: "That's no choice at all!"[6]

New Jersey mosquitoes are often mentioned in Jersey jokes. Recently I collected a joke in Albany about the ground crew at Newark airport who rushed out to refuel a large aircraft only to discover that it was a Jersey mosquito. In this example the joke takes on the characteristics of a tall tale. And there is the quip that the state legislature is going to name the mosquito the state bird. Another New Jersey mosquito joke which is also a tall tale is the one about a duck hunter along the Jersey Shore who was attacked by a flock of extraordinarily large mosquitoes. He took refuge under his sneakbox (a shallow-draft boat used in duck hunting), but the mosquitoes simply drilled through the white cedar hull. Finally, the duck hunter had to use a sledgehammer to bend the mosquitoes' stingers, thereby ending the attack.

References to New Jersey mosquitoes have a long history. According to tradition, the Swedes at Nya Elfsborg in the section of New Jersey known in the 1640s and 1650s as New Sweden nicknamed their fort Myggenborg— "Mosquito Castle."[7] The historian Samuel Smith wrote in 1765: "The Musketoes were so numerous the Swedes were unable to live here, and therefore removing, named the place Musketoeburgh."[8] And in the mid-eighteenth century Peter Kalm, the Swedish traveler, wrote about New Jersey:

The gnats which are very troublesome at night here, are called mosquitoes. . . . In daytime or at night they come into the houses, and when the people have gone to bed they begin their disagreeable humming, approach nearer and nearer the bed, and at last suck up so much blood that they can hardly fly away.[9]

There are numerous contemporary examples of New Jersey jokes. A comic at a New York nightclub asks if anyone present is from New Jersey; if someone is he says: "Oh, are the bowling alleys closed tonight?" Woody Allen in his movie *Sleeper* says: "A certain intelligence governs our universe, except in certain parts of New Jersey." John Belushi on the television comedy program "Saturday Night Live" says: "Don't you hate it when you wake up in the morning and go to put on your shirt and it smells like New Jersey?" And Gilda Radner portraying Roseanne Roseannadana on the same television program mentions an unexplained itch she suffered from: "My father called a doctor in Fort Lee, New Jersey, and he asked me if I had had any contact with New Jersey and I realized that maybe a New Jersey person had touched me."[10]

These jokes, of course, are not unique to New Jersey. Similar jokes have been told about Philadelphia, Brooklyn, Terre Haute, and Peoria. Jokes that are told about places, like the Jersey joke, or people, like ethnic jokes, function as vehicles for stereotypes. The Jersey joke reflects a serious problem in the way New Jersey is perceived by the rest of the country. Protestations will not eliminate the Jersey joke, any more than they will eliminate ethnic jokes. The only solution is to educate people about the real history and traditions of the state. No matter how upsetting it may be to New Jerseyans, the Jersey joke is part of the folklore of the state. It shows something very important about folklore. While folklore is often viewed as trivial, in reality it often deals with extremely personal and even explosive notions about the very identity of people and places.

A Lenape Indian Myth

MANY PEOPLE think that myth means fallacy. But this is not how folklorists define the term. Myths are oral narratives set outside historic time and addressing ultimate questions. This is in contrast to legends, which are oral narratives set in historic time. Myths deal with such topics as creation, the origin of of agriculture, the nature of man, and prehistoric happenings. For the Europeans who settled in New Jersey, the Bible provided a substitute for the mythology of oral tradition. This is why there are so few European myths in the folklore of New Jersey. But for one group especially, myths were the main component of its religion. These were people who called themselves the Lenape, which means "people" in their language. Europeans called them the Delaware Indians after the river named for the governor of Virginia, Sir Thomas West, Lord de la Warr.

At the time that Europeans first made contact with them, the Lenape were a loose geographic grouping of Indians who spoke two dialects related to the Algonkian language family. They occupied what is now New Jersey, eastern Pennsylvania, and northern Delaware. By the time of the War of 1812, they had been pushed into the Midwest into what is now Indiana and Ohio. Today, the few surviving Lenape live either in Oklahoma or in Canada. Most of what is known of their myths and ceremonies was collected in places outside New Jersey after their departure from the state. We do not know for sure whether those Lenape who lived in New Jersey shared all of the myths collected after their departure.

For example, the Walam Olum, or "Red Score," is a combination creation myth, deluge myth, and migration myth in the form of ideographs (memory pictures) drawn on flat, wooden sticks. The sticks were discovered in the 1820s in Indiana and the ideographs translated in 1833 by Constantine Samuel Rafinesque, a professor of historical and natural sciences at Transylvania University in Kentucky. The myth describes the creation of land and sky out of primal fog and the creation of men and animals. They lived in harmony until an evil Manito (spirit) in the guise of a giant serpent brought a flood. Some survivors escaped onto the back of a turtle, where they were protected by the culture hero Nanbush. After this primordial flood, the tribe migrated from a cold, northern climate southwest to a warmer climate in the Snake Land, where they conquered the Snake people. There they learned how to cultivate maize. After other wars with other peoples, they migrated east to the Salt Sea, where they subdivided into three groups. The myth ends with the arrival of the white man.

The authenticity of the Walam Olum has been disputed. Daniel Brinton, the anthropologist, noted that the Walam Olum was "slightly colored by European teachings," but he concluded: "It is a genuine native production which was repeated orally to someone indifferently conversant with the Delaware language, who wrote it down to the best of his ability."[1] William W. Newcomb, Jr., an anthropologist at the University of Texas, has, however, questioned whether it was an aboriginal narrative. He hypothesizes that the Walam Olum might have been a late eighteenth- or early nineteenth-century creation of a nativistic move-

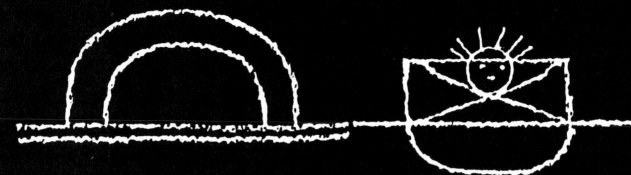

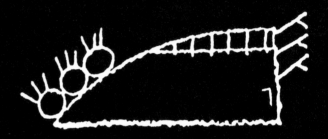

*Sayewi talli wemiguma wokgetaki*
"There at the edge of all the water where the land ends . . ."

*Hackung kewlik owanaku wak yutali
Kitanitowit-essop*
". . . the fog over the earth was plentiful, and this was where the Great Spirit stayed."

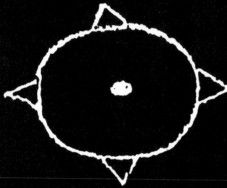

*Sayewis hallemiwis nolemiwi elemamik
Kitanitowit-essop*
"It began to be invisible everywhere, even at the place where the Great Spirit stayed."[2]

*Witehen wemiluen wemaken nihillen*
"All of them said they would go together to the land there, all who were free . . ."

*Nguttichin lowaniwi Nguttichin wapaniwi
Agamunk topanpek Wulliton epannek*
". . . the Northerners were of one mind and the Easterners were of one mind; it would be good to live on the other side of the frozen water."

*Wulelemil w'shakuppek Wemopannek
hakhsinipek Kitahikan pokhakhopek*
"Things turned out well for all those who stayed at the shore of water frozen hard as rocks, and for those at the great hollow well."

Examples of the pictographs from the Walam Olum, with accompanying verses.
*Based on Daniel G. Brinton,* The Lenape and Their Legends. *D. G. Brinton.*

ment seeking to establish a previous claim to the territories of the Midwest.[2] If that is the case, the Walam Olum should not be included in the folklore of New Jersey, because of the likelihood it was created after the Lenape had left the state.

The first part of the Walam Olum, however, is similar to an authentic Lenape creation myth recorded in 1679 by the Dutch traveler Jasper Danckaerts.

> In the morning there came an Indian to our house, a man about eighty years of age, whom our people call Jasper, who lived in Ahakinsack or at Ackinon [Hackensack] . . . We asked him where he believed he came from, he answered from his father. "And where did your father come from?" we said, "and your grandfather and greatgrandfather, and so on to the first of the race?" He was silent for a little while, either as if unable to climb up at once so high with his thoughts, or to express them without help, and then took a piece of coal out of the fire, where he sat, and began to write upon the floor. He first drew a circle, a little oval, to which he made four paws or feet, a head and a tail. "This," said he, "is a tortoise, lying in the water around it," and he moved his hand round the figure, continuing, "this was or is all water, and so at first was the world or the earth, when the tortoise gradually raised its round back up high, and the water ran off of it, and thus the earth became dry." He then took a little straw and placed it on end in the middle of the figure, and proceeded, "the earth was now dry, and there grew a tree in the middle of the earth, and the root of this tree sent forth a sprout beside and there grew upon it a man, who was the first male. This man was then alone, and would have remained alone; but the tree bent over until its top touched the earth, and there it shot therein another root, from which came forth another root, from which came forth another sprout, and there grew upon it the woman, and from these two were all men produced.[3]

Later upon returning to Achter Col in the lower Hackensack River Valley, Danckaerts asked his translator and guide, an Indian named Hans, who was from the vicinity of Constables Hook, to confirm the creation myth he had heard from Jasper.

> I told him I had conversed with Jasper or Tantaque, another old Indian, on the subject, from whence all things had come, and he had told me they came from a tortoise; that this tortoise had brought forth the world, or that all things had come from it; that from the middle of the

tortoise there had sprung up a tree, upon whose branches men had grown. That was true, he replied, but Kickeron made the tortoise, and the tortoise had a power and a nature to produce all things, such as earth, trees, and the like, which God wished through it to produce, or have produced.[4]

Hans explained that Kickeron was the name of the "Supreme Being, the first and great beginning of all things, . . . who is the origin of all, who has not only once produced or made all things, but produces every day."[5] He noted that this Supreme Being also was known as Sackamacher, which was the term for chief.

It should be noted that this version of the creation myth was filtered through the perceptions of the European who wrote it down. Thus it is not a pure Indian expression in form, language, or style. In terminology and cadence it is reminiscent of the Bible. There is even some European condescension toward the Indian named Jasper in the reference to his being "unable to climb up at once so high with his thoughts, or to express them without help." This in itself makes the written version of this myth a useful document showing European attitudes toward the Indians.

What makes this myth important is that it contains the world view of the Lenape Indians. The earth is visualized as being the back of a turtle, the horizon being the curvature of its shell. But the myth also contains some universal themes or motifs, such as the reference to a primordial flood, mentioned in the mythologies of many different cultures. Some of these similarities might result from cultural borrowing. By the time this myth was recorded, the Lenape had been in contact with Europeans for more than fifty years, so some cultural borrowing is likely. In this myth, for example, the creation of man before woman probably reflects the influence of Christianity. Other similarities may be archetypes, that is, universal themes, created independently. And finally, this version of the myth proves that at least one part of the Walam Olum can be traced back to when the Lenape inhabited New Jersey.

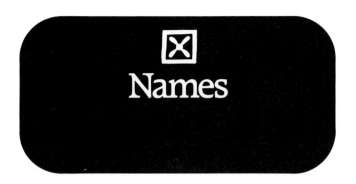

# Names

PLACE NAMES, personal names, and group names are part of the folklore of New Jersey for several reasons. First, naming traditions are customs handed down from generation to generation. The Dutch had a particular naming tradition that differed from that of the English. And place-name traditions in America differ from those in Europe and the British Isles. Second, certain types of names and the lore associated with them are traditional. For example, nicknames are folklore because they are normally used in informal, spoken communication, rather than in formal, written communication. Often there are legends associated with either place names or nicknames. Third, there is a particular kind of folklore associated with names, that is, folk etymologies. These are explanations of name origins that are widely believed, but are not necessarily linguistically true.

Place names provide an insight into local history. Some, such as Sandy Hook, Stillwater, Green Brook, Long Beach, Little Falls, and Barrentown, reflect the physical geography of the locality. Others, for example, Bear Swamp, Beaver Brook, Goose Creek, and Rattle Snake Run, reflect the wildlife that once inhabited the place. Some reflect the dominant occupations or industry of the region. Crabtown, Fishing Creek, Bivalve, and Oyster Creek testify to the importance of fishing in the waters of New Jersey. Mine Mountain, Dover Forge, Colliers Mills, and Hanover Furnace survive from the bog-iron industry of South Jersey and the deep shaft mining in the northwestern part of the state. Cedar Creek, Tarkiln Creek, Turpentine, Shingle Landing (Millville today), and Lumberton survive from the days when lumbering, naval stores, and cedar-shingle production were integral parts of South Jersey's economy; just as Glassboro does from the era of the glassblowing industry.

Many places are named after people. Toms River, for example, was named after Captain William Tom, who surveyed that part of New Jersey. There is also a folk etymology that Toms River was named after an "Indian Tom," but this latter explanation is doubtful.[1] According to W.F.H. Nicolaisen, a folklorist who specializes in studying place names, the naming of places after people was more common in America than in Europe.

Place names also tell us which groups settled where. Some names pertain to people who no longer reside in the state. I refer to the numerous Indian place names in New Jersey. Hohokus, Manahocking, Musconetcong, Hopatcong, Moonachie, Piscataway, Hackensack, Weehawken, and Towaco are examples. Contrary to popular misconception, these are not the names of Indian tribes. Rather they represent the Europeans' attempt to record the place names used by the Lenape Indians. Early travel accounts show that there was no uniformity to these place names, and many of those that existed in the past did not survive to the present. Furthermore, many of the alleged translations of these names in local history books are in fact folk etymologies that are not linguistically accurate. There is another kind of Indian place name typified by such names as Indian Mills, Indian Lake, and Indian Run. These, of course, are not Indian names, but English designations referring to Indians.

Dutch place names abound in New Jersey. Some English names are direct translations from the original Dutch. For example, Egg Harbor is a literal translation of Eyerhaven, which is found on seventeenth-century Dutch maps. We do not really know why the Dutch named it that. The folk etymology is that the seventeenth-century Dutch explorers found numerous sea-gull eggs there, but this is not confirmable.[2] Attempts at direct translation of Dutch place names can be misleading. For example, it has been suggested that the name Barnegat came from the Dutch verb *barnen* ("to burn") after the Indian practice of burning the underbrush which the Dutch allegedly saw from the sea. Thus, it is posited, the name means "burning hole." Another theory is that the name came from a different meaning of the verb *barnen* ("to break upon the shore"), referring to the waves breaking on the barrier island. So, it has been suggested, the name literally means "breakers' inlet." But in modern Dutch the word *gat* means "gate." The most probable explanation is that it was named after a place in the province of Holland named Barndegat.[3]

Most folk etymologies of Dutch place names appear only in written sources. I know of two folk etymologies, however, from oral tradition. The first was told by a second-generation Russian-Jewish American, who was born in the Hell's Kitchen section of New York City and who lived as a young man on Staten Island. Two immigrants were coming in on a ship to Ellis Island. One pointed to the land and said: "What's that?" The other answered: "Stat an island" (Staten Island). In fact, the island, whose name appeared on early Dutch maps as Staten

Eyland, was named in honor of the Estates-General, the parliament of the Netherlands. The second etymology is of Kill Van Kull, the body of water separating Staten Island from New Jersey. It was told by a young man who was born and raised along the Jersey Shore. He learned it from his father, who was from Bayonne, and who in turn had learned it from his father. When Henry Hudson first came into New York Harbor, one of his crew took out a gun and shot a bird and turned to Henry Hudson and said: "I just killed one gull."

Folk etymologies like the above examples are generally relegated to the realm of trivia. But I would argue that they have broader cultural significance. Their significance is linguistic. When the English conquered New Netherland in 1664, they inherited a landscape already named by the Dutch. While the English did rename many places, numerous Dutch place names remained. These folk etymologies are largely attempts by non–Dutch-speaking people to make sense of these Dutch place names.

Most of the folk etymologies can be explained by the process of substitution. That is, a phoneme (basic unit of sound) in one language is substituted for a similar-sounding phoneme in the other language. Sometimes the substitution happens to be an accurate translation. This is because English and Dutch are Germanic languages, so there is some shared vocabulary. In other cases, the folk etymologies are intentional puns designed to produce humor. Still others demonstrate the process of correction in which a familiar or understandable phrase is substituted for an unfamiliar or misunderstood phrase, as in Achter Col becoming Arthur Kill.

In order to understand these linguistic changes, one must become familiar with the topographic morphemes (basic units of meaning) in Dutch place names. These include: *kill*, stream or creek; *bos* or *bosch*, woods; *gat*, passage (Barnegat); *vly* or *valey*, flat or salt meadow (Tenafly, Polifly); *hoek*, a point of land (Sandy Hook and Corlaer's Hook); *rack*, reach; *vlachte* or *vlacke*, meadow; *wyck*, town; *dorp*, village; *boght*, bay; *zee*, sea; *vliet*, stream; *veld*, field; *cobble*, hill; *neus*, high promontory; *haven*, harbor (Beach Haven, Eyerhaven, or Egg Harbor); *punt*, point (Sant Punt); and *dael*, dale.

The Swedes also tried to establish a settlement in New Jersey. Their colony of New Sweden, founded in 1638, occupied the lower reaches of the Delaware River Valley on both the New Jersey and the Pennsylvania-Delaware sides. In 1655 the Dutch regained control, putting an end to this colony. But a few Swedish settlers remained, and several place names provide evidence of the existence of the colony. One such place is Elsinboro Point, in Salem County, the site of the Swedish Fort Elfsborg founded in 1643. Another is Swedesboro, although it was founded well after the conquest of New Sweden and was originally named Raccoon.

The English, as we know, also changed place names. New Netherland became New York and East and West Jersey. Names such as English Neighborhood (Ridgefield, Leonia, and Englewood), Englishtown, and English Creek are obvious in their references. Many of the counties of New Jersey, established under the English colonial government were given English county names, such as Middlesex, Gloucester, Essex, Cumberland, Somerset, and Sussex. Cities and towns were also given English names. Newark was named after Newark-on-Trent in East Anglia. Westfield reflects the English open field system in which various fields around the farming town were given names.

The Quakers were very much involved in the English proprietary colonies of East and West Jersey, especially West Jersey. Such place names as Penn's Neck in Mercer and Salem counties, Upper Penn's Neck and Penn's Grove in Salem County, and Quaker Bridge and Quakertown (Fairview) in Burlington County reflect their influence. And the Scots became involved in the East Jersey proprietary colony, as is attested by the place names Perth Amboy (named after Perth in Scotland) and Edinburgh, both in Middlesex County. The German influence in the western part of New Jersey is reflected in the names Frankford in Sussex County, New Hamburg and New Germantown in Hunterdon County, Friesburg in Salem County, and German Valley in Morris County. The Moravians who settled in New Jersey tended to use biblical and inspirational names, hence Bethlehem in Hunterdon County and Hope in Warren County.

There are also many unusual place names about which folk etymologies have developed. For example, a section of Piscataway Township is known as Quibbletown. According to tradition, the name came from the "quibbling" between the Orthodox Baptists and the Seventh Day Baptists about which day should be observed as the true Sabbath.[4] In Warren County there is a ridge of mountains known as Jenny Jump, and legends abound about who Jenny was and why she jumped. The Pine Barrens contain New Jersey's equivalent of ghost towns, that is, towns that were founded as part of the bog-iron, glassblowing, or shingle-making industries, but that have long since been abandoned. One of these is Ong's Hat. One folk etymology has it that the town was named after a tavern keeper named Ong who had a picture of a hat on his tavern sign. Another folk etymology is that the name came from a young woman who was slighted by Ong and so threw his hat into a tree.[5] The fact that there are variations indicates that these etymologies are folklore. Ocean County has a place known as

18

Double Trouble. The legend about this name is that it refers to two simultaneous breaks that allegedly occurred in a dam there.[6]

Many folk etymologies are plausible, but we may never know whether they are true. Until they are proven or disproven, they must be considered folklore. Other folk etymologies are dubious. For example, it is said that Bedminster was named after the custom of "bedding the minister" in the days when preachers traveled from congregation to congregation as circuit riders.[7] This etymology is basically a pun, similar to the Dutch folk etymologies mentioned above. Another example is the folk etymology of Amwell and Hopewell: two neighbors were exchanging greetings over the boundary line; one said, "Hope well," and the other answered, "Am well."[8] Whether these folk etymologies were ever considered anything but jokes is hard to tell.

Personal names also have cultural significance. As mentioned, different cultures have different naming traditions, and a comparison gives us some insight into differences in their kinship systems. For example, the Dutch naming system tells us much about the nature of the family. Gradually from the late seventeenth through the mid-eighteenth centuries the Dutch in America adopted a system of fixed surnames. This was in part the result of acculturation, with the Dutch adapting to life in a colony controlled by the English. Previously the Dutch had used patronymics instead of fixed surnames. A child took the name of his father, adding the suffix *zoon*, *sen* (anglicized to "son"), *se, z,* or *s,* meaning "son of." For example, Hendrick Jansen means Hendrick the son of Jan. If Hendrick's son was named Teunis, he would be known as Teunis Hendrickson. Thus the patronymic would change with each generation, rather than being a fixed surname.

A person might also be known by a personal characteristic, occupation, or place of origin. For example, the name Teunis Hendrickson Brouwer would indicate a brewer, and William Teunison Bleeker would be a bleacher. Other names that literally stand for occupations are Coster (sexton), Shoemaker (shoemaker), Stryker (ironer), Snediker (cutter), and Dykeman (dike keeper). The prefixes Van (of), Vander (of the), Ver (a contraction of Vander), or Ten (at the) are used to indicate where someone is from. For example the Van Wycks, Van Schaacks, and Van Bergens are from towns with those names in Holland; the Van Burens, Van Dyks, and Van Linderns are from towns in Gelderland; the Van Winkles from Winkle in Utrecht; the Van Nesses from Ness in Friesland; the Van Duynes from Duyne in Zeeland; the Vanderbilts from the Bildt (certain elevations of land in Gelderland and Utrecht); the Van Cowenhovens from a farm known as Cowenhoven near Amersfoot in Utrecht.[9] This doesn't necessarily mean that all members of the family came from that place, but rather that there was some ancestral connection.

This patronymic system applied to daughters as well as sons. Thus, Gerriti Brants and Lysbeth Brants were the daughters of Brant Peelen van Rykerck. The fact that a daughter took her father's name indicates a degree of patrilinear descent. However, there is also an indication of bilateral descent in this naming system. It was traditional for the first son in Dutch families to be named after the paternal grandfather, but the second son was named after the maternal grandfather. Similarly, the first daughter was named after the paternal grandmother, and the second daughter after the maternal grandmother. Furthermore, the early baptismal records indicate that in the absence of surnames women did not assume the names of their husbands. Instead the father was listed by his Christian name followed by his patronymic and the mother by her Christian name followed by her patronymic. Once the surnames became fixed, women used their husbands' surnames when they got married. Another aspect of the Dutch naming system was that when a child died it was the custom to give the name to the next-born child of the same sex so as to perpetuate the ancestral name. This custom took precedence over that of naming successive children after paternal and maternal relatives.

Nicknames also help us to understand the complicated sociological, psychological, and historical functions of naming. Nicknames are often used in families or small communities to distinguish between individuals of the same name. This is especially helpful in families in which there is a tradition of naming children after living relatives, especially a son after his father or a daughter after her mother. And in communities, such as the Ramapo Mountain People, in which there has been a pattern of marrying within a relatively small group over a long period, it is common for many people to have both the same Christian name and the same surname, and nicknames help distinguish among them.

But this is not the only function of nicknames. I know a family in northern New Jersey that has used so many different nicknames for each other that the family members have trouble keeping track of them. Everyone in this family has many different nicknames, some of which function as socially acceptable ways to violate the rules of kinship behavior. For example, in this family the children use nicknames for their father ("Heps" and "Pops") and mother ("Effie Mae," "Mammette," "Twirlacurl") as a socially acceptable way of expressing feelings of disrespect. In the same way, feelings of antagonism can be dealt with by means short of fighting, by using nicknames expressing animal imagery ("Rin-Tin-Tin," "Ri-Bit"), ridicule of physical traits ("Daddy Long Legs," "Toothless Wonder," "Lard"), mocking references to high status ("The Duke," "Saint Sniffles," "Her Highness"), or ridicule of lack of intelligence ("Space Cadet," "Rockethead," "The Vac"). Nicknames are also used to express affection ("Pooh Bear," "Little Duffer"). Thus even within a single family nicknames can have complicated psychological and social functions.

Group names are also of interest to folklorists, because these names often convey stereotypes and attitudes not readily available from other sources. For example, until recently the name "Jackson Whites" was used to refer to the racially mixed people who live in the Ramapo Mountains of northern New Jersey and southeastern New York State. The name is considered derogatory by the Ramapo Mountain People, supposedly because it is associated with a folk legend about a Captain Jackson who allegedly supplied prostitutes to British soldiers during the Revolutionary War (see "Legend"). I found in my research that the name actually preceded the legend by almost fifty years. The first appearance of the name in print was in a local newspaper in 1878, but the legend of Captain Jackson did not show up in print until the 1920s. The name probably was originally a phrase—"jacks and whites," in which "jacks" was a derogatory reference to free blacks. Over the years the meaning of "jacks" became less well known, and "jacks and whites" became "Jackson Whites," by the process of homonymous substitution. In other words, a similar-sounding sensible term ("Jackson Whites") was substituted for a term that had no meaning to the listener ("jacks and whites").[10] A descendant of one of the old Dutch families of the area recently told me that her grandfather used to refer to the Ramapo Mountain People as "jacks and whites."

Another example is the name "Piney," referring to the people who live in the Pine Barrens of South Jersey. It was originally a derogatory name like "Jackson Whites." The earliest written record I could find of the name was in the "Report on Social Conditions in the Pine Belt" written in 1913 by Elizabeth Kite of the Vineland Training School.[11] This report was done in conjunction with the now discredited Kallikak study of the heredity of "feeblemindedness," although the name "Piney" does not appear in the Kallikak study itself.[12] While the Kallikak study was important in the development of the field of criminology, its genetic approach has long since been repudiated, but the stigma it left on the "Pineys" remained. The name, however, does not appear in an 1893 article "Jerseyisms" in *Dialect Notes*; instead the innocuous term "Piners" is used to refer to "those who live in the Jersey Pines."[13] A Burlington County newspaper in 1891 used the term "Pine-hawkers."[14] But an article in the *Atlantic Monthly* in 1859 used the obviously derogatory name "Pine Rats."[15] From Pine

Rat to Pine-hawker to Piner to Piney—no wonder the name had a pejorative connotation.

When Herbert Halpert collected folklore in the Pine Barrens in the 1930s and 1940s he kept asking people where the Pineys were. He was told again and again that they were farther south, until he reached a point where people started to say that the Pineys were farther north. Nobody wanted to be a Piney. Definitions would beg the question of whom the name referred to. For example, a Piney was defined as someone who lives "just a little deeper in the Pines than you live." Nevertheless, social distinctions were made by the slang names "Piney," "Clam Diggers," and "Rock Jumpers." The "Pineys" lived in the interior, the "Clam Diggers" were the baymen along the coast, and the "Rock Jumpers" were the farmers of South Jersey. But today people from all over South Jersey are calling themselves "Pineys," and there are even bumper stickers with the slogan "Piney Power." The transformation of a negative stereotype into a positive one is a well-known phenomenon. For example, the term "Yankee" was originally associated with a negative British stereotype of Americans as bumpkins, as in the song "Yankee Doodle." But Americans embraced the stereotype and turned it into something positive. The same has happened with the name "Piney."

Folklorists are well aware of the importance of names. The modern Delaware Indians know each other only by nicknames, because to know a person's real name, which is given in a naming ceremony, is to be able to work magic against that person. Besides this association of names with magic, we have seen how names are an important part of the identity of people and places.

T HE LANGUAGE that is used to communicate folklore is itself a kind of folklore. Folk speech or conversational language differs from written language in that it tends to be less rigid and less arbitrary than the hard and fast rules of grammar, spelling, and pronunciation would dictate. Folk speech tends toward greater variation over space and time than written language. It takes years for a new word to enter the dictionary, but slang expressions are added to folk speech all the time. Because it is so responsive, folk speech provides much useful historical and cultural information that is unavailable from other sources. For example, the boundaries of culture areas are determined by mapping differences in pronunciation and word usage. Acculturation is studied through trade jargon and loanwords. The intensity of ethnic groups' cultural identity is seen in the persistence or decline of native languages. And regional, occupational, and class differences in society are revealed by slang expressions and special terminology.

The geographic area of New Jersey does not represent a single linguistic area. This is the case with spoken English today, and it was the case with the Indian dialects spoken here before the first Europeans arrived. The Lenape Indians spoke a language in the Algonkian language family, which had the same relationship to the languages of most other Eastern Woodland Indians as French, Italian, and Spanish, all members of the Romance language family, have to each other, or as Dutch, Flemish, and High German, members of the Germanic language family, have to one another. Indians speaking Algonkian languages occupied most of the eastern woodland region of North America at the time of the first contact with Europeans.

According to Ives Goddard, a linguist, there were two dialects spoken by the Lenape Indians—a northern and a southern dialect which more or less corresponded to the northern (Munsee) and southern (Unami) geographic groupings of these Indians. He maintains that these dialects were sufficiently different that a speaker of one could not understand a speaker of the other. The northern dialect was spoken in northeastern New Jersey, the middle and lower Hudson River Valley, western Long Island, and Staten Island. The southern dialect was spoken in southeastern Pennsylvania as far north as the Lehigh Valley, most of Delaware, and the southern three-quarters of New Jersey, including the area of Trenton, which had its own variety that the Dutch called *Sankhikan*. Goddard notes that this linguistic boundary corresponded with the major political boundary between Indian groups during historic time, running up the Raritan River to the Delaware River in the vicinity of the Water Gap, as recognized in the 1758 conferences in which the Indians relinquished their land claims in New Jersey. The Delaware Indians no longer live as a tribe in New Jersey; their descendants live in Canada and Oklahoma. Goddard notes that the Canadian Delaware speak the northern and the Oklahoma Delaware the southern dialect.[1]

When the Dutch first came into contact with the Indians of New Jersey, they communicated with each other by means of signs and gestures. As trade between them developed, a special trade jargon or lingua franca, which was based on a simplified form of the Indian dialects and sufficed for the conduct of trade, was created.[2] According to Goddard, "the jargon avoided all of the tremendous complexities of Delaware grammar by simply stringing along the words in baby-talk fashion."[3]

In 1912 John Dyneley Prince, a linguist at Columbia University who was then acting governor of New Jersey, found in the vaults of the Department of State, in a manuscript volume of Salem County deeds dated 1684, a list of 261 words in the trade jargon. Some of the words, such as *moos*, "cow," were based on onomatopoeia (the naming of a thing or action by a vocal imitation of the sound associated with it). Other words were closely related to the Munsee dialect, such as *sewan*, "wampum"; *manitto*, "the Devil"; and *pone*, "bread" (which survives in the American South in corn pone, "corn bread"). Still others had no basis in the Delaware dialects, such as *squaw*, "wife," and *papouse*, "a sucking child."[4] Goddard has warned that "jargon words cannot be used as direct evidence for the dialect actually spoken by the Indians of a given place, since the Dutch and their colonial successors used the jargon over a considerably larger area than that in which it originated."[5]

The Dutch developed their own dialects in America, of which there were at least two: "Jersey Dutch" in northeastern New Jersey and southeastern New York State and "Albany Dutch" in the Mohawk and upper Hudson River valleys. According to Prince, "Jersey Dutch was originally the South Holland or Flemish language, which, in the course of centuries (ca. 1630–1880), became mixed with and partially influenced by English, having borrowed also from the Munsi (Lenape-Delaware) Indian language a few animal and plant names."[6] Some examples cited by Goddard of Munsee words that entered Jersey Dutch include: *spanspak*, "cantaloup," from Munsee *špánšpe·kw*; *spaon*, "cornmeal mush," from Munsee *nsá·pa·n*; and *tahæ:im*, "strawberries," from Munsee *wté:hi:m*.[7] Not only did the Dutch borrow words from the Indians, the Indians borrowed words from the Dutch as well. Some examples Goddard cited are: *kašt*, "box, chest, coffin," from Dutch *kist*; *pán'ko:k*, "pancake," from Dutch *pannekoek*; and *kó:way*, "cow," from Dutch *koei*.[8] Some of the loanwords were the calls for the animals, rather than the words denoting the animals. For example, the Munsee *kí:kí:pạš*, "chicken," comes from the Dutch call *kiep! kiep!*; and the Munsee *kó:ško:š*, "pig," comes from the hog call in the dialect of Hasselt *kuš-kuš-kuš*.[9]

In 1794 a British traveler named William Strickland commented on the Jersey Dutch dialect in Bergen County as follows: "The people here universally speak English to those who address them in that language, but among themselves only Dutch, though greatly corrupted."[10] Jersey Dutch should not be considered a corruption of Dutch any more than American English should be considered a corruption of English as spoken in England. Change and variation are part of the nature of the oral tradition. Similarly, there existed a variant of Jersey Dutch that was spoken by free blacks and slaves in northern New Jersey. Prince noted that "the negro slaves of the old settlers used an idiom tinged with their own peculiarities."[11] And in his *A Jersey Dutch Vocabulary*, James B. H. Storms wrote: "Even the colored people, for the most part children of slaves, without any education, were proficient in the use of Jersey Dutch and had enough knowledge of English to converse in either."[12]

The spoken Dutch language in New Jersey began to die out in the nineteenth century. One of its last refuges was the Dutch Reformed churches, where services were conducted in Dutch until the middle of the nineteenth century. By the turn of the twentieth century, there were only a few people left in Bergen County who spoke the dialect. Today, Jersey Dutch is no longer a spoken language, but there are still local people who remember fragments of it. The following nursery rhyme was collected from a descendant of Jersey Dutch settlers in Bergen County.

| | |
|---|---|
| Trip a trop a tronjes, | Trip a trop a tronjes [nonsense words] |
| De varkens in de boonjes | The pigs are in the bean row |
| De koejes in de klaver, | The cows are in the meadow, |
| De paarden in de haver, | The horses are in the oats, |
| De eenjes in de waterplass, | The ducks upon the waterways, |
| Zoo grott mijn kleine Joris was. | So great my darling Juris is.[13] |

This nursery rhyme is one of the most common pieces of Dutch folklore. It can be traced back to the Netherlands and has been collected in New York and New Jersey.

A similar process occurred with other spoken languages in New Jersey. Around 1750 the Swedish visitor Peter Kalm commented on the impending disappearance of the Swedish language in South Jersey.

In the morning we continued our journey from near Maurice River down to Cape May. We had a Swedish guide along who was probably born of Swedish parents, and was married to a Swedish woman but who could not, himself, speak Swedish. There are many such here of both sexes; for since English is the principal language in the land all people gradually get to speak that, and they become ashamed to talk in their own tongue, because they fear they may not in such a case be real English. Consequently many Swedish women are married to English-men, and although they can speak Swedish very well it is impossible to make them do so, and when they are spoken to in Swedish they always answer in English. The same condition obtains among the men; so that it is easy to see that the Swedish language is doomed to extinction in America; and in fifty or sixty years time there will not be many left who can understand Swedish, and still less of those who can converse in it.[14]

He noted that "the present language and method of speaking in New Sweden . . . [have] already deviated from the Swedish that is used in the Old Country. Soon it will be a new tongue and we can see that Swedish will in a short time die out."[15] Ives Goddard found several Lenape Indian loanwords in the Swedish spoken in South Jersey, such as *ässpann*, "raccoon," from the Munsee *é:span*; and *hopiss*, "ground nut, Indian potato (Apios tuberosa)," from Unami *h'pani:s*.[16]

The same can be said of the spoken languages of more recent immigrants to New Jersey. Whether it be Yiddish, Italian, Spanish, or Ukrainian, the spoken language changes as a result of isolation from the mother tongue and contact with other languages. But not all ethnic groups have the same tendency toward language retention at all times. For some groups, such as the Hispanics in New Jersey, their language has become an element in their sense of ethnic identity. In the recent revival of ethnic consciousness there has been a strong interest in preserving the native language (e.g. Yiddish, Italian, Polish) on the part of second- and third-generation members, who formerly were anxious only to learn English and cast off the mother language. Folklorists and linguists need to study the variants of these languages spoken in New Jersey.

Even English is spoken differently in different parts of New Jersey. Certain words are pronounced differently in places just a few miles apart. For example, the place name "Newark" is pronounced *'nuark* (sounds like *new-uhk*) in Bergen County, but in Essex County it is pronounced *nɔrk* (sounds like *nork*). Linguistic boundaries can also be determined from the usage of different expressions. In fact, a major linguistic boundary dividing the Northern dialect from the Midland dialect cuts across the center of the state. These dialect areas extend far beyond the political boundaries of New Jersey. The boundary line is surprisingly similar to that described by Goddard (discussed earlier in this chapter) as dividing the Munsee and the Unami dialects of the Lenape Indians. These two major dialect areas in New Jersey are divided into three subregions, which also extend beyond the state. Parts of northern New Jersey fall into the Hudson Valley subregion and other parts into the Metropolitan New York subregion of the Inland Northern dialect area; South Jersey is part of the Delaware Valley (Philadelphia area) subregion of the Midland dialect area.[17] Cape May County is a special case. It was founded by Yankee whalers in the late seventeenth century. Consequently, there are survivals of New England expressions there.

Some examples show the differences among these regions and subregions. In the Northern dialect area the expression "brook" is used for a "small stream"; in the Midland area the term is "run," as in Six-Mile Run or Bull Run. The Dutch term *kill* is found in the Hudson River Valley and northeastern New Jersey.[18] The Northern term for cottage cheese is "Dutch cheese," except in the Hudson Valley subregion, where it is called "pot cheese" from the Dutch term *pot kees*. The Midland term, however, is "smear case" ("schmear case" or "smear cheese") from the Pennsylvania German *schmierkas*.[19] The wooden bar on a horse's harness is called a "whiffletree" or "whipple tree" in the Northern dialect and a "singletree" or "swingletree" in the Midland dialect. Parts of central New Jersey have their own local expression for it—a "swiveltree."[20] In New England, upstate New York, and northern Pennsylvania cows in the pasture are called by yelling "Boss! Bossie!" But in eastern New England, Long Island, and South Jersey the call is "co!" And in northern New Jersey cows are called by yelling "kush! kushie!" and calves by yelling "tye!"[21] In most of the Northern and Midland regions it is said that "school lets out," except in the New York Metropolitan region, where it is said that "school gets out."[22]

There are certain expressions that appear to be unique to New Jersey. In an article in *Dialect Notes* in 1893 Francis B. Lee referred to these expressions as "Jerseyisms." For example, in Salem, Sussex, and Burlington counties, apple whiskey was called "jack." The term "Jersey lightning" was not used by natives of New Jersey, according to the author. In New England apple whiskey was called "cider brandy." When someone drank too much jack, he was said to be suffering from "apple palsy." In Cape May County people from the southern part of the county were referred to as "down felowyers," which was thought to be a "corruption" of "down belowyers." Along the Jersey Coast, to "go by water" meant "to follow the Sea as a calling."[23]

Traditional occupations have their own terminology. New Jersey had two major canals in the nineteenth century: the Morris Canal in the north and the Delaware and Raritan Canal in the central part of the state. On the Morris Canal the coal boats were called "chunkers." To "snub" meant to tie the boat to a post known as a "snubbin' post" while it was in lock.[24] Dredging for oysters was an important maritime occupation in the Delaware Bay, where it was done with sailing schooners as recently as the 1940s. An oyster smaller than a quarter was known as a "blister" from Barnegat south to Cape May. To sort oysters was to "cull" them, and poor oysters were known as "cullings." A long thin oyster was called a "stickup" in Cape May County because the oystermen say that it sticks up in the mud. For an oyster to be "milchy" or in "milch" referred to its being about to spawn.[25]

Glassblowing was one of the early industries in South Jersey, making use of the sandy soil of the Pine Barrens. "All aboard" was the cry to begin work in the flint glassworks. The "batch" was the term for the mixture of soda and sand from which the glass was made. To "shear to" was "to heat up the furnace," and the "melt" was the "process of reducing the batch to molten glass." A young boy employed in the glassworks would be called a "snapper up." "Tempo" was the cry to stop work.[26]

Charcoal burning was another traditional industry both in the Pine Barrens of South Jersey and in the mountains of North Jersey. Woodcutters would partially burn the timber they cut to produce charcoal to be used in furnaces, foundries, and home heating. They too had their own terminology. The "firing place" was a location suitable for charcoal burning. Irregular sods, called "floats," were laid on four-foot lengths, over which sand was placed. The center pole in the charcoal pit was called a "fergen," and horizontal sticks of cordwood, known as the "crib," were piled triangularly around the fergen. Sticks of cordwood were placed at right angles to form a column against which cordwood would be piled in ranks.[27] South Jersey also had a shingle industry for marketing the white cedar of the Pine Barrens. "Shingling" was the term used to refer to this occupation. Shingles made from buried logs were called "dug ups." Shingles made from trees that were twisted by the wind so as to result in twisted grain in the wood were called "wind shakes."[28]

The folk speech of New Jersey is rich and varied, from the two dialects of the Lenape to the Dutch, Swedish, and English of the early settlers to the variety of European and Asian languages of the immigrants and ethnics. Even within the dominant English language, regional, occupational, and class differences abound. Linguistic culture areas tend to have the same boundaries as other culture areas in New Jersey.

We must reject the notion that folk speech is a debased or bastardized form of language. While the written language changes at a much slower rate, it demonstrates the same kinds of changes that we see in folk speech. We must remind ourselves that the English language evolved out of Celtic, Germanic, and Norman influences and that American usage eventually differentiated itself from "the King's English." It was not until the early nineteenth century that there was any standardization of spelling in American English. Folk speech is a valid form of language which should be appreciated, studied, and preserved. That is why folklorists and oral historians use tape recorders rather than rewriting the accounts in their own words.

# Legend

LEGENDS ARE folktales that have a historical setting. They may be told about either real or fictional people, but they must be placed in a historical context.[1] The difference between legend and myth is the same as the difference between history and prehistory: legends are folk history; myths are folk prehistory.

The difference between history and legend is that history is based on documentary (mostly written) records, whereas legend is based on oral tradition. The defining characteristic of legend is not its truth or falseness but whether it has been in an oral tradition.[2] Some legends are basically true accounts of past events, and some are complete fabrications. Most contain at least some elaboration resulting from the chain of oral transmission.

In New Jersey historical time begins relatively recently with the coming of the Europeans circa 1600, and thus the Lenape Indian legends take place in the relatively recent past. The Grasshopper War folktale is such a legend. According to John Witthoft, the anthropologist, "it is the only Indian folktale which to my knowledge has become part of the oral tradition of a white community. It has not survived among its Indian originators, but it is known at present only from American white informants."[3] The legend is about an eighteenth-century battle between the Lenape and Shawnee Indians over a trifling incident—a quarrel between children over the possession of a dead grasshopper. Variants of the legend place the battle in different localities; several claim that it occurred in Hunterdon County. Witthoft quotes an account dated about 1870 from the notebooks of John Ruth of Bucks County, Pennsylvania, an amateur naturalist and collector of Indian relics. While this version was collected in Pennsylvania, the legend was set in New Jersey.

> Tradition tells us that a great battle was fought by the aborigines in the vicinity of Holland, Hunterdon Co., N.J. Three tribes (so the story tells it) were at that time living on the Jersey side of the Delaware in this vicinity. One occupied a position near Holland Station, probably the village on Mrs. Hager's farm about a mile north of the station and opposite the northern end of the island; the second tribe had its village at the mouth of the Musconetcong, now the farm of Isaac Riegel, and the third tribe lived some distance up the Musconetcong. The children of these tribes coming together, they got into a quarrel about a grasshopper. The quarrel was taken up by the older ones and was sufficient cause for making an attack on each other. They met each other at some intermediate place and fought a terrible battle in which one tribe was completely destroyed. The site of the battle is pointed out on the farm of Mr. Snyder, a short distance below Holland church. If the tradition concerning this battle is true, this was the place where it was fought. We have picked up a number of arrow points and other weapons at the place. Many of the points are broken. That the place was not a village site is evident from the fact that there is not to be found any of the broken cobble stones and other refuse found on the sites of ancient villages. It is stated that a person witnessed this conflict from the Pennsylvania shore.[4]

Another variant of the legend also found in Ruth's notebooks mentions two tribes (the Shawnees and the Lenapes) living on opposite banks of the Delaware River; rather than being totally destroyed, the Shawnees fled into the wilderness.

> The Shawnees occupied the west bank of the Delaware, and the Lenape the east bank. For a number of years they lived in peace with each other, and the Shawnees became a powerful people. A very trifling incident finally involved the two tribes in a war. Some of the Shawnee

women wandering over to the east side of the river, met a party of women and children of the Lenape. One of the children found a large grasshopper, which a squaw snatched from the child's hand and gave to her own child. This led to war which resulted in the defeat of the Shawnees, who fled to the wilderness of the Susquehanna. The final battle of this was was fought in the vicinity of Holland Station, Hunterdon County, New Jersey. A white man is said to have witnessed it from the narrows, or palisades on the Pennsylvania side. Broken spear-points, arrow heads, and stone axes are still found in the vicinity.[5]

Other variants of the legend collected elsewhere in Pennsylvania place the battle in the Juniata Valley, the Susquehanna Valley, and the Wyoming Valley. According to Witthoft, the function of this folk legend in Indian culture was to explain why the Lenape and the Shawnee spoke similar languages, although they were different people. This was because, according to the legend, they were once the same people. In white culture, Witthoft argues, the legend functions as a "rationalization of why the Indians left the area during the frontier period (absolving Whites of any guilt)."[6]

The legend of the Old Mine Road is an example of folklore that happens to be historically untrue. The Old Mine Road runs from the New Jersey side of the Delaware Water Gap to Kingston (formerly Esopus), New York. According to legend, the road was used to transport ore from copper mines at Pahaquarry said to be worked by the Dutch in the mid-seventeenth century. There was an oral tradition about the Old Mine Road as early as the 1780s, according to a letter written in 1828 by Samuel Preston, a Pennsylvania Quaker who helped survey this region. In 1787 Preston interviewed Nicholas Dupuis, a resident of the upper Delaware Valley, who told him

> that he had well known the Mine Road to Esopus, and used, before he opened the boat channel through Foul Rift, to drive on it several times every Winter with loads of wheat and cider, as also did his neighbors, to purchase their salt and necessaries in Esopus, having then no other market or knowledge where the river ran to.[7]

Preston continued with an account of why the Mine Road was so named, which constitutes the earliest known version of the legend.

> This interview with the amiable Nicholas Dupuis, Esq., was in June, 1787. He then appeared about sixty years of age. I interrogated as to the particulars of what he knew, as to when and by whom the

Mine Road was made, what was the ore they dug and hauled on it, what was the date, and from whence, or how, came the first settlers of Minisink in such great numbers as to take up all the flats on both sides of the river for forty miles. He could only give traditionary accounts of what he had heard from older people, without date, in substance as follows:—

That in some former age there came a company of miners from Holland; supposed, from the great labor expended in making that road, about one hundred miles long, that they were very rich or great people, in working two mines,—one on the Delaware River where the mountain nearly approaches the lower point of Pahaquarry Flat, the other at the north foot of the same mountain, near half way from the Delaware and Esopus. He ever understood that abundance of ore had been hauled on that road, but never could learn whether lead or silver.[8]

That this legend was not the creation of Nicholas Dupuis but was already in the oral tradition is indicated by Preston's postscript: "The other old men I conversed with gave their traditions similar to N. Dupuis, and they all appeared to be grandsons of the first settlers, and very ignorant as to the dates and things related to chronology."[9]

Don McTernan of the National Park Service and Herbert C. Kraft of Seton Hall University believe that this legend about seventeenth-century Dutch mines and a mine road is unfounded in historical fact. Kraft notes that the earliest European settlers of the upper Delaware Valley came by this route, but he questions the date. He notes that the earliest documented visit to the region was in 1692 by Arent Schuyler, who made no reference to a Mine Road, copper mines, or any European residents other than an itinerant trader and interpreter named Vielle.[10] On the basis of an extensive study of maps and documents, McTernan has concluded that while an Indian trail existed along this route in the early seventeenth century, there was no wagon road along the length of the Esopus-Minisink Way until the early eighteenth century. He finds no evidence for any mining at Pahaquarry to the colonial period.[11]

To many people folk legends are innocuous anecdotes about the past that have little importance. But when a folk legend deals with the origins of a group of people it can become very personal; and when a legend becomes the vehicle for conveying derogatory stereotypes, the result can be explosive. I have mentioned the legend about the origin of the "Jackson Whites" (see "Names"). The

Legend

Ramapo Mountain People think of themselves as having Indian and white ancestry, but many whites in the vicinity see them as having black ancestry. I found that there were two variants of the legend about their origins: one told by the Mountain People themselves and the other told by outsiders. The outside version had four parts, each part associated with a different alleged strain in their ancestry. The first strain was said to be Tuscarora Indians migrating from North Carolina to the province of New York in the eighteenth century. The second strain was supposedly escaped slaves who sought refuge in the Ramapo Mountains and intermarried with the Indians. The third and fourth parts of the legend were set during the Revolutionary War. The third strain consisted of Hessian soldiers who deserted the British and went to the mountains, and the fourth prostitutes procured by a man named Jackson for the British forces occupying New York City. After the war these prostitutes somehow crossed the Hudson River and supposedly migrated to the Ramapo Mountains. The Mountain People only told the parts about the Tuscarora Indians and the Hessian soldiers.

When I did a genealogical study of the oldest family names (Van Dunk, De Freese, De Groat, and Mann), I found that although the legend was based on fragments of accurate historical information, it was totally inaccurate as an account of the origins of the group. There was no evidence that the Tuscarora Indians ever came as far east as the Ramapo Mountains, their migration being mainly through Pennsylvania. While New York and New Jersey farmers owned slaves, some of whom escaped, there is no evidence that they went to the Ramapo Mountains and intermarried with Indians. The surnames of the Mountain People turned out to be mostly Dutch surnames, not German, as would be the case had they descended from Hessians. And no documentary evidence has been found to substantiate the existence either of Captain Jackson or of a group of prostitutes who found their way to the Ramapo Mountains.

Instead, I found a documented genealogical history that traced back to a settlement of free blacks living on the outskirts of New York during the 1670s. They were racially black and mulatto but culturally Dutch. They had Dutch surnames, spoke the Dutch dialect, and attended the Dutch Reformed church. During the 1680s they were among the first non-Indian settlers in the Hackensack River Valley on the west side of the Hudson River. They moved there as landowners, not as squatters or refugees. They and their descendants lived and farmed in this valley throughout the eighteenth century. Around 1800 they began to sell their land and move northwest to the Ramapo Mountains. One probable reason for this migration was that New Jersey passed a law in 1798 that restricted the interstate travel rights of free blacks. Since they were living on either

33

side of the New York and New Jersey boundary, their move to the mountains could have been an attempt to live completely within New Jersey. Another possible reason was that they had divided their property among all their offspring, so that their landholdings got smaller and smaller in each generation until it was necessary to find more land.[12]

Like the legend about the Grasshopper War, this legend has two different functions. For outsiders it confirmed a derogatory stereotype they had of the Mountain People as renegades, outcasts, and degenerates. But for the Mountain People parts of the same legend were used to confirm their self-image as having Indian and white ancestry. The legend is so important to their self-image that they have persisted in believing it to be true, despite documented, historical evidence to the contrary. In fact, they recently incorporated as The Ramapough Indian Tribe, Inc., and the state legislature memorialized Congress to recognize them as an Indian tribe.

A similar legend might be involved in the various accounts of the origin of the so-called Pineys in the Pine Barrens of South Jersey. They are said to be descended variously from Tories, "disowned" Quakers, Indians from the Brotherton Reservation, Hessian soldiers, Pine Robbers (Revolutionary War bandits in the Pine Barrens), escaped slaves, criminals, smugglers, and even pirates. Nathaniel R. Ewan suggested in 1947 that this image is a stereotype and that "undoubtedly" many originated as workers in the bog-iron, glass, and paper industries of South Jersey.[13] But no one to my knowledge has done a genealogical study to separate fact from fiction in this legend.

One of the most common types of legend is the tall tale. These stories are often told about people who actually lived, but their feats have become exaggerated with repeated telling, to the point that some people refer to these stories as "lies." Herbert Halpert collected in the Pine Barrens a cycle of legends about Sammy Giberson (1808–1884) who was such a great fiddler and dancer that he thought he could defeat the devil himself in a competition. In some versions he wins and in others he loses. The following legend was told on June 23, 1940, by Elven Sweet, age sixty-eight, from Magnolia, Burlington County, who worked in the cranberry bogs his entire life.

> Old Sammy Giberson he was playin' to a dance, and after he got done, he said he could beat the Devil. So—on his road home, he come to a bridge—he had to cross a bridge. And the Old Man appeared to him right on the bridge—that's the Devil hisself. "I understand," he says, "You can beat the Devil playin' the fiddle." "Well," Old Sammy says,

"that's what I said and that's what I meant." So they went at it and, by God, Old Sammy played every piece the Devil did, and the Devil played every one that he did, except one, and old Sammy heard the tune comin' through the air, and that's where he beat him. The Devil couldn't play it and old Sammy could. That's it, that's all of it.[14]

This motif of "beating the devil" can be traced back to European folklore. Similar stories have been told about the Italian violinist Niccolò Paganini (1782–1840) and the Norwegian violinist Ole Bull (1810–1880).

Halpert also collected legends about Jerry Munyhun, wizard of Hanover Furnace who sold his soul to the devil. Tom Test of Browns Mills, Burlington County told Halpert on June 27, 1940, the following account of Munyhun's death.

I believe it was a lie. It don't sound right, does it? They told and said it was the truth—Jerry Munyhun. He lived at Plumley Lot over here between Brindletown and Hanover Furnace. He was taken sick, and one night at about twelve o'clock, a knock come to the door, and his wife she went to the door to see who it was. There was a man there at the door when she opened the door, and she asked him what he wanted. He says he wanted to see Jerry. And she said, "Jerry, there's a man wants to see you." And Jerry says, "What kind of a lookin' man is it?" She said, "I don't know, it's a little black man." And Jerry said, "I know who it 'tis. It's the Devil. Tell him I'm ready." He died right there and then—and that was the last of Jerry. Never heard tell of him from that day to this. They claim he had sold hisself to the Devil, and I guess he had.[15]

Readers will recognize this as the Faust theme that appears in European literature and folklore.

In the Ramapo Mountains I collected a cycle of tall tales about Uncle Rob Milligan, a strong man who worked in the Ringwood iron mines. These legends were told to me by John and Madge Morgan and their family, who were related to him.

JOHN MORGAN: And right down here—this mine hole I heard my father and them say—they was there—that they snugged him fast with a rope around his body to a tree until he reached down and pulled a mule up out of that mine hole down there, right by the halter. Yes.
COHEN: How big was he?

35

JOHN: Oh, he was—he was a regular giant. I don't know. He must of been pretty near eight feet tall. Yeah. He was three feet or more across the shoulder. He was! He couldn't get in the door without—when he coming through an ordinary door, he had to—he had to bend down to walk through door.

MADGE: He must have been seven feet tall.

JOHN: He was that big. He could take—I've seen him working in the mines. I know this is true. I've seen him from the mines, when the boys would be tightening up pipes—I've seen him take one hand on the pipe and tighten it. Two men would get on one of them long wrenches to break it loose. See. That's how powerful he was.[16]

Uncle Rob Milligan was supposed to have killed a balky horse by striking it with his fist and breaking its neck. He died trying to lift a car back on to the road.

MADGE: His car run off the road up there. He was going up to Hewitt. His car run off in the snow bank. He was all alone, and he went to lift the car out of the ditch, and they think that he musta taken all that weight to just lift the car up on the road—that it musta put him in cerebral hemorrhage to him. He went right in the coma, like, and he never came out of it. He musta bursted a vein of some kind.[17]

These tall tales about Uncle Rob contain traditional motifs that have been collected elsewhere. For example, the folklorist Richard Dorson collected an account telling how the Maine coast fisherman Barney Beal killed a horse by hitting it with his fist. Barney Beal allegedly died when he tried to haul a dory ashore by himself.[18] In the heroic-legend formula the death of the strong man usually occurs under extraordinary circumstances.

It is useful to distinguish between the popular culture hero and the folk hero. The legends about the folk hero must have an oral tradition; legends about popular culture heroes are conveyed via the mass media, in local history books and magazine articles, on radio and television. Molly Pitcher, for example, is a popular culture heroine, because everything we know about her comes from written sources. The same might be said about Paul Bunyan, Johnny Appleseed, and Davy Crockett. Dorson called legends about these heroes "fakelore" but this is a misnomer; they are authentic popular culture heroes.[19] Usually folk heroes are unknown local characters who are celebrated in their families or their local communities. But the motifs are universal. Their function is to be ideal-type personalities embodying the physical and character traits admired and emulated by the community.

It is sometimes hard to tell the difference between the popular culture hero and the folk hero. Take for example Tom Quick, the legendary Indian fighter of the upper Delaware Valley. He was a real person who was born in 1734 in Milford, Pennsylvania, and died in 1796. After his father was killed by Indians in 1756, he supposedly vowed to take revenge by killing 100 Indians. The legends about him contain motifs that have been collected elsewhere. For example, one account tells how he tricked some Indians who wanted to kill him into helping him split logs. When their fingers were in the log, he knocked out the wedge, thereby trapping them, and then killed them. There are different accounts of his death. One is that he died of smallpox before he could fulfill his vow, having killed only 99 Indians. But the legend is that the Indians dug up his grave, and contracted the disease. And so he ended up killing more than 100 Indians after his death. According to his biographer Frederick W. Crumb, "stories [about Tom Quick] have been told around firesides of the Delaware Valley for one hundred and fifty years."[20] Crumb may have been stretching the truth. The Tom Quick legends may never have been in oral tradition.

Perhaps the most famous figure in New Jersey folklore is the Jersey Devil. Originally known as the Leeds Devil, his story is in part legend and in part a folk belief. The earliest known version of the legend is the following written account, which appeared in the *Atlantic Monthly* in 1859.

There lived, in the year 1735, in the Township of Burlington, a woman. Her name was Leeds, and she was shrewdly suspected of a little amateur witchcraft. Be that as it may, it is well established, that, one stormy gusty night, when the wind was howling in turret and tree, Mother Leeds gave birth to a son, whose father could have been no other than the Prince of Darkness. No sooner did he see the light than he assumed the form of a fiend, with a horse's head, wings of a bat, and a serpent's tail. The first thought of the newborn Caliban [the brutal, monstrous, and deformed slave in Shakespeare's *Tempest*] was to fall foul of his mother, whom he scratched and bepommelled soundly, and then flew through the window out into the village, where he played the mischief generally. Little children he devoured, maidens he abused, young men he mauled and battered; and it was many days before a holy man succeeded in repeating the enchantment of Prospero [the sorcerer in Shakespeare's *Tempest,* who controls Caliban by magic]. At length, however, Leed's devil was laid—but only for one hundred years.

During an entire century, the memory of that awful monster was preserved, and, as 1835 drew nigh, the denizens of Burlington and the Pines looked tremblingly for his rising. Strange to say, however, no one but Hannah Butler has had a personal interview with the fiend; though, since 1835, he has frequently been heard howling and screaming in the forest at night, to the terror of the Rats in their encampments. Hannah Butler saw the devil, one stormy night, long ago; though skeptical individuals affirm, that very possibly she may have been led, under the influence of liquid Jersey Lightning, to invest a pine-stump, or, possibly, a belated bear, with diabolic attributes and a Satanic voice. However that may be, you cannot induce a Rat to leave his hut after dark,—nor, indeed, will you find many Jerseymen, though of a higher order of intelligence, who will brave the supernatural terrors of the gloomy forest at night, unless secure in the strength of numbers.[21]

This account obviously is not a folk text reflecting the true style of oral tradition. People who believe in the Jersey Devil normally don't make literary references to Shakespeare. Rather this text reflects the nineteenth-century prejudices of the writer toward the people of the Pines, who are referred to in the text as "Pine Rats." Furthermore, the writer himself obviously did not believe in the Jersey Devil, because like most of those who have written about it he explains its sightings as hallucinations. These sightings fall into the genre of unexplained happenings that befuddle the scientific establishment, like Bigfoot in the Pacific Northwest, the Abominable Snowman in the Himalayas, and unidentified flying objects. Most of the published accounts of the Jersey Devil have been written by unbelievers. These writers have trivialized what was originally an authentic folk legend and folk belief. This is one of the differences between the treatment of such topics in popular culture and folk culture.

One might ask why study legends, especially when they may not be true accounts of past events? Legends are important not as evidence of what actually happened, but of what people think happened. They are examples of what has been called "the usable past," that is, how people make the past relevant in the present. Some people use the past to provide themselves with a sense of identity. Some use it to reinforce stereotypes they have about other people. Some use it to celebrate their ancestors or legitimate their origins. Some people use the past to support a belief in a golden age that they would like to believe once existed, and some use it solely for entertainment. All of these are the uses of history; they are also the uses of legend.

# Folk Belief

**F**OLK BELIEFS are those beliefs that are communicated through an oral tradition; they are often at odds with the belief system of the scientific and religious establishment. Folk beliefs pertain to two main areas: religion and science. Folk religion is related to but different from organized religion,[1] and the relationship has often been an adversary one. For example, the European folk belief in witchcraft was based in part upon Christianity, the covenant with the devil being the reverse of the covenant with God. Yet the church repeatedly tried to stamp out the witchcraft cult. However, organized religions have risen on a foundation of folk belief. Most successful religions began as sects, and most enduring religions are those that most successfully amalgamate formal theology and folk belief. Folk science refers to beliefs about cause and effect in secular areas of life, such as physics, biology, and the like. It includes folk medicine, which constitutes a separate chapter in this book.

Some scholars distinguish between folk belief and "primitive" religion, but among tribal people such as the Lenape Indians there was no such distinction. Their religion was an oral tradition. Among the best sources for Lenape folk belief are those who have tried to eradicate it. The Reverend David Brainerd was a Presbyterian missionary sent by the Society for Propagating Christian Knowledge to convert the Indians. From 1745 to 1747 he brought his mission to New Jersey, working first at Crossweeksung (present-day Crosswicks) and then at Cranberry (present-day Cranbury). In recording the folk beliefs of the Lenapes, he noted that they believed in "a plurality of invisible deities." He added that

> those who yet remain Pagans, pay some kind of superstitious reverence to beasts, birds, fishes, and even reptiles; that is, some to one kind of animal, and some to another. . . . I have known a Pagan burn fine tobacco for incense, in order to appease the anger of that invisible power, which he supposed presided over rattle-snakes, because one of these animals was killed by another Indian near his house.[2]

39

Brainerd wrote that before the coming of Europeans some Lenape Indians believed in four invisible powers that inhabited the four corners of the earth. Others considered the sun to be the only deity. Still others worshipped a fountainhead deity that was present in various animals and inanimate things. After the coming of Europeans, he noted, the Lenape adopted the idea that "there were three deities, and three only, because they saw people of three different kinds of complexion, viz. English, Negroes, and Indians." He found that they believed they were not made by the same God that made white people, but rather that they were made after white people were. "I fancy," he wrote,

> that they suppose their God gained some special skill by seeing the white people made, and so made them better; for it is certain they look upon themselves, and their method of living, which, they say, their God expressly prescribed for them, vastly preferable to the white people, and their method.[3]

Brainerd reported that the Lenape believed in life after death. What they called the *chichung* "shadow" survived the body after death and journeyed southward to an unknown place where those who were good would enjoy some kind of happiness, such as hunting, feasting, or dancing.[4] They offered sacrifices to their deities for success in hunting or in other affairs, and to prevent sickness and other calamities. They believed that neglect of these sacrifices might lead to punishment in this life, but not in the afterlife. By the time Brainerd was writing, the Indians of New Jersey had been in contact with Europeans for over 100 years, and it is difficult to know whether these beliefs in reward and punishment and an afterlife were influenced by Christianity.

The Lenape also believed that through dreams the invisible powers communicated with them and sometimes told them which animal to worship. Brainerd summarized some of these dreams that were told him.

> One I remember affirmed to me, that himself had once been dead four days, that most of his friends in that time were gathered together to his funeral, and that he should have been buried, but that some of his relations at a great distance, who were sent for upon that occasion were not arrived, before whose coming he came to life again. In this time, he says, he went to the place where the sun rises; imagining the earth to be a plain; and directly over that place, at a great height in the air, he was admitted, he says, into a great house, which he supposes was several miles in length, and saw many wonderful things, too tedious as well as

ridiculous to mention.—Another person, a woman, whom I have not seen, but of whom I have been credibly informed by the Indians, declares, that she was dead several days, that her soul went *southward*, and feasted and danced with the happy spirits, and that she found all things exactly agreeable to the Indian notions of a future state.[5]

This is strikingly similar to what has recently been called the "out-of-body experience" of people who were medically dead for a short time.

Brainerd also wrote of the so-called *powaws* or powwows (conjurers or diviners) among the Lenape. They were people who had the power to foretell the future, heal the sick, or cause illnesses by means of charms, chants, and magic. Normally the powwow had no choice in acquiring this power; some acquired it in infancy and others as adults. There were, however, exceptions: "It is supposed to be given to children sometimes in consequence of some means which the parents use with them for that purpose; one of which is to make the child swallow a small living frog, after having performed some superstitious rites and ceremonies upon it."[6]

European settlers brought with them not only their organized religion but also their folk beliefs. Folk religion in the past is harder to study than organized religion. We have many sermons written by ministers that give us insights into the beliefs of organized religion. But folk religion is transmitted orally and is rarely written down. Nevertheless, folk beliefs sometimes find their way into historical documents. Here, for example, is the report of a coroner's inquest into a murder:

> On the 22 day of September in the year of our Lord 1767 I John Demarest Coroner of the County of Bergen and province of New Jersey was present at the view of the body of one Nicholas Tuers then lying dead, together with the Jury which summoned to inquire of the death of the said Nicholas Tuers. At the same time a negro man named Harry belonging to Hendrick Christian Zabriski was suspected of having murdered the said Tuers but there was no proof of it, and the negro denied it. I asked if he was not afraid to touch Tuers? He said no he had not hurt him and immediately came up to the corpse lying in the coffin; and then Staats Storm one of the jurors said "I am not afraid of him" and stroked the dead man's face with his hand which made no alteration in the dead person and (as I did not put any faith in any of these trials) my back was turned toward the dead body when the jury or-

dered the negro to touch the dead man's face with his hand and then I heard a cry in the room of the people saying "he is the man" and I was desired to come to the dead body and was told that the said negro Harry had put his hand on Tuers' face and that the blood immediately run out of the nose of the dead man Tuers. I saw the blood on his face, and ordered the negro to rub his hand again on Tuers' face, he did so and immediately the blood again ran out of the said Tuers nostrils near a common table spoon at each nostril, as well as I can judge. Whereupon the people all charged him with being the murderer but he denied it for a few minutes and then confessed that he had murdered the said Nicholas Tuers by first striking him on the head with a ax, and then driving a wooden pin in his ear, though afterwards he said he struck him a second time, with the ax and then held him fast until he had done struggling. When that was done he awakened some of the family and said Tuers was dying he believed.—JOHANNES DEMEREST, Cor.[7]

This account is important as a historical document. For a slave to take the life of a white man in eighteenth-century New Jersey was a daring form of rebellion. Taken with other evidence (see "Folk Music, Folk Song, and Folk Dance") it shows that some slaves in New Jersey were not content with their condition of servitude. In a sense, this is evidence on a smaller scale of what took place in Virginia in 1831 during Nat Turner's rebellion.

But to folklorists this document has another significance. They recognize in it the "bleeding corpse" motif, which is found throughout the western world.[8] It shows up, for example, in New England in 1646 and 1674 in the writings of Cotton Mather, in the English and Scottish traditional ballad "Young Hunting," in the *Niebelungenlied* in Germany, in Shakespeare's *Richard III*, in Scottish court records in 1687, in North Carolina newspapers in 1875, and in current oral tradition from Ashe County, North Carolina.[9] That this kind of evidence was used in New Jersey in 1767 reveals the persistence and power of folk belief.

Folk beliefs are often contained in local legends. In fact, some folklorists consider legend to be a form of folk belief and use the term "belief legend."[10] The Jersey Devil legend is one example (see "Legend"). Another is legends about ghosts. In Burlington there is a tree known as the Pirate Tree. According to legend, Blackbeard the pirate buried his treasure under this tree and murdered one of his crew so that the dead man's ghost would stand guard over it. Some believe that a black dog was buried with the pirate, because a doglike apparition has also been seen in the vicinity. A written version of this belief legend appeared in 1844 in Barber and Howe's *Historical Collections of the State of New Jersey*.[11] It is a common folk belief that the ghost of a murdered person will haunt the scene of the crime.

The ghost of Hannah Caldwell is the subject of a legend based on a true incident of the Revolutionary War. The wife of the Reverend James Caldwell, minister of the Presbyterian church at Connecticut Farms (now Union), was killed by British soldiers on June 7, 1780, during the hostilities surrounding the Battle of Springfield. Ever since, her ghost has been reported at various places in the vicinity. One of the earliest written versions of the ghost story was in Theodore Sedgwick's *A Memoir of the Life of William Livingston* (1833). In this account, on the night after the shooting several drunken British soldiers broke into Liberty Hall, the mansion of Governor Livingston in Elizabeth, but they mistook one of the governor's daughters, who wore a white dress, for the ghost of Hannah Caldwell and retreated in fear.[12]

In the 1890s when Stephen Crane was a free-lance newspaper writer in New York City, he wrote two feature articles about New Jersey ghosts. One of them, "Ghosts on the Jersey Coast" (Sunday *Press*, November 11, 1894), contained six ghost stories: they dealt with the appearance of a ghostly light above the graves of shipwreck victims at Branchburg; the specter of a pirate ship with skeletons dangling from the mastheads at Shark River; a spectral Indian who in life had accidently poisoned his bride; a young man and a maiden who keep a ghostly lovers' tryst at Deal Beach; the ghost of a Tory at Long Beach who threatens fishermen with his knife; and a phantom black dog sighted along the Jersey Shore that dragged his dead master ashore from a shipwreck only to be killed by the pirates who caused the wreck. In another story, "The Ghostly Sphinx of Metedeconk" (New York *Press*, January 13, 1895), Crane wrote about a lady dressed in white who walks along the beach at midnight in search of the body of her lover who drowned at sea.[13]

Some ghost stories collected in New Jersey are associated with specific ethnic groups. For example, Anne H. Sidwa of Newark collected two legends pertaining to the Polish folk belief in the *topielce* (the soul of a drowned creature). The nasty owner of the paper mill in the town of Żywiec committed suicide by drowning himself in the River Soła. Once when Mrs. Sidwa's grandmother was crossing the bridge over the river she found herself being drawn irresistibly to the edge. This was believed to be the result of the *topielce* trying to lure her into the water with sirenlike music. What saved her was the fact that she was pregnant and accompanied by a young child; the *topielce* is afraid of unborn babes and innocent children.[14] Mrs. Sidwa's grandfather, who took over the operation of the paper mill after the suicide of its previous owner, also had an encounter with the *topielce*. Once when he was working late in his office he heard the door open at midnight, felt a blast of cold air, and heard the sound of footsteps behind him. He did not turn around but saw in the window the reflection of a form. It seemed to be made of light and was an unearthly color. The air felt cold and clammy. It then departed, leaving small rusty puddles. The experience turned his hair white.[15]

When people think about witchcraft what comes to mind is the witchcraft trials in Salem, Massachusetts, in the late seventeenth century. But the folk belief in witchcraft is not an isolated phenomenon that can be explained away in terms of the special circumstances of the time or the peculiar prejudices of the Puritans. There has been a continuous tradition of folk belief in witchcraft in Europe and America from the Middle Ages to the present.[16]

In 1730 the *Pennsylvania Gazette* described a trial by ordeal for witchcraft in Mount Holly, Burlington County. The defendants, a man and a woman, were accused of "making their Neighbours' Sheep dance in an uncommon Manner, and with causing Hogs to speak, and sing Psalms, &c." It was thought that "if the Accused were weighed in Scales against the Bible, the Bible would prove too heavy for them; or that, if they were bound and put into the River, they would swim." They were tested along with two of their accusers. The reported outcome was that both accused and accusers proved too heavy for the Bible. In the trial by water the male accuser sank, and everyone else floated. The story concluded:

> The more thinking Part of the Spectators were of [the] Opinion that any Person so bound and plac'd in the Water (unless they were mere Skin and Bones) would swim till their Breath was gone and their Lungs fill'd with Water. But it being the general Belief of the Populace, that the Womens Shifts, and the Garters with which they were bound help'd to support them; it is said they are to be tried again the next warm Weather, naked.[17]

However, this account has all the earmarks of a hoax. While the author is unknown, Benjamin Franklin was the owner of the *Pennsylvania Gazette* at that time, and he, of course, was known for this kind of satire.

Authentic examples of folk belief in witchcraft abound in the history of New Jersey. In 1668 the General Assembly of East New Jersey included as one of the "Capital Laws": "If any person be found to be a witch, either male or female, they shall be put to death."[18] This law was reenacted in 1675. A lawsuit filed by Abigail Sharp against Abraham Shotwell in the New Jersey Supreme Court charged that in 1727 in Woodbridge he falsely accused her of being "an old witch & had been flying all night & that he saw her . . . as he was coming home early in the morning and she was just lighted in a patch of beans." He was also accused of saying that "he heard a Noise on the top of his house & he Saw her . . . in the Shape of a Cat," and that she "bewitched that horse that Lies Dead in my field."[19]

A book published in 1792 about the "Morristown Ghost" was actually not about a ghost but about a hoax perpetrated by a Yankee trickster named Ransford Rogers. To set the stage by showing how superstitious the local people were, the anonymous author mentioned some authentic folk beliefs associated with witchcraft.

I was in Morristown, and happened to be in conversation with some gentlemen, who had, as it were, the faith of assurance in witchcraft. They informed me that there were several young women who were bewitched; and they had been harassed so much by witches for a long time, and all their experiments proved abortive, and the young women were so much debilitated they were fearful they would never recover their healths. They related several occurrences, that I think too simple to mention; but one instance was, "That an old lady was churning and being much fatigued, and unable to obtain butter, she at last concluded that the witches were in the churn, and immediately had recourse to experiments, which were, that of heating several horse-shoes, and putting them into the churn alternately: she burnt the devil out, and immediately obtained butter."

I perceived that the generality were apprehensive of witches riding them, and the greatest evidence of a witch was if a woman had any deformity, or had lived to that age to cause wrinkles in her face, she had appellation of a witch. There was another occurrence that happened on Sunday. They informed me, a man was driving his sheep from his grain, and an accident happened as they were jumping over a fence, one of the sheep broke its leg. The man for some time before supposed that the same sheep was bewitched. About the same time, an aged old lady returning from church, her horse unfortunately stumbled, she fell to the ground and broke her leg—. This was received as an indication that she was a witch: and in fact, if a horse had the belly-ache, or any beast was in agony of pain and behaved uncommon, the general opinion was that the creature was bewitched.[20]

This passage contains a number of traditional motifs associated with the folk belief in witchcraft that can be traced back to the Middle Ages in Europe. These include the belief that witches can prevent milk from being churned into butter, and that they can metamorphose into animals. Similar testimony was taken at the witchcraft trials in Salem, Massachusetts.

The belief in witches continued strong throughout the nineteenth century. Barber and Howe's *Historical Collections* cites a lecture given at the Camden Lyceum in the winter of 1841–1842 that described various charms used in Cumberland County to counteract witchcraft, among them that "it was customary to hang upon the neck by a string a piece of dried beef cut in the shape of a heart, with two needles stuck on in the form of a cross, as a protection against witches." The speaker continued:

Another safeguard was in the horse-shoe, which originally was nailed boldly over doors, and in places open to the eye; but as superstition dispelled before the light of a later day, those who pertinaciously clung to the ways of their fathers placed it out of sight, under the doorsteps, or in some other covert spot; or else they would apply it to some ostensibly useful purpose, such as a hook in the well-sweep, or as a catch to receive the gate-latch. . . . Another favorite place for the shoe, was on the inside of the hinder axle of wagons; and even to the present day it may be found nailed to the under side of the wheelbarrows of the negros in the Philadelphia market.[21]

Witches could be men as well as women. In 1889 such a case came to light in Bergen County. It was reported in an amateur newspaper, the *Landscape*, published by Alfred P. Smith, a black, out of his home in Saddle River.

Some weeks ago household goods in the blacksmith's John Bell's at Park Ridge, were frequently disarranged or moved from place to place by some unseen agency, and the suspicion that the disturbance was owing to the diabolical influence of witches was fully confirmed by the repeated appearance of the "witch" himself (a strange man) to a fifteen year old daughter threatening a dreadful vengeance for alleged unfriendliness to the witch. Day after day the residence of Bell was thronged with inquisitive persons, and the reports they spread raised the hair upright on Park Ridge heads and sent shivers down Park Ridge spines. The knives and forks jumped up on the table and danced. The contents of the match boxes and hairpins flew about the room and circled around the head of a voracious visitor. An almanac, a work which played an interesting part in the proceedings, pursued the inhabitants of the house, in spite of attempts to confine it by nailing it to the floor, from room to room wherever they went. A soothing-iron wafted through the air, followed in the same manner, an empty pair of trousers were seen by an intelligent observer walking down the stairway behind its owner, &c.[22]

Such a spirit, which causes strange happenings, is known as a poltergeist. It has become transmuted in popular culture into the haunted house. Testimony similar to the account in the *Landscape* was given at the Salem witchcraft trials almost 200 years earlier.

The folk belief in witchcraft continues in the twentieth century. In the early 1940s Herbert Halpert collected in the Pine Barrens a cycle of stories about the witch Peggy Clevenger, who supposedly kept a hotel named the Half-Way Place near Red Oak Grove. Halpert noted that in these folktales there was no mention of the compacts with the devil or witches' Sabbaths common in the European witchcraft tradition. Rather the tales tended to deal with the power of the witch to transform herself into an animal and to cause and cure illnesses.[23] In the late 1960s I collected in the Ramapo Mountains similar stories about the alleged witches Handsome Abbey and Black Mag. Sam Van Dunk of Livingston Manor, New York, told me how one night his cousin injured a white cat that crossed his path, and the next morning Jake De Groat couldn't get out of bed. The suspicion was the Jake De Groat was the cat that was injured the night before.[24]

Among Hispanics the belief in witchcraft takes the form of a folk religion known as *santería*. This is a syncretistic folk religion in which Catholic saints are associated with African deities. For example, Changò, the Yoruban god of fire and war, is associated with John the Baptist, and Elegguá, the messenger of the gods who also protects entrances to homes, is associated with Saint Peter. Part of this folk religion is the belief in possession by evil spirits and illnesses caused by witchcraft. *Santeros* (traditional practitioners) have the power to cure these illnesses, often by prescribing charms, amulets, and herbs available in *botánicas* (herb stores) (see "Folk Medicine").

Folk beliefs vary from one ethnic group to another. In 1975 Cynthia Joy Skibo of Edison, a student at Douglass College, collected Hungarian folk beliefs

47

from her maternal grandmother, Mary Rozman, who was born in Hungary in 1903. Mrs. Rozman, who came from a peasant family, migrated to New Jersey and worked as a farm cook in Dayton, in a cigar factory in Perth Amboy, and in a leather factory in New Brunswick. Among the folk beliefs she contributed are the following:

- On the New Year's morning you not supposed to take out the garbage because you take out the luck.
- On New Year's day, if a man comes to your house, you gonna have luck all year. If a lady comes, that's bad news.
- [When a woman is pregnant] if the baby hanging low in the front on her, it is a girl.
- Thirteen names you put in a hat. You do it on December 13. What name you pull out, that's who your boyfriend gonna be.
- On December 13, you clean the floor, you sweep. After you sweep, you take the dustpan and at 12 o'clock you throw the dirt into the yard. The way the dust flies, that way you going to marry, a man from that country.[25]

These folk beliefs are not simply ethnic, they also represent a form of women's folklore. They reflect the concerns, biology, and work roles of the traditional Hungarian peasant woman. They also reflect the special importance of certain dates, certain numbers, and certain hours of the day.

Another aspect of folk belief pertains to weather lore—traditional ways of predicting the weather or its effects on human affairs. In the mid-eighteenth century Peter Kalm recorded several examples in New Sweden.

I was told, that it was a very certain forecast of bad weather, when you saw clouds on the horizon in the southwest, about sunset, and that if those clouds sank below the horizon a while later it would rain the next day, though all the forenoon were fair and clear. But if some clouds were seen in the southwest on the horizon at sunset, and they rose some time later, one could expect fair weather the next day. . . .

An old Swede foretold a change in the weather, because it was calm today; for when there had been wind for a few days and a calm followed, they said there would be rain or snow, or some other change in the weather. I was likewise told that some people here were of the opinion that the weather commonly altered on Friday. In case it had rained or blown hard all week and a change was to happen, it would commonly fall on Friday.—How far the forecast has been true appears from my own observations of the weather, to which I refer.[26]

Several Polish "weather notions" were collected in 1959 from the Sidwa family of Newark.

> When it begins to rain, fix your attention on a small puddle of water. If large bubbles form, *and float about*, you are in for an all-day rain. If bubbles form, but break at once, you will have only a shower.
>
> On washday, if it is cloudy but doesn't actually rain, and if the sun peeks through now and then, you may know the boys still love you. But if it rains, you will know you have gone by, and the boys are for you a lost cause.[27]

This kind of weather lore tends to be more common among agricultural and seafaring people than among those whose occupations and activities are pursued indoors.

There is much ethnic folk belief associated with the eyes. One example is the evil eye, a tradition in many cultures. Anne H. Sidwa describes a Polish folk belief: "If your eye itches or smarts, note whether it is the right one or the left. If the right, there are tears ahead for you, if the left, smiles."[28] (See "Folk Medicine.") In Polish folklore collected in New Jersey there are "Talking Eyes" and "Devil Eyes," associated with the idea that it is bad luck to look in a mirror at night for fear that you might see the devil. According to Mrs. Sidwa:

> "Look out," my mother would say, repeating her own mother's warning (got from a gypsy in Hungary!), "you might see a Devil if you look. Not in the mirror will he appear, but *in your own eyes*. Then your eyes will change to Devil Eyes, and you will be lost."
>
> Talking Eyes, though good eyes, most readily become Devil Eyes. Talking Eyes can comment with no word spoken, and read your whole life simply by looking hard at you. The danger time for the Devil to appear is that *zła godzina*, that evil hour the Devil so loves. If he catches you looking in the mirror in that hour, he will possess you on the spot, and it will be very hard for you to get free. For a second you will see the Devil *in your own eyes*, and you will know you are in his power.[29]

The symbolic fascination with this particular body organ is subject to several different interpretations. Some scholars associate the gaze of the eye with vanity, envy, or narcissism. Others see the eye as a cross-cultural archetype symbolizing the window to the soul. It was an important symbol in ancient

Egypt.[30] Symbols, however, are not restricted to single meanings, and it is these many possible meanings that make the study of folklore so psychologically informative.

Folk beliefs reflect the world view prevalent in certain subcultures. Too often our understanding of particular periods is informed solely by intellectual history. Those historians who write about the *Zeitgeist*, the spirit of an age, tend to base their statements on the world view of intellectuals and those influenced by them. A more comprehensive history of human culture must take into account that for many people there has been a continuous tradition of folk belief that bears little relationship to the beliefs and thoughts of intellectuals or of the literary elites of society. The study of folk belief reminds us that there is not a single "American mind" that holds true for all people in all places at all times. Nor was there ever a single New Jersey "mind."

FOLK MEDICINE refers to the etiology (notions about causation) and treatment of illnesses and injuries, which lie outside the framework of modern, professional, scientific medicine and pharmacy. According to Don Yoder, the folklorist, folk medicine has existed in an uneasy relationship with professional medicine since the eighteenth century. Certain ideas once accepted in the canon of professional medicine—such as the four humors—remain part of folk medicine. On the other hand, some folk herb cures have come to be accepted by professional pharmacists and doctors. Yoder defines two branches of folk medicine: "natural" remedies, such as herb cures, and magical and religious beliefs about healing.[1] Thus some aspects of folk medicine overlap with folk belief (see "Folk Belief"). In the folk mentality, however, no distinction is made between herb cures and magic; they are considered equally effective.

Yoder considers American Indian medicinal beliefs and practices as a separate category, which he calls "primitive" medicine. However, he finds that primitive" medicine and folk medicine have the same world view and the same magical techniques.[2] Throughout this book I include the Lenape Indians in my definition of folk. By doing so in this chapter we get a fuller idea of the variety of folk medicine beliefs and practices in New Jersey.

The Reverend John Heckewelder was a missionary to the Lenape in the late eighteenth century shortly after they were forced to move from Pennsylvania and New Jersey to Ohio. In 1819 he wrote about the Lenape Indian practitioners of folk medicine in the Ohio Valley.

> There are physicians of both sexes, who take considerable pains to acquire a correct knowledge of the properties and medicinal virtues of plants, roots and barks, for the benefit of their fellow-man. They are very careful to have at all times a full assortment of their medicines on hand, which they gather and collect at the proper seasons, sometimes fetching them from the distance of several days' journey from their homes, then they cure or dry them properly, tie them up in small bundles, and preserve them for use.[3]

He learned that the tribal healers were not the only ones who had a knowledge of the healing properties of roots and plants; each warrior was also made acquainted with them in case he was wounded in battle. Heckewelder attested to the effectiveness of these cures.

> I have myself been benefited and cured by taking their emetics and their medicines in fevers, and by being sweated after their manner while labouring under a stubborn rheumatism. I have also known many, both whites and Indians, who have with the same success resorted to Indian physicians while labouring under diseases. . . . I firmly believe that there is no wound, unless it should be absolutely mortal, or beyond the skill of our own good practitioners, which an Indian surgeon (I mean the best of them) will not succeed in healing.[4]

What Heckewelder wrote about the Lenape Indians after they had left New Jersey is supported by earlier descriptions of the Indians while they were still here. In 1638 David Pietersz. de Vries, the Dutch patroon of Staten Island, described their sweat lodges.

> When they wish to cleanse themselves of their foulness they go in the autumn, when it begins to grow cold, and make, away off, near a running brook, a small oven, large enough for three or four men to lie in

it. In making it they first take twigs of trees, and then cover them tight with clay, so that smoke cannot escape. This being done, they take a parcel of stones, which they heat in a fire and then put in the oven, and when they think it is sufficiently hot, they take the stones out again, and go and lie in it, men and women, boys and girls and come out so perspiring, that every hair has a drop of sweat on it. In this state they plunge into the cold water; saying that it is healthy, but I let its healthfulness pass; they then become entirely clean, and are more attractive than before.[5]

De Vries explained this ritual as being related to cleanliness, but Heckewelder said it was considered by the Indians to be beneficial to health. The two are, of course, related.

In the 1740s the Reverend David Brainerd described the Indian powwows as "a sort of persons who are supposed to have a power of foretelling future events, or recovering the sick, at least oftentimes, and of charming, enchanting, or poisoning persons to death by their magic divinations."[6] He mentioned one case in particular:

The Indian was bitten with a snake, and was in extreme pain with the bite. Whereupon the diviner, who was applied to for his recovery, told him, that at such a time he had promised, that the next deer he killed, he would sacrifice it to some great power, but had broken his promise. Now, said he, that great power has ordered this snake to bite you for your neglect. The Indian confessed it was so, but said he had never told any body of it.[7]

Brainerd considered the influence of the Indian powwows a hindrance to his efforts to convert the Indians to Christianity. Yet European settlers in America had their own folk medicine, including both herb cures and magic, some of which they brought with them and some of which they borrowed from the Indians.

In the seventeenth century Adriaen van der Donck, the patroon of Colendonck (present-day Yonkers), wrote of the healing herbs used by both the Dutch and the Indians in New Netherland.

No reasonable person will doubt that there are not many medicinal and healing plants in the New Netherlands. A certain chirurgeon who was also a botanist, had a beautiful garden there, wherein a great variety of medicinal wild plants were collected, but the owner has removed and the garden lies neglected. Because sickness does not prevail much, I suppose the subject has received less attention. . . . The land is full of different kinds of herbs and trees besides those enumerated, among which there undoubtedly are good simplicia, with which discreet persons would do much good; for we know that the Indians with roots, bulbs, leaves, &c. cure dangerous wounds and old sores, of which we have seen many instances.[8]

When Peter Kalm visited Raccoon (present-day Swedesboro in Gloucester County) in the mid-eighteenth century he wrote:

The Swedes had this winter told me the agricultural and medical uses of many plants, to which they gave names unknown to me; they could not then show me those plants on account of the season and by their deficient and erroneous descriptions I was not able to guess what plants they meant.[9]

If Kalm, who was a naturalist, was unfamiliar with these plant names, we can probably conclude that there were some differences between the Old World and the New World herbal lore.

By the time of the Revolution folk medicine was commonly practiced in the homes of New Jersey. In *Medicine in Revolutionary New Jersey*, David L. Cowen says that some home remedies may have been learned from the Indians. He mentions a commonplace book of the Hankinson family of Reading, dated 1787, which contains sundry "infalible," "efectual," "Indian Squaw's" cures. One of these was to use "buternut" bark from the north side of the tree, steeped in vinegar for half an hour, to cure a fever.[10]

With the professionalization of medicine and pharmacy, folk medicine and professional medicine began to diverge. In 1766 the Medical Society of New Jersey was established, and in 1772 New Jersey became the first province to require the examination and licensing of physicians.[11] Despite attempts to limit the practice of medicine to professionals, the folk practitioners continued to effect their cures.

In the eighteenth and nineteenth centuries some of these folk practitioners were called "Indian doctors." *The Indian Doctor's Dispensatory*, by Peter Smith (1753–1816), was published in Cincinnati in 1812. Smith lived in Ohio; his father, Hezekiah Smith, had lived in New Jersey. The author described himself and his father as Indian doctors. "I call myself an *Indian doctor*, because I have incidentally obtained a knowledge of many of the simples used by the Indians; but chiefly because I have obtained my knowledge generally in the like manner that the Indians do."[12] He wrote that he had had a "slight classical education" in his early life and had read some medical and anatomy books.

> But as I never pretended to live by my practice, I kept very little of the medicine of the shops; consequently my advices to my friends mostly were simples; and by this means I have by continued observation come to be of the opinion, that our best medicines grow in the woods and gardens.[13]

His book contains a mixture of herb cures and magic cures. He gave uses for such herbs as black snake root, squaw root, and butternut bark pills. He recommended applying a dead toad to a wen (a type of cyst) and curing a toothache by discarding at an isolated place a rag containing fingernail and toenail clippings, a lock of hair, and some blood from the gums of the mouth. He mentioned a cure for venomous bites and stings.

> To cure any of these, you may only wet a thimbleful of indigo with good vinegar to make it into mud, and apply it to the bite or sting. . . .
>
> The above is a discovery lately made in Sussex County, New Jersey, where the snake called the pilot, or copper-head, was so common and bit so many, that the mowers would scarcely venture into the meadows, until the discovery was made. They then kept some of the indigo mud by them, and found that they could cure themselves at once by this simple application.[14]

One of the most fascinating figures in New Jersey folk medicine was a self-educated black doctor from Medford, James Still. He was known as "the doctor of the Pines," but since he was not a professionally trained physician his cures qualify as folk medicine. In his autobiography, published in 1877, he gave an account of a lady in Mount Holly who suffered from an inflammation of the uterus after giving birth. Professional doctors were called in, but their treatments were ineffective. After seven weeks the woman's husband went to Dr. Still for help. Still warned the husband that one of the doctors would not continue to treat the woman if he knew that Dr. Still had seen her, but the husband insisted that Dr. Still treat his wife nevertheless. Dr. Still first prescribed some medicine, the specific name of which he does not provide in his account. The man showed the medicine to the physicians without telling them it came from Dr. Still, and they said that it was as good as anything they knew. After a few more days and repeated entreaties Dr. Still finally agreed to see the woman.

I went over in the train on Friday afternoon, took with me such preparations as I thought needful, and on my arrival at the house found the lady prostrate upon the bed. She extended her hand, and, with tears in her eyes, exclaimed, "Oh doctor, I wish you would do something to relieve me!"

On investigation of the case, I made application to the diseased parts, left medicine, also an external application, gave orders to the nurse how to proceed, bade her good-by, and left. On the following Sunday she was able to sit up and eat some breakfast. The family doctor had called on Saturday morning, and, upon being told that I had visited the house, quietly left, without so much as asking after his patient. Upon a certain occasion the wife of this same physician remarked to a friend of mine, "That black man can't know anything, because he had no education." This was the remark of an Eastern lady with a fair share of education, herself, brains small, prejudice and ignorance large.[15]

This incident is revealing not only of racial hostility but also of the clash between practitioners of folk medicine and professional doctors that resulted from the professionalization of medicine in the nineteenth century. This was a cause of much concern to Dr. Still, as he wrote in his autobiography.

I am sorry to say that most of those cures which are effected outside of the medical faculty are reproachfully spoken of by them, although they be performed by men of candor and honesty. They cry "quack," and teach their adherents that it is better to die soon by their treatment than to live long by that of one who has not been to college or won a diploma. As though the keys of knowledge were exclusively within the university walls! As though nature had not written truth and science in every root of the forest and in every leaf that grows.[16]

Indeed, many of Dr. Still's medicines were in fact herb cures, involving such medicinal plants as horehound, bloodroot, catnip, and skunk cabbage.[17]

Midwives might also be considered practitioners of folk medicine. Until recently they learned their techniques through oral tradition, rather than in medical or nursing schools. Martha Austin Reeves (1760–1832) of Cumberland County was a midwife whose record book was fortunately preserved. When her husband John died in 1811, she became a midwife. Her record book consists mostly of a registry of births, but it also contains some folk remedies, including the following "receipt" for the "bloody flux" (a discharge of blood):

As soon as you find the flux is bad, if possible before it comes to the dissentery, drink three or four teacupsfull of melted mutton suet dayly, say one every four hours; let the food be the flour of well parched Corn, made into a paze [a variant of "pease," here probably referring to a porridge or pudding] with new milk, sweetened with loaf sugar; let the drink be nothing else but a strong tea made of chipped log wood or red oak bark, sweetened with loaf sugar; when you find it is checked make the tea weaker; should you stop it too soon take a little salts or senea; the cure is perfected in five, six or seven days.[18]

Midwives no longer use such folk remedies, but in earlier generations there was a close relationship between folk beliefs about childbirth and folk medicine (see "Folk Belief").

Folk medicine continues to be practiced in both rural and urban areas of New Jersey. In 1969 I collected an account of "taking the fire [pain] out of a burn" from one of the Ramapo Mountain People. James De Groat of Spring Valley, New York, told me that as a young man working as a molder in a foundry in Mahwah he had burned himself seriously one day. His wife convinced him to send for a neighbor named Steve De Groat who knew how to "take the fire out of the burn."

> JAMES DE GROAT: So he came over. And he said, "Well, take the bandage off." So my wife did. So he got down on his knees. Right on to the ground. He was in my yard. And, ah, he took his finger and he circled it, first one way and then back the other way around, and he kept blowing with the breath of his mouth over it. He did that a few times, and while he was doing it, all the pain left, and I slept like a log. And I guarantee you, I do say that I'll swear by that method that this Steve De Groat did for me.[19]

This cure has been widely reported in Europe and the United States. Mr. De Groat informed me that the ability to perform this cure could only be learned from a member of the opposite sex—a common rule in folk cures. Often verses from the Bible are recited when effecting the cure.

Another modern example of folk medicine is curing the evil eye. In 1977 a Rutgers University student, Barbara Schulz, tape-recorded an interview with Anna Vaccaro of Paramus, who explained how her Italian mother could cure the evil eye.

> ANNA VACCARO: The evil eye. Like my mother used to do the evil eye, not do it but take it away from someone who had it. People would

come and ask her to please do this, and she would do it. She could also tell who gave it to them. The horns. That's what the evil eye is. The horns. My mother would do whatever she had to do. She could teach us if she wanted this one prayer. It had to be taught to you Christmas Eve for five minutes. If you didn't learn it in five minutes, you had to wait until next year. That's the only time you are allowed to learn it.

She would do it with water, you put it in a bowl with oil and salt, and she would say the prayer. One time when she did it for a woman who had it really bad, a cross appeared in the bowl. I was only a young girl at the time. I ran.

She then narrated an incident in which her mother cured a sick baby girl, who had had a temperature of 105 degrees. The doctor wanted to put her in the hospital.

ANNA VACCARO: He said there was nothing more that they could do at home for her. She had pneumonia. They asked my mother to come and take the evil eye away. My mother said that she could not come, that she had to do it in her own home. She told her to bring a piece of the clothing the girl was wearing. The woman brought the girl's clothes. My mother said the prayer, and before the woman got home, the baby was up and playing around.

Mrs. Vaccaro corrected herself, saying, "But it had to be done for three days at the same time. The woman came for the three days, and the girl never went into the hospital."

Mrs. Vaccaro went on to explain that the evil eye could be given accidentally. "It can be given without even meaning to. It's done. Sometimes you say, 'God bless her; she's so cute!' Sometimes by just staring at a person they can get a headache." When asked how to avoid being afflicted, she answered, "Wear the horns! I have two big ones; my sister gave them to me. You are supposed to hang one at the back door."[20] The evil eye is found in many cultures. In Italian it is called the *malocchio*. In Yiddish, the term *keyn eyn nehore* (literally, "no evil eye") is used to ward off the evil eye. The expression is used, for example, after complimenting a baby, which is similar to the traditional Italian practice, or after any compliment or statement of optimistic expectations. It is approximately equivalent to "knock on wood."

Herb cures are still practiced in many New Jersey cities. Several years ago I had a black student whose grandmother used to make yearly trips from Newark to her former home in Virginia to gather herbs for home remedies. In the Iron-bound section of Newark some of the grocery stores sell herbs shipped from Portugal in specially packaged boxes with handwritten labels. It is believed that they are more effective in healing illnesses.

Many New Jersey cities, including Union City, Trenton, Paterson, Newark, New Brunswick, and Vineland, have *botánicas* that sell religious articles and herbs to a largely Hispanic clientele. The *botánica* is the adjunct of two folk religions among Hispanics: *santería*, the worship of Catholic saints who have become associated with various African deities, and *espiritísmo*, which involves the belief in possession by and communication with spirits. Both involve a folk medicine. A study issued in 1977 based on eighty interviews with Puerto Rican adults in Vineland, most of whom came from Utuado and its vicinity in Puerto Rico, showed that one out of four went to the *botánica* after the doctor gave them a prescription for the pharmacist, and 65 percent said that "they know of and practice home remedies." Some herb cures included teas, potions, and syrups made from various combinations of garlic (*ajo*), ginger (*jengibre*), clover (*clavo*), and cinnamon (*canela*). A potion of rue (*ruda*) and sweet marjoram (*mejorana*) mixed with olive oil was used for labor pain; warm teas made from lettuce leaves and wild flowers to soothe the stomach of a fretful infant; a syrupy blend of onions and sugar administered daily for asthma; hot teas made from lemon and camomile (*manzanilla*) for stomach aches; and a hot tea made from the leaves of the sour orange tree (*naranjo*) for nervousness. The conclusion was that Puerto Ricans in Vineland were adhering to and transmitting to their children both modern medicine and Puerto Rican folk medicine.[21]

The study of folk medicine helps us to understand the historical process of acculturation. When European immigrants came to live and work in American industrial cities they had to adjust to a whole new way of life. Part of this adjustment occurred when they confronted the doctors and nurses in big city hospitals. In 1938, in *South Italian Folkways in Europe and America*, Phyllis H. Williams documented this clash between cultures as experienced by one group of transplanted peasants.[22] A similar clash occurred when people migrated from a rural area to an urban area within the United States. This was the case with the Great Migration of American blacks from the rural South to the urban North. In 1971 Ellen J. Stekert, the folklorist, showed that the same problem existed for southern Appalachian mountain people who migrated to Detroit.[23] Thus folk medicine has implications for the study of social history and current social problems. Medical schools have begun to take account of the folk medical beliefs of their patients; some have engaged folklorists and medical anthropologists to help in training a new generation of doctors.

# Folk Music, Folk Song, and Folk Dance

I T IS useful to divide music into three types: folk music, popular music, and art music. Folk music has an oral tradition and is usually performed by non-professionals in small group settings. Art music or what some people call classical music is generally composed by academically trained composers. It is usually published and copyrighted, and performed by academically trained musicians. Popular music is also usually composed and performed by professionals. It is generally published and copyrighted, and is designed to have broad appeal and to be distributed through the mass media.

At a certain level these distinctions break down. For example, a folk song originally in the oral tradition might be recorded by a professional singer. Or a traditional folk singer might be asked to perform before a large audience at a folk festival. Field recordings of folk music, such as those produced by Folkways Records or the Library of Congress Archive of Folk Song, might be made available for sale on phonograph records. Despite this, the music remains folk music. The point is that there are stylistic differences between folk, popular, and art music. These differences should be appreciated on their own terms, rather than being the subject of invidious comparisons. This is especially true when one tries not only to enjoy music as entertainment, but to study it as an integral part of culture.

The tribal music of the American Indians is often considered as something other than folk music. Generally folk music is restricted to the Euro-American and Afro-American musical traditions. But just as Lenape myths and legends should be considered part of New Jersey folklore, so too should Lenape music. The Lenape Indians had a singing and dancing tradition, which was associated with their religious and secular celebrations. Adriaen van der Donck wrote about them in 1656.

Feasts and great assemblages are not common among the Indians, yet they occur sometimes, and on special occasions, as on the subjects of peace, war, alliances, treaties, and devotions, or to counsel the devil on some approaching event, or in relation to the fruitfulness of the seasons, or to celebrate some successful occurrence by frolicking and dancing, as at the conclusion of peace, or to make war with some neighbouring people.[1]

Unfortunately we have no detailed descriptions of their singing and dancing dating from the period in which they inhabited New Jersey. There are descriptions of the Big House Ceremony, including details about dances, songs, and musical instruments, but these pertain to the time after the Delaware Indians settled in the Indian Territory in Oklahoma. It is conceivable that by then they had adopted many traditions that they did not have in New Jersey.

We also have John Heckewelder's description of their singing dating from shortly after their move to Ohio.

> Their songs are by no means unharmonious. They sing in chorus; first the men and then the women. At times the women join in the general song, or repeat the strain which the men have just finished. It seems like two parties singing in questions and answers, and is upon the whole very agreeable and enlivening. After thus singing for about a quarter of an hour, they conclude each song with a loud yell, which I must confess is not in concord with the rest of the music; it is not unlike the cat-bird which closes its pretty song with mewing like a cat. . . . The singing always begins by one person only, but others soon fall in successively until the general chorus begins, the drum beating all the while to mark the time. The voices of the women are clear and full, and their intonations generally correct.[2]

Heckewelder also described their warlike songs, which were associated with the war dance. This dance imitated the movements of combat.

> They are dressed and painted, or rather bedaubed with paint, in a manner suitable to the occasion. They hold the murderous weapon in their hand, and imitate in their dance all the warlike attitudes, motions and actions which are usual in an engagement with the enemy, and strive to excel each other by their terrific looks and gestures. They generally perform round a painted post set up for that purpose, in a large room or place enclosed or surrounded with posts, and roofed with the bark of trees; sometimes also this dance is executed in the open air. There every man presents himself in warrior's array, contemptuously looking upon the painted post, as if it was the enemy whom he was about to engage;

as he passes by it he strikes, stabs, grasps, pretends to scalp, to cut, to run through; in short, endeavors to show what he would do to a real enemy, if he had him in his power.[3]

Whoever joins the dance is considered to have enlisted for the battle. Heckewelder described the dance as the Indian mode of military recruiting. The war songs were sung in short lines or sentences as detached parts, rather than completely through in their entirety. Thus they resembled the formulas common in the Afro-American blues. Heckewelder translated one of these war songs.

> O poor me!
> Who am going out to fight the enemy,
> And know not whether I shall return again,
> To enjoy the embraces of my children
> And my wife.
> O poor creature!
> Whose life is not in his own hands,
> Who has no power over his own body,
> But tries to do his duty
> For the welfare of his nation.
> O! thou Great Spirit above!
> Take pity on my children
> And on my wife!
> Prevent their mourning on my account!
> Grant that I may be successful in this attempt—
> That I may slay my enemy,
> And bring home the trophies of war
> To my dear family and friends,
> That we may rejoice together.
> O! take pity on me!
> Give me strength and courage to meet my enemy,
> Suffer me to return again to my children,
> To my wife
> And to my relations!
> Take pity on me and preserve my life
> And I will make to thee a sacrifice.[4]

The plaintive tone of this song contradicts the stereotype we have of Indian war dances and songs. It enables us to empathize with the universal theme of young men going off to war.

Another kind of song recounted the singer's personal exploits in war. It was done in a kind of half-singing recitative to the accompaniment of a drum. The order of recitation was determined by seniority, the oldest warrior going first. They would go around the group several times with their short recitals in what Heckewelder described as "a kind of alternate chant." It was considered an insult if the order of recitation did not reflect the seniority of each warrior. Heckewelder witnessed an occasion when an insulted warrior stepped out of the circle in which he was dancing and killed an upstart who had usurped his position.

The ethnomusicologist Charles Kaufman has shown that the strict religious principles of the Dutch, the Puritans, and the Quakers who settled in New Jersey discouraged the development of music during the colonial period.[5] He noted that in 1677 the General Assembly of East Jersey banned the following behavior on the Sabbath: "namely, staggering, realing, drinking, cursing, swearing, quarreling, or singing any vain Songs, or Tunes of the same."[6] In 1716 the Philadelphia Yearly Meeting, which had jurisdiction over Quakers in New Jersey, advised "that care be taken to prevent Friends, Children, and all professing Truth from going to, or being in anyways concerned in plays, games, lotteries, music, and dancing."[7] An Immorality Act passed by the New Jersey legislature in 1798 banned "interludes or plays, dancing, singing, fiddling, or other music for the sake of merriment . . . on the Christian Sabbath, or first day of the week called Sunday."[8] And an account in 1801 of the conversion of the Quaker Edward Andrews refers to him as a resident "in the Jersey, near the sea-shore, among a wild sort of people, Indians and others—vain and loose in their conversation; fond of frolicking, music, and dancing; among these he acted the part of fiddler." Upon his conversion he resolved "to break the fiddle in pieces, which when done his heart rejoiced, and he felt a strength of hope rising in him, that God would give him further power over all his vanities."[9]

Despite the ban on secular singing, especially on the Sabbath, the Quakers and the Dutch had a form of religious folk music. For the Quakers this took the form of a singsong preaching style, which Peter Kalm described in the mid-eighteenth century.

In their preaching the Quakers have a peculiar mode of expression, which is half singing, with a strange cadence and accent, and ending each cadence, as it were, with a full or partial sob. Each cadence consists of from two to four syllables, but sometimes more, according to the demand of the words and meaning; i.e. my friends // put in your mind // we can // do nothing // good of our self // without God's // help and assistance // etc. In the beginning the sobbing is not heard so plainly, but the deeper and farther the reader or preacher gets into his sermon the more violent is the sobbing between the cadences. The speaker to-day had no gestures, but turned in various directions; sometimes he placed a hand on his chin; and during most of the sermon kept buttoning and unbuttoning his vest. The gist of his sermon was that we can do nothing of ourselves without the help of our Savior. When he had stood for a while using his sing-song method he changed his manner of delivery and spoke in a more natural way, or as ministers do when they read a prayer. Shortly afterwards, however, he reverted to his former practice, and at the end, just as he seemed to have attained a certain momentum he stopped abruptly, sat down and put on his hat.[10]

This Quaker singsong preaching style was recorded in West New Jersey as well as eastern Pennsylvania.

Margaret Van Brunt Moore Gausman, born in 1839 of Dutch parents in English Neighborhood, remembered how the *dominies* (ministers) of the Dutch Reformed church would "line" the hymns in the traditional folk manner.

Before we had hymn books, the Dominie used to line the hymns. One time he began:
> "The light iss dim, I cannot see.
> I haf not brought my specks mit me."
And the congregation repeated,
> "The light iss dim, I cannot see.
> I haf not brought my specks mit me."
While the Dominie continued,
> "I did not say to line this hymn,
> I only said the light was dim."[11]

With the migration of other ethnic groups, such as the Scots, Scotch-Irish, Irish, Germans, and Africans, folk music and folk dance began to flourish. In fact, folk singing and dancing even began to take hold among the conservative Jersey Dutch. Mrs. Gausman told the following short narrative: "Young Dr. Poppin was a minister at the True Reform Church. At supper at my home one time he was telling me about the lively game he had been playing. He described the Virginia Reel. 'You've been dancing!' I told him. 'Was that dancing?'"[12]

Mrs. Gausman knew numerous Anglo-American and native American ballads, including "Roy's Wife of Aldivalloch," "Polly Won't You Ki' Me, Oh," "The Battle of the Constitution and the Guerriere," "Jimmy Polk," "Yankee Doodle," "Poor Old Horse," and a cante fable (half-story, half-song) about the battle of Tripoli.[13] These songs are indications of acculturation on the part of the Jersey Dutch.

Little if any research has been done on Afro-American folk music in New Jersey. According to Charles Kaufman,

New Jersey's slaves must have carried with them the complex music of their African homeland, an art that remains only as an influence on our popular music. Like other folk music, it rarely appears in print and depends for its survival on word-of-mouth and imitative transmission from singer to singer, from performer to performer. Because of this we have little specific information about folk music of our early days; therefore it can be discussed with little degree of certainty.[14]

There is, however, a fragment of a song that indicates the existence of a slave-song tradition in New Jersey. It was remembered in 1888 by Alfred P. Smith, the black editor of the *Landscape*. He wrote that it was sung by slaves in Bergen County.

> Cold, frosty morning
> Nigger berry good.
> Wid his axe on his shoulder,
> And way to the wood,
> Wid a piece of cold pancake,
> And a little hog's fat,
> And de grumble like de debble,
> If you get too much of dat.[15]

The caricature of the Afro-American dialect in this song fragment was a publication convention of the time, but the song is also interesting in that it documents a dissatisfaction of slaves with their situation.

A reminiscence by Margaret Gausman seems to indicate the existence of a blues tradition in New Jersey in the late nineteenth century.

At the same corner two colored men killed a store keeper. His name was Alfred Myers. He had spent his last evening with my sister, Elizabeth, on our front stoop. Then that night he got terribly cut up and mangled. They caught them both. One got twenty years in prison in Trenton. One got hung. As he rode along in an open cart, he sang out—

> Hi-jim-along, I'm tired of waiting.
> Hi-jim-along, why don't they come?
> Hi-jim-along, I'm tired of waiting.
> Hi-jim-along, why don't they come?[16]

Unfortunately we have no records of this music that can enable us to view it from an Afro-American perspective.

There is evidence that, as elsewhere in America, during the nineteenth century blacks in New Jersey played European instruments to accompany whites dancing at frolics and other such gatherings. In John Hosey Osborn's *Life in the Old Dutch Homesteads* there is a photograph captioned "Yon, the fiddler, and Sam, the Witch Doctor." It shows two black men standing in a barnyard with a hay barracks (a haystack with a movable roof) in the rear. Yon has a fiddle under his chin, and Sam is holding a shotgun in his arms.[17]

Some southern blacks settled in South Jersey prior to the Civil War, attracted by the presence of Quaker abolitionists in that area. Lydia Parrish, author of *Slave Songs of the Georgia Sea Islands*, who grew up in the late nineteenth century as a Quaker in Salem County, commented upon the paradox of southern blacks known for their singing living among Quakers known for their silent meditation. "I was born in a Quaker community, thirty miles south of Philadelphia, where descendants of slaves—and some ex-slaves themselves—were the only singers. Theirs was the only music worthy of the name that I heard in my youth."[18] While this slave-song tradition in South Jersey flourished for a while, it was short-lived.

> For many generations prior to the War Between the States, colored people—mostly from tide-water Virginia—had secretly crossed the river from Delaware into Salem County, New Jersey, where they found sanctuary among the Friends. . . . In my childhood they so greatly outnumbered the white voters that we had a colored overseer of the roads. At that time there was no lack of spontaneous music and laughter among them. However, in the late eighties, when a railroad was put through their village, the sophisticated Philadelphia Negroes were enabled to show the country cousins that they were hopelessly out-of-date. Then it was that the dull but stylish hymns of the white man sup-

planted those of the old regime, and standardized behavior became the rule.[19]

She noted that she did not hear slave songs again until she visited Georgia in 1909.

With the Great Migration of rural blacks from the South to northern cities such as Newark after World War I, there was a fresh infusion of Afro-American folk music into New Jersey. Traditional call and response preaching and gospel singing in storefront churches became common. Today Springfield Avenue in Newark probably has more storefront churches than any other street in New Jersey. Folk blues played by nonprofessional musicians on acoustic guitars can still be heard at family barbecues in Newark and Orange. But whereas urban blues developed in midwestern cities like Chicago and Detroit, the cosmopolitan atmosphere of northern New Jersey cities, with their proximity to New York City, soon made jazz the vehicle for blues expression.

Folk music and folk dance also thrived in various enclaves. Despite their black pioneer ancestry, the Ramapo Mountain People of northern New Jersey rejected the Afro-American blues tradition in favor of the "hillbilly" music common throughout the Appalachian culture area. Years ago the oldtimers used to have jug bands, using such musical instruments as guitars, banjos (Afro-American in origin but quickly becoming part of the Anglo-American folk music tradition), sweet potato whistles, jugs, washboards, Jew's harps, fiddles, accordions, and drums made out of hollowed logs. Additional rhythm was supplied by slapping hands against the body, in what is known in the South as the hambone. These jug bands accompanied dancers who danced the buck and wing, a shuffling type of tap dance in which the upper part of the body is kept loose and the arms swing freely. It is related to English clog dancing, Scottish step dancing, and Irish jigs.[20]

In 1967 Charles Kaufman collected several fiddle tunes in Ringwood from Jimmy De Freese, who played the fiddle in the traditional folk manner, holding it against his side rather than under his chin. The tunes included "Fisher's Hornpipe" (an Irish reel), "Nigger Wench," "Sailor's Hornpipe," "Irish Washerwoman," "Jordan Is a Hard Road to Travel," "Poppa Kicked Me Out of Bed Before I Got My Britches On" (a Scottish reel known as the "Devil's Dream" elsewhere in the United States), and "Buck and Wing" (better known as "Turkey in the Straw").[21] Today most of this folk music has been supplanted by popular country and western music.

A similar Anglo-American folk music tradition survived among the Pineys of South Jersey well into the twentieth century. In 1940 Cornelius Weygandt, author of *Down Jersey*, described how Elven Sweet from Pemberton would sit in a low chair, tuck a fiddle under his chin, announce the title of the tune, and play it, while he beat time with his foot. He played such old tunes as "The Chicken Reel," "Miss MacLeod's Reel," "The Devil's Dream," "How Dry I Am," "Trotting Horse," "The Fisher's Hornpipe," "Up the Road to Lancaster," "The Bummer's Reel," "Pop Goes the Weasel," and "Turkey in the Straw," as well as many reels, hornpipes, and jigs that he couldn't name.[22]

Fiddle playing was intended primarily to accompany dancing. Elven Sweet also told Weygandt about the square dances in the Pine Barrens around the turn of the century. He said that the boys would be loafing around the country store or hotel and someone would suggest: "It wouldn't be sweaty dancing tonight." They would send Sweet home for his fiddle, and five or six boys and some girls would go down the street while he played the fiddle. Eventually, someone would invite them into his house. They would carry out the furniture, take up the carpet, and have a dance. Sweet bragged that he "played right through the night on dark winter evenings and midnights and the small hours, from dark to day, played without repeating a tune from five in the evening to six in the morning."[23]

In 1936 Herbert Halpert began collecting several hundred folk songs from people in South Jersey. Mrs. Mary Parks of Job's Swamp near Whiting told him in 1938: "We used to get together and have regular singin' parties, four or five get together. Everyone would sing a piece."[24] In the same year the wife of Tom Test of Brown's Mill told Halpert:

> When neighbors come in maybe this one sing a song, maybe that one sing. She was a good singer (Tom's mother). They used to go around to houses and say "You sing a song," and then "You sing a song." They used to get around and make quilts. I heard about them days many a time.[25]

Among the songs Halpert collected in South Jersey were "Jolly Sailor," "This Colliers Mill's a Very Fine Place," "The Unquiet Grave," "The Bailer's Daughter of Ireland Town," "Shooting of His Dear," "Jimmy Randall," "A-Rolling in the Dew Makes the Milkmaid So Fair," "Jolly Thrasher," "Major Andre," "The Boatman and the Chest," "The Indian Lass," "Hard Times in the Mount Holly Jail," "Nottingham's Fair," and "Dear Mothers Ain't You Glad."[26] These songs are a mixture of Anglo-American ballads (also known as Child ballads after Francis J. Child who collected and indexed them), British broadsides (ballads published on broadsides in England), and native American ballads (i.e. created in America). This folk music tradition suggests British origins for the Pineys.

Some folk music in New Jersey might be described as occupational rather than regional or ethnic. For example, folk music was part of life on the Morris Canal. In 1976 James Lee of Stewartsville interviewed Isabelle Lenstrohn Mann, the daughter of a canal-boat captain, about this folk music.

> JAMES LEE: Did you ever do any singing on the canal on Sunday?
> ISABELLE MANN: Oh yes, all kinds of singing. And they would have little parties on Sunday and play music. They played the accordion, the violin and the Jew's harp and on the empty boats they used to make their own music, Jim. They would have a couple of bottles—I imagine they were beer bottles—and they would fasten wire to them somehow or other on the bottom of the boat and they played music with them with their fingers and with a stick. I don't know what they called that but they used to do that.
> JAMES LEE: Was your father musically inclined?
> ISABELLE MANN: Yes, he played the accordion, harmonica, Jew's harp and the violin—they called it a fiddle.
> JAMES LEE: How about the brothers, were they?
> ISABELLE MANN: Oh, yes. They were all musically inclined. They played banjo, violin, guitar. My mother too. She played accordion and the fiddle and the Jew's harp.
> JAMES LEE: Did they have any dances at different times?
> ISABELLE MANN: Oh, yes. If we were tied up at Port Delaware or any good place where there was a good place to dance—an old barn or something—why, they would have square dances.[27]

Florence Van Horn told Lee about informal music and dancing at the stores along the canal.

> At closing time for the boats when you put your mules in the company stables, well, generally at those locks or planes most of them had a little store where they sold soda and candy and stuff for the boatmen. Whenever we got there around the stores I was right with the gang. We was all out there. They had jew's harps, mouth organs, and bones. . . . And they would get out there by the store and play that music and all us girls would dance.[28]

One of the folk songs associated with the Morris Canal was "Going down to Cooper's." Cooper's referred to Peter Cooper's furnace at Phillipsburg. The song went in part:

> Going down to Cooper's just six o'clock.
> Who did I see, but old Aaron on the dock.
> And he said me jolly driver; Now whose a team is that?
> Sure 'tis old Mike Cavanaugh's, just a getting fat.
> Fal-ra-di-aiedo, Far-al-de-ya.
> Fal-ra-di-aiedo, A-hum-de-dally-dae.[29]

The Jersey Shore had its own tradition of folk songs associated with fishing, whaling, and oystering. In 1971 Donald H. Rolfs composed the following "oyster chanty" inspired by his interviews with the oystermen of Delaware Bay.

> The rails awash with a scupper breeze
>     and we're beatin up the Bay;
> Ready the drudge for the grounds me boys,
>     it sure is an oysterin day.
> Reef her down lads for the winds up high,
>     reef her while ye may,
> While the drudge goes a rumblin over the side
>     gatherin oysters for our pay.
> Cull em out boys and giver a try
>     under the watchboats leeward eye,
> Fore and aft is the deck piled high
>     with oysters a reachun to the sky.[30]

Songs like this were not truly work songs. They did not provide the cadence for the joint effort of the crew. Like the songs on the Morris Canal, they functioned to provide entertainment during leisure time.

Folk songs about rafting on the Delaware River were often legendary accounts about legendary men. "Boney" Quillan was a riverman who also was a songwriter. In 1934 Leslie C. Wood wrote about him as follows:

> Of the thousands of men who followed rafting as an occupation and of all the famed characters on the river, Robert "Boney" Quillan is remembered as the most witty; the most comical and the cleverest of them all, he being possessed of a keen wit, with just enough deviltry mixed in, to be the chief jokester the full length of the Delaware River

and cause more grief to hotel and saloon keepers than a whole regiment of his fellow watermen. Unusually smart, he could compose a piece of poetry almost as fast as the words could leave his mouth or put together a comical song in less time than it takes the ordinary person to think of a line or two—and many were the supposedly clever, well educated men put to shame by some of "Boney's" witty retorts or one of his humorous compositions, usually sung or recited after the luckless one had offended Quillan or one of his rafting partners.[31]

Wood quotes the lyrics from one of Quillan's songs about an incident in which a raft struck a bridge pier near a place known as Sawmill Rift.

> We sailed around Old Butler's,
>   And little did we fear;
> Until we came to Sawmill Rift—
>   And slam against the pier.
> *Chorus:*
> And shove around the grog boys,
>   The chorus around the room;
> For we are the boys that fear no noise,
>   Although we're far from home.[32]

Folk music and folk dances were brought to New Jersey in the late nineteenth and early twentieth centuries by various immigrant groups. The Italians who settled in Newark during this period brought folk songs sung to the accompaniment of mandolins and guitars. These included two main types: Neapolitan songs and the *stornelli romani*. The Neapolitan songs were originally associated with the annual festival in the Piedigrotta in Naples. These songs are very romantic and sentimental. The *stornelli*, which are sung to a single tune, are extemporaneously composed insult songs in which two singers try to outdo each other. The Italian folk dances include the tarantella, the *purlana* (from Venice), the *mazzucca* (adopted from the Polish mazurka by early Italian immigrants), the *ruggiera*, and the *siciliana*. They are danced to the accompaniment of the mandolin, guitar, and tambourine. But Charles W. Churchill noted that the traditional music and dances were not being continued by the second- and third-generation Italian-Americans in Newark.[33]

In 1933 Louis Mounier described an eastern European Jewish wedding from the first decade of this century that took place in Carmel, Cumberland County, one of the South Jersey agricultural colonies founded by the Jewish Agricultural Society with funds from the Baron De Hirsch Society. The guests gathered at the bride's home and escorted the bride and groom in a candlelight procession to the synagogue, accompanied by two musicians "who played on instruments strangely unrelated, namely a violin and a sort of flageolet, or yellow boxwood clarionet, played by a Jewish man hired from Philadelphia for this occasion."[34] Mounier continued: "As soon as the religious ceremony was over the musicians, who had so far played in a minor key, burst out gayly and vigorously, with perhaps the only Jewish tune in the major mode that the Russian Jews play."[35] The procession went from the synagogue to the hall where the reception was held.

> The two musicians during the banquet came to each guest and played his favorite tune to him, receiving a coin as pay. This music with the harsh and disagreeable sound of that yellow clarionet, continued during the banquet, and also during the dances which followed. In these, everyone young or old participated, at first in round dances, eight or ten men and women holding each other's hands, lifting one foot, then the other, if this can be called dancing, and the ring turning while the dancers either laughed, sang or shouted. I was dragged into one of those circles, and my wife into another, and there was no way of refusing. We were the only "goyim" the others who had been invited having left after they had had their fill of beer and victuals. . . .
>
> We had one room in the Hall in which to stay over night if necessary. On that occasion we stayed, but we could not sleep, for that shrieking clarionet, and its fiddle accompaniment, sounded all the night, either in the Hall or in the street. The curious part of this strange duet was that in spite of the coarseness of the wind instrument, the violin was heard distinctly above it. In the stillness of the night, the crescendos and diminuendos due to the musicians walking toward, or away from the Hall, were very effective, indeed could not have been so well rendered by playing crescendo and diminuendo in the usual manner.[36]

While this description is from the perspective of a not totally sympathetic outsider, it documents the existence in South Jersey of what is known as *klezmer* music. The *klezmerim* were roving musicians in the Jewish villages of eastern Europe. This music and dance began to die out among the second generation of Jewish-Americans, but in recent years a *klezmer* music revival has been taking place.

Since World War II various Hispanic groups in New Jersey have become important contributors to New Jersey folk music and folk dance. The Puerto Rican, Dominican, and Afro-Cuban music today known as *salsa* (soul) stems from Euro-Afro-American folk music sources. The guitar and Puerto Rican *cuarto* (ten-string guitar) can be traced back to Spain, as can the *décimas* (ballads with ten-line stanzas), *plenas* (love songs), and *aguinaldos* (Christmas carols). Other instruments are African in origin, such as the bongó (a pair of small drums covered with sheepskin on top but open at the bottom and attached together) and the *claves* (two small cylindrical sticks which are struck against each other). The *güiro* (a gourd with notches cut in the flat side which are scraped with a small stick) and maraca (gourd rattle) are instruments from the Caribbean Indian tradition.

There are certain differences among the music and dance traditions of various New Jersey Hispanic groups, which are documented in a film produced by New Jersey Public Television entitled *Aquí Se Habla Español*. For example, the characteristic type of Dominican traditional music and dance is known as the *merengue*. In Afro-Cuban music there are the rumba, the conga, the mambo, and the more recent *charanga* (played by two violins and a flute). The traditional Puerto Rican folk music is known as *jíbaro* (peasant) music, and the traditional folk dance as the *bomba*. The rhythms of these kinds of folk music can be heard on city streets and in county parks in New Jersey, especially during the summer months.

We might ask whether there is a unique folk music tradition in New Jersey. The answer is suggested by two traditional ballads. In the 1940s the folklorist Anne Lutz from Ramsey collected in the Ramapo Mountains a version of the ballad "The Butcher Boy from Jersey City." She noted that this was a local version of the English ballad "The Butcher Boy." The English version begins:

> In London town where I did dwell,
> A butcher boy whom I knew well.
> He courted all my life away,
> And now with me he will not stay.[37]

The local version she collected begins instead:

> In Jersey City where I did dwell,
> A butcher boy I loved so well;
> He courted me my heart away,
> And now with me he will not stay.[38]

And in 1936 Herbert Halpert collected in the Pine Barrens a native American ballad entitled "Hard Times in the Mount Holly Jail," which goes in part:

> When you go to Mount Holly,
> It's there where you're set,
> It's whiskey and tobacco you get damned a bit,
> And it's hard times in Mount Holly Jail,
> And it's hard times in Mount Holly Jail.
> Your hands and feet chained down to the floor,
> God damn their old souls why can't they do more.
> *Refrain (after each verse):*
> And it's hard times in Mount Holly Jail,
> And it's hard times in Mount Holly Jail.[39]

Halpert noted that the same song had been collected in New Hampshire under the title "Hard Times in Lancaster Jail." This shows that much of New Jersey folk music is in fact localizations of songs found elsewhere. The songs are made New Jersey folk songs by being sung about New Jersey people and places. The song is sung today by a band known as the Pine Coners based in Waretown. They are associated with an organization named the Pinelands Cultural Society, which is dedicated to preserving Piney folk traditions endangered by suburban development.[40] But their version of the song is done in a bittersweet nostalgic tone unlike the resentful tone of the original prison song. Thus the same song serves different functions at different times.

In 1976 Bruno Nettl, the ethnomusicologist, wrote about American folk music.

> Folk music in the United States reflects the history and composition of American society. It stands as a testament to the diverse cultures of millions of immigrants who have crossed the Atlantic to the New World. . . . If we restrict the concept of a nation's folk music to the creations of that country's indigenous inhabitants . . . American Indian music would be our only genuine tradition. But ironically, most Americans do not regard Indian music as part of their experience, nor do they understand it. We may conclude that many borrowed, nonindigenous traditions are the basis for most folk music in the United States. It is the mixing and blending of these that [are] characteristically American.[41]

We might say the same about the folk music of New Jersey.

# Part II
# New Jersey Folklife

# Folk Painting

**F**OLK PAINTING is generally defined as the art of self-taught painters. John Michael Vlach, the folklorist, has recently challenged this definition, which, he notes, was developed by fine art scholars, not folklorists. Vlach argues that whether someone should be termed a folk artist should depend on the source of his themes and on whether he embodies community values and esthetics.[1] There is, however, one problem with Vlach's formulation. There are many examples of folk songs and folktales that originated in written sources and then went into oral tradition. The fact that a painter may have derived his ideas from nonfolk sources doesn't disqualify him from exhibiting a folk esthetic.

Folk art is different from folklore. Folk art is not a tradition handed down from generation to generation by word of mouth. Folk painters, unlike craftsmen, do not learn their skill through an apprenticeship. Also, unlike crafts, folk painting is not primarily utilitarian. While fraktur may have a utilitarian function as birth, baptismal, and marriage certificates, portraits and landscapes are primarily works of art.

The main point is that folk painting expresses an esthetic sufficiently different from fine art, on the one hand, and commercial art, on the other, to allow us to distinguish among the three. In fact, most folk paintings demonstrate a remarkable similarity of style. In part, of course, this is because we have tended to define folk artists as those whose work is characterized by this particular style. But the fact remains that artists who were not in communication with one another do exhibit a preference for certain techniques. Their works have a two-dimensional quality, owing to the fact that they do not use the rules of perspective that have characterized realistic drawing since the Renaissance. As a result landscapes seem more like diagrams, and portraits have a stiff, doll-like appearance. The colors tend to be bright and flat, and there is not the interplay between color and light common in fine art painting.

Art historians and museum curators tend to view these characteristics as resulting from the folk artists' lack of formal training. That is what is implied in the condescending labels "primitive" and "naive." They often describe folk

Catharine Hendrickson, by an unknown artist, 1770.
*National Gallery of Art, Washington, D.C. Gift of Edgar William and Bernice Chrysler Garbisch*

painting as "charming," "delightful," and "childlike."[2] The implication is that folk artists do not know how to draw. One writer on the subject repeatedly says that folk artists had trouble drawing hands.[3] But Henry Glassie notes that folk art simply embodies a different esthetic.

> Figuratively folk art is not crude popular art; it is the improvement of reality. It is the result of drawing the real world or the illusionistic popular artwork through a traditional filter that improves the figure, that is, renders it more in keeping with the folk esthetic philosophy held by the artist and his audience.[4]

In the eighteenth and nineteenth centuries folk painters were called "limners" (from the Latin *illuminare*, to outline or delineate). In America local limners were often itinerants, painting portraits or farmsteads for individual patrons wherever they went. It was long believed that they painted the bodies and backgrounds beforehand and painted only the faces in the presence of their subject.[5] That is no longer thought to be true. No one has discovered faceless portraits, but incomplete portraits, with a head but no body or background, have been found.[6] The similarity of portrait poses derives from the artistic conventions of the period, both in folk painting and in fine art painting. The subject is seated formally in the foreground, and the background is a landscape or scene associated with his or her interests or occupation. Another misconception is that limners were all anonymous.[7] Often they signed their portraits or at least put their initials on them. Research by art historians over the many years that folk art has been fashionable has enabled us to know a good deal about the lives of many of these painters.

New Jersey has enjoyed a certain distinction in the history of folk painting. In 1930–1931 the Newark Museum held an exhibition entitled "American Primitives," assembled by Holger Cahill, the museum curator.[8] This was one of the first folk art exhibitions in the country.

New Jersey's most famous folk painter was Micah Williams (1782–1837). Several of his portraits are in the possession of the Abby Aldrich Rockefeller Folk Art Collection in Williamsburg, Virginia, the Monmouth County Historical Association, and the New Jersey Historical Society. For years his identity was unknown until it was established in the 1950s through the research of Mrs. Irwin F. Cortelyou. Williams was a native of the Paterson area, and he was described in the Paterson *Chronicle* in 1823 as "self-taught, having never been instructed by the masters of the art."[9] About 1811 he began to work as an itinerant artist, based at different times in New Brunswick and New York City and traveling extensively in Monmouth County. He painted in pastels, and used local newspapers to line the backs of his portraits. Often he would inscribe on the back the name of the subject, the date the "likeness was taken," and "by Micah Williams."

In the work of Susan C. Waters (1823–1900) there is an evolution from one style to another. She was born Susan Catherine Moore in Binghamton, New York. Her father was a cooper. Her family moved to the town of Friendsville in northern Pennsylvania, where she attended the Friendsville Boarding School for Females. In 1841 she married a local Hicksite Quaker, William C. Waters. She became an itinerant painter, traveling to small towns in northern Pennsylvania and the southern tier of New York, and as far as the Berkshire Mountains of Massachusetts. In 1852 William and Susan Waters moved to Bordentown, and although they lived for brief periods after that in Iowa and Pennsylvania, New Jersey became her home until her death. There was a distinct change of style in her paintings after she moved to Bordentown. Her early portraits were very much in the folk style of other itinerant limners. But after her move she stopped painting portraits and began to do animals and still lifes. Her style became more influenced by the fine art style of romantic realism and less by the folk esthetic. In all her paintings there are a gentleness and peacefulness that reflect her Quaker outlook.[10]

Folk painting is not merely a remnant of the distant past; it is a tradition that continues into our own times. Henry Thomas Gulick (1872–1964) was a New Jersey farmer who took up painting as a hobby when he retired in 1946. He was born, raised, and lived his entire life in Monmouth County, and his family was descended from some of its first settlers. He ran a dairy, fruit, and vegetable farm for fifty-five years, until he had to retire because of arthritis. "I thought I was done for that Christmastime," he recalled years later. "My sons gave me a set of paints for a gift with a note saying that it wasn't a joke. They really expected me to use them. Well, I started using them and I haven't quit yet."[11] His work is best described by Barbara Wahl Kaufman, the art historian.

He was the complete amateur. In part, he attributed his success to the very fact that he was untutored. He said that it left his art unconfused, and so it is. With sure line and bold color and precise design he painted what he saw around him. His work reflects the harmony between man and nature in the farmland of Monmouth County. He limned the rolling fields, his farmhouse and the homes of his neighbors, a curtained window festooned with potted plants, frosty fields slumbering in the

Mrs. Jonathan R. Schanck (Sarah Peacock, 1797–1861), attributed to Micah Williams, 1821. *Monmouth County Historical Association. Gift of William C. Riker*

winter-time, and the stark white walls of his church. Gulick laid on his paint evenly, his colors were outspoken, unshaded and direct. Each object stands out in its own right, treated with equal intensity and vigor no matter how distant it is. The result is as lively and gay as an American quilt.[12]

This description captures not only the local interests and specific style of Gulick but also the underlying esthetic of American folk art.

Folk paintings have value both as art and as historical documents. They contain all kinds of information about changes in fashion, family life, domestic architecture, interior decoration, the cultural landscape, and moral and political values. This is also true of much fine art painting, but folk paintings tend to reflect a different level of society from fine art paintings. They tend to depict common people, simple things, and everyday life.

Folk portraits are not quite as democratic as folk painting generally. Not everyone can afford to have his portrait painted. While fine art portraitists tended to paint the very wealthy and the very influential, the country gentry had their likenesses done by local limners. These folk portraits show some interesting things about that level of society.

Take, for example, the portrait of Catharine Hendrickson done by an anonymous folk artist in 1770, which is part of the collection of Edgar William and Bernice Chrysler Garbisch. She is very fashionably dressed in the style of the period. She wears a high-bodiced dress and a tall coiffure, which were in vogue among the upper classes in England and France.[13] She holds flowers in one hand and a closed fan in the other. Beside her is a vase containing carnations, and behind her is a landscape with trees and birds, including a robin, a cardinal, and a dove. Clearly we are dealing here with aristocratic pretensions among the Dutch-American country gentry.

The portrait of Sarah Peacock Schanck (1797–1861), the wife of Jonathan R. Schanck, thought to have been painted by Micah Williams in 1821, shows the fashionable style of dress and hair that followed the French and American revolutions and continued through the empire period in Europe. Her dress is a chemise with a high bodice, and her hair is arranged with ringlets on her forehead and a coiffure of loops of hair in a style known then as *à la girafe*.[14] This style was a reaction against the aristocrats of England and France, and a celebration of democratic Greece and Rome. According to Alice Morse Earle, the social historian, you can tell whether a man or woman was a Federalist or a Republican by the way he or she dressed.[15]

*Rebecca Hubbard,*
by Micah Williams, circa 1825.
*Monmouth County
Historical Association*

*Opposite:*
"Girl in White with Cherries,"
attributed to Micah Williams,
circa 1832. *The Jane Voorhees
Zimmerli Art Museum, Rutgers,
The State University
of New Jersey.
Gift of Miss Anna I. Morgan*

Micah Williams's portrait of Rebecca Hubbard, circa 1825, shows the little girl seated in a child's chair. In her hand she holds a peach. Her ringlet hairdo and long toga-style chemise show the same sense of fashion on the part of her mother as we saw in the portrait of Mrs. Schanck. It also shows that little girls were dressed very much like adult women—or, at any rate, that it was thought proper for them to be so attired when having their portraits painted. Philippe Ariès, the historian, has shown that the depiction of children in art can give insights into the changing nature of the family.[16] Arthur W. Calhoun, the historian, has used the phrase "the emancipation of childhood" to refer to the change in the image of children from the colonial Puritan notion that they were tainted by original sin and had to be strictly disciplined to the nineteenth-century notion of childhood innocence.[17] If ever there were a picture of nineteenth-century childhood innocence, it is the portrait of Rebecca Hubbard.

The portrait "Girl in White with Cherries," attributed to Micah Williams circa 1832, depicts an older girl who is also dressed exactly like an adult woman

Rachel Brinkerhoff, born April 10, 1776, aged 39 years.
*Monmouth County Historical Association*

of the period. She too is fashionably dressed. She wears a high-bodiced dress with pantaloons. Pantaloons for women, like pants for men, were a byproduct of the French Revolution; previously only the lower classes wore pants. They remained in style for women well into the nineteenth century, and permanently changed the dress of men.[18]

In contrast to these fashionable women is the folk portrait of Rachel Brinkerhoff owned by the Monmouth County Historical Association. According to the inscription at the bottom of this watercolor, she was born in 1776 and was thirty-nine at the time the portrait was made; thus it was made in 1815. But her dress is not in keeping with the current fashion. She wears a type of head covering known as a "mobcap," which by the end of the eighteenth century was considered prudish and was ridiculed with the name "Queen's Night Cap."[19] Her dark gown is floor length with a broad white linen collar. This dress was more typical of the plain style of the Hicksite Quakers. She sits on a banister-back, rush-bottom chair and holds a book in her hand. Since she was thirty-nine, her conservative dress cannot be attributed to the taste of a very old woman whose eye was fixed on the fashion of an earlier period. Rather, this portrait captures certain social values as expressed in dress.

How accurate are folk paintings as historical documents? There is no simple answer. Some were done by memory years after the scene was experienced. For example, in 1971 I interviewed Ed Morgan of Haskell, a self-taught artist who was then eighty-one. We talked about his painting, "Old Iron Furnace, 1776." He had done several versions of this scene, one of which is in the Montclair Art Museum.

COHEN: What is this a painting of?

MORGAN: This is the old iron works at Hewitt, New Jersey. This was in the early part of the 1700s. This was in operation before the railroad went through. . . . What they did in those days was they built a dam. Greenwood Lake was a man-made pond. . . . Greenwood Lake would be back up here. [He points.] In the back there. And down here [he points] a couple of years ago—three or four years ago—that's where they found that forge. They claimed the forge was 250 years old. . . .

COHEN: Do you remember ever seeing it work?

MORGAN: My mother does. This was all in nice shape when I was a boy. We used to go up here. Everything you see here when I was a boy was still in perfect shape. It hadn't been shut down for long. We used to call it [Greenwood Lake] Long Pond. . . .

"Old Iron Furnace, 1776," Hewitt, by Ed Morgan, 1971.
*Owned by David S. Cohen*

COHEN: Did you go to the site of the furnace to draw this, or did you do it by memory?

MORGAN: I did it by memory. I didn't have to go there to see it. No. You can take that picture up there and see. You can go in there on this road and see where the water used to come down here and down in there. . . .

COHEN: Do you ever rearrange buildings to make it look nicer?

MORGAN: No. No. No. No. No sir. No sir. I didn't do that.

86

COHEN: Everything is in the right place?

MORGAN: Yes, sir.

COHEN: Never leave a building out?

MORGAN: Oh, no. . . . I know these places by heart—I know them good. I was born and raised there by them, and things like that, and I know where they are. . . . When I work like that on something like that I try to make it just as near as I possibly can to what it really is. That's the way I work that. . . .

This was here. That's the way it was then. That's the way I know it. That's the way I paint it. I couldn't change it. I couldn't paint something that wasn't there, because that wouldn't be right. I mean, I paint it according to the way it is.[20]

When Mr. Morgan talks about his painting he talks about how the furnace operated, not about abstract ideas of art, composition, and color. For him to rearrange the locations of things in his painting for the sake of composition would border on dishonesty.

However, when a picture is filtered through memory discrepancies between what is depicted and what actually existed are likely to occur. Take, for example, the folk painting in the Salem County Historical Society collection of John Fenwick's first home at Ivy Point. The house was built about 1677 and was demolished about 1830. The painting was done about 1867 by William Patterson, on the basis of a description supplied by his father James. The image in the painting is idyllic and somewhat incongruous. Fenwick stands looking out over Delaware Bay. An Indian woman sits under a tree nearby, and an Indian man paddles a dugout canoe. Offshore is a nineteenth-century schooner under full sail. Yet there are some authentic elements in the painting. The house has an English gambrel roof and patterned brickwork (see "Folk Architecture"), and the stumps of trees left in the fields are evidence of the gird and burn method of clearing the land. One cannot assume that folk paintings supply a literal picture of the past, or on the other hand that they are totally inaccurate. Like other types of historical documents they must be critically analyzed.

Folk paintings, like folk tales, sometimes have different versions. I have already mentioned the several versions of Ed Morgan's "Old Iron Furnace, 1776," which are substantially the same except in size. There are two variants of the painting of the house and shop of David Alling, chairmaker of Newark, both painted about 1840 and attributed to Johan Heinrich Jenny. One is owned by the Newark Museum and the other by the New Jersey Historical Society. In

John Fenwick's home, by William Patterson, circa 1867.
*Salem County Historical Society and Salem County Tercentenary Committee*

both variants a horse and carriage are tied to a hitching post in the street. But the sidewalk scene is different. In the Newark Museum painting two men stand talking on the far left, a chair is placed in front of Alling's shop, a woman and a young girl are walking in front of the house, the open doorway of the shop is empty, and a black laborer pushes a wheelbarrow on the far right. In the Historical Society's version the black laborer with the wheelbarrow appears on the left, the chair is missing from the sidewalk, the two men are now standing in front of the house, a man (possibly Alling) stands in the open doorway, and the little girl stands on the right. Are these two different moments in the passing street scene? Probably not. Although the location of the two men has been shifted, their postures are almost the same in both paintings. Are they two different studies for the scene? Probably not, because both are finished paintings.

88

House and shop of David Alling, attributed to Johan Heinrich Jenny, circa 1840.
*The Newark Museum Collection* (top) and *New Jersey Historical Society, Newark* (bottom)

Gulick farm in 1880, by Henry Thomas Gulick.
*Montclair Art Museum. Owned by Mr. and Mrs. Henry G. Gulick*

On rare occasions we have multiple interior and exterior visions of the same environment. That is the case in Henry Thomas Gulick's paintings of his family's farm. One view is of the farm as he remembered it as a boy in 1880. The house and the side addition are seen from the front. There is a white picket fence in front of the house and a log snake fence zigzagging down the hill. Behind the farmhouse are the barns and outbuildings, including a Dutch barn. Gulick also

90

painted a present-day view of the farm as seen from the side of the house. The picket fence and the snake fence are gone and so is the Dutch barn, replaced by newer barns and sheds. Another of his pictures is a view of the barns and sheds in the snow, with the cows in the barnyard, two horses, a sleigh, a farm wagon in the barn door, and a partially filled corncrib. Gulick painted several interior views of the farmhouse. They included such features as the front door, the main hall showing the double parlor on the right and the dining room in the addition on the left, the corner cupboard in the dining room with a ladder-back chair beside it and the folk painting of the Gulick barns on the wall, and a view across the hall as seen from the dining room with part of the fireplace mantel in the parlor and part of a Dutch *kas* in the hall. It is as if he had set out to make a visual inventory of his estate.

Main hall, Gulick farmhouse, by Henry Thomas Gulick.
*Montclair Art Museum. Owned by David B. Johnson*

An important ethnic form of folk painting is fraktur, a survival of the medieval illuminated manuscript. In the eighteenth and early nineteenth centuries it was primarily associated with the Pennsylvania Germans. The German word *fraktur* comes from the Latin *fractura,* an old style of penmanship with breaks between the strokes of the letters. In Pennsylvania fraktur took different forms—birth and baptismal certificates (*taufscheinen*), house blessings (*haussegen*), and copybooks (*vorschriften*). The German fraktur has elaborate symbolic motifs, which, according to John Joseph Stoudt, a Pennsylvania local historian, are primarily religious in meaning. The flower, according to Stoudt, is "the chief symbol of Pennsylvania folk art" and symbolizes "human hope and longing."[21] It is related to the biblical rose of Sharon and the lilies of the valley in the Song of Songs. The eagle is the symbol of the ascending Lord, the peacock of resurrection and rebirth, and the dove of the Holy Spirit. Two doves standing by a beaker of water are the symbol of baptism, and the bird of paradise represents the longing of the soul for Christ.[22]

New Jersey has its own tradition of fraktur, according to David McGrail, a literary scholar who has studied this subject. Pennsylvania Germans settled in the northwestern counties of New Jersey and brought with them this folk art tradition. McGrail argues that the English and the Dutch had their own decorated family manuscript traditions with lettering very different from the German.[23] Some of the New Jersey examples, however, show a mixture of German and English printing styles. One example is a watercolor fraktur of the Schuyler family genealogy dated 1804, inscribed "done by James Anson." It depicts a pair of birds facing each other in the tradition of the Pennsylvania German doves, but they are referred to as "India Pheasants." Another New Jersey fraktur is patriotic rather than religious—a stylized version of the federal coat of arms inscribed with the name Aaron Schuyler, the motto *E Pluribus Unum,*" and the date "february 6, 1804." Patriotic themes also occur in Pennsylvania German fraktur of this period.

A birth certificate owned by the Monmouth County Historical Association is a fine example of English fraktur in New Jersey. It shows a man and a woman, decorative flower designs, and the inscription "John Mason / Son of Solomon Mason and Anna his wife / Was born January the 3rd Anno Domini 1767." It too is different in lettering and design style from the Pennsylvania German fraktur. What makes New Jersey fraktur so interesting is that it exemplifies the kind of cross-cultural borrowings that occur at the boundaries of culture areas.

Birth certificate of John Mason, January 3, 1767.
*Monmouth County Historical Association*

In summary, while folk paintings are intended primarily as art, they lend themselves to interpretation as historical documents. They represent a source of historical information not readily available in printed sources. Despite the fact that not all folk paintings are accurate in the historical information they contain, we can learn much from them about family life, fashion, architecture, interior decoration, and the cultural landscape of past periods. They also can be seen as evidence of cultural borrowings between ethnic groups.

# Folk Sculpture

FOLK SCULPTURE refers to traditional figures and patterns in three dimensions or relief, carved from wood, chipped from stone, or wrought in metal. Like much of folk art, folk sculpture is really a craft. That is, its primary function is utilitarian. Duck decoys, for example, were intended to lure ducks so that they might be hunted, and trade signs were intended to advertise goods and services. Their design, however, embodies an esthetic, which qualifies them as art. The craftsmen who make folk sculpture generally do not call themselves "sculptors." Rather they identify themselves by their specific craft—decoy maker, tombstone carver, blacksmith. They usually learn their craft through apprenticeships, rather than in art schools. Although craftsmen have their own individual styles, the emphasis in folk sculpture is on traditional figures and patterns. This means that these works can be traced to places of origin, usually in the Old World. Originality is there, but within the context of tradition. In fine art sculpture originality is primary and tradition secondary; in folk sculpture the opposite is true.

The Newark Museum has the distinction of having sponsored one of the first folk sculpture exhibitions in America.[1] It opened in 1931, the year after the museum's first exhibition of folk painting. Like its predecessor it was organized by Holger Cahill, the museum curator. This exhibition featured some New Jersey objects, including duck decoys, cigar-store figures, and spoon racks.

One of the best-known examples of folk sculpture is the weathervane. In the colonial era and well into the nineteenth century weathervanes were found on American barns and public buildings. They are descended from medieval English heraldic banners known as fanes (an archaic word, meaning both flag and weathervane), which were flown from the castle rooftops. Made of metal, the fane displayed the family crest. It was made so that it would swivel in the wind and show the wind direction, important information in an age that relied heavily on archery. In addition, buildings in medieval and Renaissance Europe had finials on their roofs, the most common of which was the gilded sphere. Even the crosses on the top of churches were placed on spheres.[2]

There were few regional differences among American weathervanes. One of the most common designs was the swallow-tailed banner. Another was the cock, a symbolic figure of "the vigilant bird, the first voice of the morning."[3] It was regarded "as the symbol of watchfulness—a reminder of the immortal chanticleer whose shrill admonitory crowing woke Peter's guilty conscience the night he thrice denied his Lord."[4]

Colonial weathervanes were made of wood, copper, or iron. New Jersey had a colonial iron industry, with mines and foundries in both northern and southern parts of the state. Blacksmiths would shape the iron by heating and hammering it on anvils. Copper vanes were made by coppersmiths, who would shape the vane around a rounded wooden model. In the nineteenth century new methods were developed to mass-produce weathervanes. Beginning in the 1820s and 1830s cast-iron weathervanes were made, and in the 1850s copper vanes were made in iron molds. The copper vanes still had to be handcrafted, however. The copper was beaten with a mallet into a negative mold in sections, and then the sections were soldered together. This made possible a greater variety of shapes, but at the same time vanes were becoming more of a uniform mass-produced commodity. The motifs of these nineteenth-century vanes included the grasshopper, the Indian king, the serpent, the fish, the eagle, Liberty or Columbia, the trotting horse, the Angel Gabriel, sailors, the cow, and the pig. In the late nineteenth century trade catalogs began to show weathervanes from specific manufacturers.[5]

Trade signs come in two forms, painted or sculptured. A tavern sign, for example, might be considered folk painting, a shoemaker's boot sign folk sculpture. In this chapter I deal with both kinds of trade signs as a single genre. The use of signs and signboards by tradesmen has been traced at least as far back as the Roman Empire. Most of the symbols and motifs that appear on trade signs in America originated in medieval England. They often took the form of a rebus, an enigmatic representation of a word or phrase by pictures or symbols. These signs advertised the nature of the business at a time when many people could not read.[6] People would meet "under the sign of," that is, at a certain tavern. Trade signs were in general use well into the nineteenth century, by which time public education had reduced illiteracy; they have survived to this day, although the need for them has been virtually eliminated. In a sense, the corporate logo is the present-day embodiment of the tradition of the trade sign.

Very few original New Jersey tavern signs survive from the eighteenth and nineteenth centuries. One example is the Washington House tavern sign, depicting George Washington on horseback with sword in one hand and hat in the other. There were many taverns and inns in New Jersey and elsewhere in the early nineteenth century called Washington House or Washington Tavern, a reflection of Washington's status as a symbol of American nationalism. It was in this period that Parson Mason L. Weems wrote his legend-making biography of Washington.[7]

Other tavern signs we know about from historical prints and photographs. A print in Barber and Howe's *Historical Collections of the State of New Jersey* shows the sign of the Eagle Tavern in Mullica Hill.[8] Charles S. Boyer, the local historian, mentions the Eagle Tavern in his book *Old Inns and Taverns in West New Jersey*: "The signboard, which hung in front of the tavern for many years, displayed a painting of an eagle with outstretched wings and on a separate panel, which hung underneath, was the name of the proprietor."[9] While the eagle is a symbol of American nationality, it also appears on English tavern signs, although not as commonly as in America.[10] Boyer also shows photographs of the Cross Keys Tavern in Gloucester County and the Blue Anchor Tavern in Camden County with their signs.[11]

Most tavern signs we know about only from the names of the taverns, but we can imagine what they looked like from the names: Black Horse Tavern, Sign of the Flag Tavern, Blue Bell Tavern, Indian Queen Tavern, Indian King Tavern, Sheaf of Wheat Tavern, Boar's Head Tavern, Pine Tavern.[12] Often more than one tavern had the same name. There were Indian Queen and Indian King taverns in several New Jersey towns. Some of the names were astrological: Rising Sun, Blazing Star, and Seven Stars.[13]

The sculptured trade sign is also an old tradition in Europe. Some of these traditional signs survive to the present. For example, the red and white barbershop pole is a survival from the days when barbers acted as surgeons and engaged in bloodletting. The three golden balls associated with pawnbrokers are said to have originated with the Lombard merchants who took this emblem from the coat of arms of the dukes of Medici.[14]

Perhaps the most famous American trade sign is the cigar-store Indian. The prototype for this advertising symbol for tobacconists has been traced back to seventeenth-century England, but it did not become common in America until the advent of the cigar in the mid-nineteenth century.[15] According to Jean Lipman, editor of *Antiques* magazine and a historian of folk art, the heyday of the cigar-store Indian lasted from the 1850s through the 1880s.[16] Lipman cites an article in the *New York Times* in 1890 that described how these statues were made. Generally they were carved from pine logs. The carver used paper patterns to outline the basic proportions of the figure. Using an axe, he blocked

Afro-American cigar-store
Indian, Freehold, reputedly
made by Job, circa 1825.
*New York State Historical
Association, Cooperstown*

out the head, the body, the legs, and the feet. Then he bored a five-inch hole
into each end of the log and inserted iron bolts, which rested against supports so
as to allow the log to hang free. He then chiseled the figure into finer form.
The hands and arms were normally made separately and attacked to the body
with screws.[17]

One of the most intriguing examples of New Jersey folk sculpture is a cigar-
store Indian princess thought to have been made about 1825 by a slave named
Job for a Freehold tobacconist. It is in the museum of the New York State Historical Association in Cooperstown. According to Lipman, "the African heritage

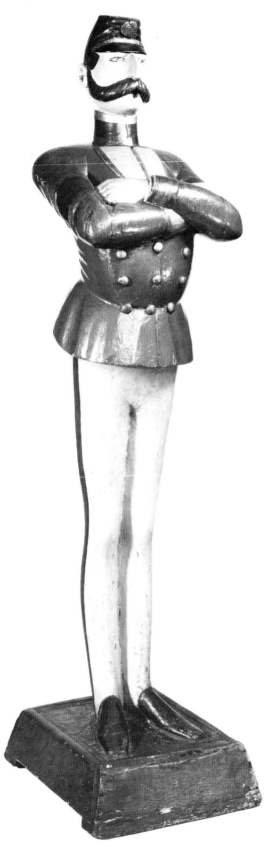

Euro-American cigar-store figure,
"Captain Jinks of the Horse Marines,"
Newark, circa 1875.
*The Newark Museum Collection*

of the carver is apparent, especially in the masklike face."[18] Other features of this sculpture that appear to be survivals of African art are the tubular, elongated arms and the enlarged hands. Furthermore, the sensuous breasts are more in keeping with the fertility statues of African art than with the rather prudish conventions of nineteenth-century European and American art. Thus, this cigar-store statue seems to be an authentic—and rare—example of Afro-American folk art in New Jersey that demonstrates African survivals.

The Indian princess is a symbol in the iconography of America. In an article in the *Winterthur Portfolio* in 1967, E. McClung Fleming traced the symbolic representations of America in prints and on maps from 1783 to 1815. In the colonial era America was portrayed as an Indian princess, but around the time of the American Revolution the image changed to that of a Greek goddess, in the form of either Columbia or Liberty. Fleming noted that the Indian princess or Indian queen continued in American folk art into the nineteenth century, but as a commercial emblem rather than as a symbol of America.[19] As we have seen in the case of the eagle on tavern signs, the use of national symbols for commercial purposes was common in the early national period.

Not all cigar-store statues were Indians. In England and America the figures of Turks, blacks, and Scottish Highlanders were used. "Captain Jinks of the Horse Marines," now owned by the Newark Museum, stood outside Feary's cigar store in Newark. The statue is attributed to Thomas J. White. Captain Jinks was named after a nineteenth-century popular song which went in part:

> I'm Captain Jinks of the Horse Marines;
> I feed my horse on corn and beans,
> And sport young ladies in their teens,
> Tho' a captain in the Army.[20]

While this was not a folk song, it was widely known in its day and is quite racy even today. The lyrics fit perfectly the image of the dapper soldier figure, which was made very much in the English tradition of trade signs.

While we usually think of the Puritans as being opposed to all artistic representations, that is not entirely true. In the late seventeenth century and throughout the eighteenth century the Puritans of New England created a religious folk art in the form of tombstone carvings. These were not, of course, uniquely American; similar motifs can be found on tombstones in England. The Puritans who migrated after 1664 from Connecticut and eastern Long Island and settled in such towns as Elizabethtown, Newark, and Connecticut Farms (today Union) brought this folk art tradition with them to New Jersey.

There was a parallel evolution of tombstone motifs in New England and in New Jersey. They were symbolic, their basic theme being the mortality of the body and the immortality of the soul. The Puritans believed that while the body dies and decays, the souls of the Elect live in eternity. This theme expressed in tombstone carvings is what Allan I. Ludwig, the art historian, has called "mystical transfigurations in stone."[21]

The mortality of the body was most commonly symbolized by the death's-head. This often took the form of the skull and crossbones, as in the tombstone of Martha Thompson of Elizabethtown, who died in 1728. This stone also contains another common motif, the hourglass. The epitaph of Elizabeth Young in Succasunna illustrates the meaning of this symbol.

> My glass is run
> My grave you see
> Prepare for death
> And follow me.[22]

On other tombstones, for example, the stone of Samuel Miller, Jr., who died in 1732 and is buried in Elizabeth, the death's-head took the form of a skull with wings. Over the death's-head appear a crown and cross and a biblical inscription (2 Tim. 4:8): "Henceforth there is laid up for me a crown of righteousness, which the Lord, the righteous judge, shall give me at that day; and not to me only, but unto all them also that love his appearing."[23]

By the late eighteenth century tombstones no longer had death's-heads but instead cherubs or soul effigies. The common gravestone of Elizabeth Charlton (died 1778), her son John (died 1752), and her daughter Elizabeth (died 1759) in Elizabeth exemplifies this later style. The epitaph reads:

> My Panting Soul ascends on High,
> To Praise my God eternally.
> In Christ alone we hope and trust
> To rise in Judgment with the Just.[24]

This stone also contains two geometric rosettes (circumscribed five-pointed stars). The same motif is found in Pennsylvania German folk art, such as fraktur, painted furniture, and "hex" signs. Ludwig and Emily Wasserman believe that this motif was merely a space-filling design,[25] but other scholars regard it as a survival of a prehistoric solar mythology.[26] The rosette is common in folk art throughout Europe.

Stone of Martha Thompson, died 1728, Elizabethtown (top) and
stone of Samuel Miller, Jr., died 1732, Elizabeth (bottom).
*From Emily Wasserman,* Gravestone Designs, *Dover Publications*

Stone of Elizabeth Charlton, died 1778, Elizabeth. *From Emily Wasserman,* Gravestone Designs, *Dover Publications*

In the early nineteenth century these motifs were replaced by the funeral urn and the tree—a result, according to Ludwig, of the influence of neoclassicism (the revival of classical influence on art and architecture).[27] The stone of Phoebe Watson, who died in 1818 and is buried in Livingston, depicts the funeral urn. The stone of Elias Osborn (died 1807) in the Connecticut Farms burial ground in Union depicts a tree with a broken branch. This is a reference, according to Wasserman, to the tree of life.[28] The tombstone of the three Wade children—Robert (died 1808, age five), William (died 1809, age eight days), and Matthias (died 1818, age two)—in Springfield combines the funeral urn with the weeping willow, a common symbol of mourning.

We should not put too much emphasis on the meanings of these symbols. The meaning was not always known by the people who commissioned them or for that matter by the stonecarvers. John Frazee was a gravestone carver who was born in 1790 in Rahway. He began as a bricklayer, but discovered that there was no stonecutter in Rahway and that headstones had to be purchased in Woodbridge, Elizabethtown, and Newark. He became an apprentice of Ward Baldwin in order to learn tombstone cutting and in 1813 went into partnership with William Dunham in New Brunswick. In his autobiography he wrote about the neoclassical tombstone designs he used.

Tombstone of Elias Osborn, died 1807, Union (top) and stone of the three Wade children: Robert, died 1808, William W., died 1809, and Matthias D., died 1818, Springfield. *From Emily Wasserman,* Gravestone Designs, *Dover Publications*

I continued to ornament my gravestones with vines, flowers, and various little devices, appropriate, as I thought to the tomb; but, in truth, there was in much of it more whim than meaning. . . . While I remained in New Jersey, I never saw a book that treated upon the arts, either historical or elementary. I knew nothing about the arts of antiquity. . . . I began my career among the tombstones, utterly igno-

103

rant of every rule of art, and of those symbols, images and attributes that had their origin in the classical ages, and that lived and breathed in the beautiful sculptures upon the tombs and sarcophagi of Egypt and Greece.[29]

It is sometimes possible to identify the craftsman who carved a tombstone. Some tombstones were signed or initialed: the tombstone of the Wade children, for example, is signed "J. C. Mooney, C. Farms."[30] Some craftsmen have recognizable styles, which can also be traced from craftsman to apprentice. For example, Ebenezer Price (1728–1788) was a tombstone carver active between 1757 and 1788 in Elizabethtown, Orange, Connecticut Farms, and Woodbridge. His style was characterized by faces with flat, square-shaped noses, distinct eyebrows, and bands of curling locks of hair. One of his apprentices, David Jeffries, adopted a similar style. The tombstone of Sarah Platt of Elizabethtown (died 1782) was made by either Price or Jeffries.[31]

The similarity of style in three tombstones enabled Wasserman to determine that they were made by the same anonymous craftsman. The style is marked by almond-shaped eyes with defined pupils and elongated, tubular noses. One tombstone is on the common grave of Elizabeth Anderson (died 1783), Mary Stewart (died 1779), and William McBride (died 1782) in Saint Paul's Church in New York City. Another is that of Caty Leonard (died 1785) in Middletown, Monmouth County. The third is the stone of Sarah Venning (died 1783) and her son John (died 1783) in Trinity Church graveyard in New York City.[32] This shows the influence on the countryside of a style originating in a nearby city. Thus northern New Jersey was part of the hinterland of New York City from an early date.

These tombstones reflect changes in popular attitudes toward death between the eighteenth and nineteenth centuries. They also provide a direct cultural link to New England and to England, clearly showing that parts of northern New Jersey were once in the Puritan culture area.

In much of American folklife we see a transplanting of European traditions in an American environment. Duck decoys, however, represent a cultural diffusion in the opposite direction. In Europe and the British Isles live birds were trained to be used as lures in hunting ducks and other wildfowl. The hunting was done originally with nets and later with guns.[33] The word decoy is said to come from the Dutch *ende-kooi*, meaning "duck cage."[34] Sometimes the term "stool," from the German word *stuhl*, meaning "seat," is used instead, especially when referring to stick-up decoys of shore birds or snipes. The original "stool pigeon" was a tame bird tied to a post to lure passing birds.[35] In

America artificial birds were first used as lures by the Indians. The Indians of the Southwest made lures out of reeds, but they are quite different from the carved wood decoys.[36] In time the American duck decoy influenced European duck-hunting techniques.

Wildfowl gunning had its heyday in the nineteenth century. The colonial flintlock musket was not sufficiently accurate, but the invention of the breech-loading shotgun made wildfowl gunning feasible. By the middle of the nineteenth century, the demand for game food in restaurants was so great that professional hunters known as "market gunners" were active throughout the Atlantic coastal region. The market gunners and the gentlemen-sportsmen created a market for duck decoys, which were made not only by folk craftsmen who hand-carved the decoys but also by factories that turned them out on lathes. There followed the unrestricted slaughter of ducks and shore birds that continued until the Federal Migratory Bird Act of 1913, which banned spring shooting, shooting at night, and the shipment of game birds, and the Migratory Bird Treaty of 1918 with Canada to protect waterfowl all along the North American flyway. This brought an end to market gunning and the shooting of shore birds. Duck hunting was allowed to continue as a sport with a carefully regulated hunting season. The new laws also ended the golden age of duck-decoy carving.

Decoys are classified according to the species of bird they are modeled after and the region in which the decoy was made. These are related factors, because certain species are found only in certain regions. Game birds are classified into two categories: waterfowl and shore birds. Waterfowl include marsh ducks (also known as river, pond, or puddle ducks) and diving ducks (also known as sea ducks). The marsh ducks (mallards, black ducks, pintails, widgeons, teal, and wood ducks) fly in small flocks of not more than fifty and congregate along lakes, small rivers, and ponds. Marsh-duck decoys are set out in "rigs" of correspondingly small numbers. The diving ducks (whistlers, redheads, canvasbacks, broadbills, ruddy ducks, eider ducks, scoter ducks, old squaws, and mergansers) fly in large flocks of 100 or more and are found over deep, open water. They are capable of diving to great depths to feed. Large numbers of decoys are used in the rigs of diving ducks.[37]

Shore birds, sometimes loosely referred to as "snipes," gather near the shore around estuaries and tidal marshes or on land. The lure that is used for them, referred to as a "snipe stool" or "stickup," has a stake that allows the lure literally to stick up in the ground. The early examples of these stick-ups were merely flat profiles or silhouettes. The species include the upland plover, the black-bellied plover, and the yellowleg. Sometimes stick-ups represent Canada geese and brant, as well as such puddle ducks as mallards, pintails, and blacks, but never sea ducks such as the canvasback.[38]

Some of these species no longer inhabit New Jersey; we know of them only from the decoys. For example, the Hudsonian godwit, also known as the ring-tailed marlin and the straight-billed curlew, is gone from the New Jersey shore. And the redheads and canvasbacks are no longer found at the Bay Head section of Barnegat Bay, even though the place name remains Redhead Bay.[39]

New Jersey has two main regional styles of duck decoys: the Barnegat Bay decoys and the Delaware River decoys. There is also a difference between the Delaware Bay decoys and the Delaware River decoys, but these are variations on a theme.[40] One of the characteristics of the Barnegat Bay decoys is that they were made of two slabs of cedar that were hollowed out. This was done to make them light enough to be transported on Barnegat Bay sneakboxes (see "Traditional Boats"). The Barnegat decoys have flatbottoms, little ornamental detail, and tightly tucked heads. The Delaware River and Bay decoys also tended to be hollow and light weight for use on the Delaware River hunting skiff or "Delaware ducker," a doubled-ended boat about sixteen feet long with a mast and half-deck. These boats accommodated two men. The Delaware River decoys have rounded bottoms and a linear shape for use in river rather than bay waters.

Barnegat Bay decoy. Drake pintail by Harry V. Shourds, Seaville. *Courtesy, Jon Frank*

They were noted for their realism and for their carved and incised wing and tail feathers. The decoys were painted after they were carved; some decoy makers painted decoys they had not themselves carved.[41]

Some of the Barnegat Bay decoy makers became famous. For example, Captain Jesse Birdsall of Barnegat Village was a coastwise skipper and decoy maker. According to legend, in the winter of 1899 he killed 115 birds in one day's shooting. Joel Barber quoted him as saying, "It took just exactly one pound of powder; the powder ran out or I'd got more."[42]

George Harvey was a decoy maker in Sea Bright. He told Richard H. Moeller, a decoy collector, the following story about a red-breasted merganser decoy he made and tried out with his gunning partner, Ed Howland, on Barnegat Bay around 1900.

On the opening day of the duck season that year Howland and Harvey were on their bleak island in the Bay. A cold, misty nor'easter was blowing up, and the predawn chore of putting out decoys was already under way. Howland was in the sneak box, and Harvey was giving directions from shore. The Merganser decoys were set at random in the middle of the rig. When the job was completed, the sneak box was hauled up on a mud flat and covered with salt hay. At sunup the wind increased and the decoys bobbed on the slate-gray water. . . .

Delaware River decoy. Drake pintail by Ridgeway Marter, Burlington. *Courtesy, Robert L. White*

Suddenly a hen Merganser was seen swimming to the drake decoy. She was circling around it, getting a little closer every second, when her mate appeared on the scene. Her doings were too much for papa Merganser, and he proceeded to make a savage attack on the decoy. He rolled it over, pecked at it, and tried to spear it with his sharp bill. The gunners were amazed at this odd battle. Finally Harvey decided it was high time to stop the fracas before he lost his new decoy. He fired a shot over the rig, but he might just as well have fired at the moon. The battle continued hotter than ever, with the decoy taking a horrible beating. Harvey became really angry, and his next shot killed the Merganser—and also sank some of the broadbill decoys.

In telling this story to me, George Harvey wound up by saying, "You know, Dick, I didn't so much mind the way that Merganser ruined the beautiful paint job on the decoy. And I didn't mind sinking several decoys when I fired that second shot. But I'm really ashamed to admit it was the first and only duck I ever shot on the water. I'll never live it down."[43]

The foremost New Jersey decoy maker was Harry V. Shourds (1861–1920) of Tuckerton. A house painter by trade, he occasionally worked as a guide for hunting and fishing parties and eventually became a full-time decoy maker. His decoys sold for six dollars a dozen. The catalog of the Shelburne Museum in Vermont refers to him as "one of the outstanding craftsmen of his time and the most prolific carver of shore bird decoys of the eastern seaboard."[44] He reportedly averaged 2,000 decoys per year over a forty-year period.[45] According to legend, he would whittle a decoy head while he was sitting in a barber's chair for a shave.[46] William Mackey, a decoy collector, has said: "In the early 1900's, because of Shourds's efforts alone, Tuckerton may be said to have been the handmade decoy capital of the United States, and therefore of the world."[47]

In 1981 I interviewed Harry V. Shourds of Seaville, who is the grandson of the Harry V. Shourds mentioned above. He explained the difference between decorative decoys and working decoys.

COHEN: For how long have you been making duck decoys?
SHOURDS: Well, I've been doing it full time for a living since 1962. So it's almost twenty years. And I've been carving since, geeze, I can remember, I guess. Making things. My grandfather carved decoys, I don't remember him, but my father—of course, he died when I was twelve years old—but he made decoys. And I used to watch him, you know. Never made anything. But I used to watch him make decoys.

COHEN: Basically, is that how you learned how to make decoys? From your father?

SHOURDS: Yeah, and I make them the same way. Basically the same type of pattern—the same construction that he used. So they are working decoys that I make. A decoy that can be used in the hunting if you want to. Most of them end up on a shelf somewhere for display.

· · · ·

COHEN: Let me ask you something about how the decoys are actually made. Could you basically describe the process from beginning to end, starting with what kind of materials are used for making duck decoys? What kind of wood?

SHOURDS: Well, the wood is a Jersey white cedar which grows in the swamp. It's a wood that's used on boats—it's used on shingles. I hear that the Independence Hall in Philadelphia and all are shingled from white cedar. So it's a good wood—a durable wood for outdoor use. And the decoys are made in two pieces—a top half and a bottom half. Both halves are hollowed out inside to make them light, and also it gives it air space so they won't check over the years. You very seldom see a hollow decoy that's checked in any way. Even an old one. Then that's put together and that's caulked—just like you would a boat—so it don't leak. The head is put on separately nailed from the top. In case it got broke with usage it could be taken off and replaced easy. There's an insert put in the bottom with a chisel where you put lead. You put about five ounces of lead in it for ballast so that when you throw the decoy out, if it lands upside down, it will roll over and sit right in the water. Just like a sailboat would do with a keel on it. And that's the thing of a decoy, you want it to ride right in the water so it swims like a duck. So actually it's really a boat that looks like a duck—in one sense of the word. And then there's a little—we usually put a little leather fold on the front of it to tie the anchor rope to. Some people put a screw eye or what not. And then you can put a line on it with an anchor—anchor it out.

· · · ·

COHEN: Aren't there some decoy carvers that make decoys just for decoration and the style's a little different?

SHOURDS: Yeah, just for decoration. And then they carve a lot of feathers in them. Really make—what they're really making is the model of a duck. You know, they make individual feathers. Insert them. They really went a long ways and carved, or sculpture. I think you get out of the carving end of it when you get into that really. I've been to shows and there's inserted feathers, they're not really a hundred percent wood anymore. There, geeze, you could find so many different materials in there, plastic wood, body putty, metal parts. So it's really a sculpture or model making I would call it—a model of a duck. And most of these guys that do that either copy off a mounted bird or a frozen bird. So's what they're doing is taking a bird and making it into a model. Where the old decoys were somebody's imagination of what a duck looked like. Which makes—to me—old—old decoy collecting really nice because you can look at a decoy and say, "Oh, Ellis Parker made that one," or "Ronny Horner made that one." You can tell the difference in their style. Where today with the decorative ducks they all look alike, you know, they're all models of real ducks. So I think they lost something along the line—for me, you know. A lot of people like them and they enjoy them and they collect them, so everybody has their own.

COHEN: So in other words with the really traditional decoys they're not neccesarily realistic looking.

SHOURDS: Not really. They look like a duck and they're realistic looking in a sense, but then there's also somebody's own idea too put in with it.[48]

New Jersey duck decoys are examples of artifacts that have become a folk art. In the 1920s private collectors began to buy them. The 1931–1932 exhibition of American folk sculpture at the Newark Museum featured a section on decoy birds. And in the 1950s the Shelburne Museum acquired the collection of over 300 New Jersey duck decoys owned by Richard H. Moeller of Rumson. It included decoys made by Henry Grant and Birdsall Ridgeway of Barnegat, Percy Grant of Osbornsville, Gideon Lippincott of Wading River, Chris Sprague and Ellis Parker of Beach Haven, Lloyd Johnson of Bay Head, Winfield White of Sea Bright, George Harvey of Rumson, Mark English of Somer's Point, and Lloyd Parker and Harry Shourds of Tuckerton. Today a Harry Shourds decoy, if you can find one for sale, will fetch a handsome price. Many contemporary carvers make decoys for decoration and artistic competition. Gone are the days when handmade decoys could be bought for six dollars a dozen.

There is a current tendency to consider weathervanes, trade signs, duck decoys, and tombstone carvings as art objects, suitable for display in galleries and museums. It is indeed welcome that connoisseurs have come to recognize the es-

Duck hunting, Forked River, 1935. Photograph by Harry Dorer.
*The Dorer Collection, Newark Public Library*

thetic qualities of folk design. But there is a danger that in taking these objects out of their proper cultural context, their true meanings may be distorted. Most of these examples of folk sculpture were utilitarian in purpose—to indicate the direction of the wind, to advertise what one had to sell, to lure ducks so that they might be shot, to mark a grave and to make a statement about life and death. While they might be appreciated as art, it is in their use that their true historical and cultural meanings are to be found.

# Traditional Boats

I N THE nineteenth century boat building was a major industry in New Jersey, especially in such South Jersey towns as Greenwich, Mauricetown, Millville, and Bridgeton. Some traditional boat types actually are indigenous to New Jersey. Just as the Chesapeake Bay has its bugeyes and skipjacks, New Jersey has its Sea Bright skiffs, Barnegat sneakboxes, and garveys. Other New Jersey boats, such as Durham boats, shallops, sloops, and schooners, are not unique to the state, but they too are a part of New Jersey's boat-building tradition.

The canoes of the Lenape Indians were the first New Jersey boats. Henry Hudson encountered these canoes on his famous exploratory voyage in 1609: "They [the Indians] soon came on board, one after another, in their canoes, which are made of a single piece of wood."[1] These canoes, which we now call dugouts, must have been fairly large, because Robert Juet, an officer on the voyage, described an incident which apparently occurred near Sandy Hook in which five crewmen from the *Half Moon* "were set upon by two Canoes, the one having twelve, and the other fourteen men."[2] Johan De Laet, a director of the Dutch West India Company, briefly described how they were constructed. "Their boats are one piece of wood, hollowed out by fire from the solid trunks of trees."[3] They were used for both transportation and fishing. Several of these dugouts have been preserved in museums. The New Jersey State Museum has a white cedar dugout, twelve feet long and three feet wide, which was found at Meisel's Pond in Belleplain State Forest. A white oak dugout, sixteen by three feet, was found in 1868 near the Hackensack River and is in the museum of the Bergen County Historical Society.[4]

Logs arranged as rafts in order to float them down the Delaware River may not technically constitute a boat type, but they are an important part of the history of the river. They were an effective way to solve the navigational problems caused by the rapids along the river above Trenton. The first person known to have constructed one of these log rafts was Daniel Skinner of Connecticut, part-owner of the Delaware Land Company. In 1764 he tried unsuccessfully to float

Delaware Bay oyster schooners under sail.
Photograph by the late Graham L. Schofield. *Courtesy, John T. Schofield*

several loose logs down the river while he followed in a canoe. He then devised a way to bind the logs together to form a raft, and floated the raft 200 miles down the Delaware from above Port Jervis to Philadelphia.[5]

Logging and rafting on the upper Delaware continued from the middle of the eighteenth century through the end of the nineteenth century. The technique basically followed that pioneered by Skinner. In the spring the lumbermen would roll the logs into the water. Holes would be made near the ends of the logs with an auger. Wooden pegs would be inserted into these holes, and then fastened to transverse "lash poles," which would hold the raft together. Sometimes sawed timbers would be used, in which case four planks with auger holes in both ends would be laid to form a rectangular frame and pinned together with sapling sprouts, known as "grubs." On this base layers of planks were placed in alternate directions to a height of two to three feet. The resulting frame was termed a "crib." Several cribs were fastened together to form a "colt," and several colts were linked together to form a "raft." When two or more rafts were joined together it was called a "double raft" or a "fleet." Then tillers or oars were attached fore and aft. Sometimes these rafts carried on their decks loads of unfloatable lumber.[6]

Each oar was handled by a man. The rear oarsman was known as the "steersman." Considerable skill was required to navigate the river, and some rivermen became legendary. The steersmen would call out changes in course direction by referring to "Jersey" for the east side of the river and "Pennsylvania" for the west side. "Jersey" was the term used even above Port Jervis where the east side of the river is New York. The largest raft was said to have been assembled near Callicoon, Pennsylvania, circa 1870. It was 210 feet long and 75 feet wide,

Durham boat.
Drawing by Joseph Crilley

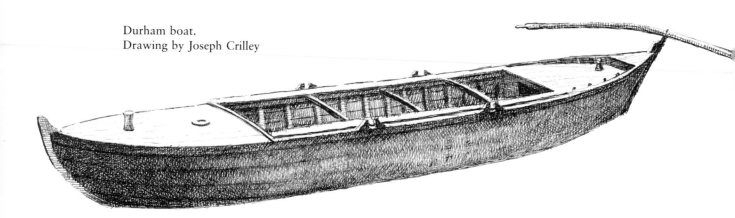

and it took eight men and eight oars to pilot it to Philadelphia. Before the Civil War the fore hands on a raft were paid ten dollars for a trip to Easton and fifteen dollars for a trip to Trenton. Steersmen made fifteen to eighteen dollars to Easton and twenty-five dollars to Trenton.[7] When the raft reached its destination it would be broken up, and the rivermen had to walk back to their point of departure.

One Delaware River boat type was made famous because Washington and his army used it in 1776 to cross the river to attack Trenton. This was the Durham boat, named after the Durham Iron Works in Bucks County, Pennsylvania. Emanuel Leutze's painting, "Washington Crossing the Delaware," depicts rowboats, not the Durham boats that were actually used in the crossing. In any case, Durham boats were used primarily for commerce. For more than a century from about 1750 to about 1850 they hauled freight on the Delaware River.

Durham boats were very large, often sixty to sixty-six feet long. A sixty-foot boat had a capacity of 150 barrels of flour or about 600 bushels of shelled corn. The boats were pointed both fore and aft. There were small cabins below deck both fore and aft. The crew slept in the forward cabin when the weather was bad. The boats were equipped with straw for sleeping and a charcoal stove for cooking. The boats had no keels. They were steered by a long "sweep" or rudder, which could be attached to either end of the boat. When going upstream, the crew would use "setting poles," which they could plant in the river bottom, propelling the boat forward by walking along the "walking planks" on either side of the deck. When going downriver, the crew set the planks on edge to prevent water from splashing aboard. Sometimes the crews pulled the boats upstream by catching hold of overhead foliage, which was known as "pulling brush." The boats had flat bottoms to enable them to negotiate the rapids above Trenton. In the mid-nineteenth century canal traffic replaced river traffic, and the last trip of a Durham boat to Philadelphia was made in 1860. Like the Conestoga wagon, which originated in Pennsylvania and spread west, the Durham boat spread to other parts of the country, such as Wisconsin, Nebraska, North Carolina, and New England.[8]

Two major canals were built in New Jersey in the nineteenth century: the Morris Canal, completed in 1831, from Jersey City to Phillipsburgh; and the Delaware and Raritan Canal, completed in 1834, from New Brunswick to Bordentown. Several types of canal boats were used on these canals. The original boats used on the Morris Canal were known as "flickers" or "stiffs." They usually had round sterns, measured seventy-five feet by nine feet, and had a capacity of eighteen to twenty-five tons. But they were too small, and when the canal was renovated in 1846 new, larger boats were used. These were called "hinge-boats," "section boats," or "lemon squeezers." They consisted of two square-sterned boats hinged together stern to stern. They measured approximately eighty-seven by ten and one-half feet and had a capacity of fifty-four to sixty tons. The Delaware and Raritan Canal used hinge-type coal barges that were ninety feet long and ten feet wide and displaced five feet of water when fully loaded. Those that carried coal from the Mauch Chunk mines in the Lehigh Valley were known as "chunkers," and those that carried coal from the mines near Reading via the Schuylkill Navigation Canal were called "skukers." On the Morris Canal the boats were officially known by numbers, but the captains also used nicknames for their boats. The name of the first boat on the canal was "Walk in the Water." The payboat was named "Katie Kellogg," after the wife of a superintendent of the canal company. James Lee interviewed the daughter of a canal-boat captain who named his boat "Rachael"; whenever it got stuck he would say, "Damn you, Rachael, what's the matter with you?"

The canal boats had small cabins below decks which contained two bunks and a table on hinges against the bulkheads, a kerosene lamp, and perhaps a corner cupboard. Generally canallers were bachelors, but some were married and even took their wives and children on trips. Small children would be tied with rope attached to the deck to prevent them from falling in the water. The boats were pulled by mule teams. A team consisting of a light and a dark mule was known as a "Jersey team." "Packet boats," used for transporting passengers and perishable goods, were pulled by horses, which were faster than mules. But they were not common on the New Jersey canals. Maintenance barges taken out on day trips to repair the canal were called "work scows." Maintenance boats called "mud-diggers" would go out for weeks at a time to dredge the canal. While the canals were used into the twentieth century, they could not compete with the railroad. In 1924 the Morris Canal was closed to navigation, and the same thing happened to the Delaware and Raritan Canal in 1933.[9]

While the Durham boat was used primarily along the upper Delaware River, the lower part of the river and Delaware Bay were home waters to the shallop. It was a European boat type, known as the *challoupe* to the French and as the *chalupa* to the Spaniards, Basques, and Portuguese. The seventeenth-century shallop was an "open" workboat; that is, it did not have an enclosed deck. It was "double-ended," which means its hull was pointed fore and aft, and it had one or two masts. The seventeenth-century Biscay shallop was primarily a whaleboat; it was used by the Dutch for whaling in the Delaware Bay as early as 1632.[10] Offshore whaling in Delaware Bay was continued by Englishmen from Long Island and New England who settled on the Cape May peninsula in the

1680s. The settlement had various names at different times: Portsmouth, Cape May Town, New England Village, and Town Bank.[11] One of the earliest ships built in the town of Greenwich in Cumberland County, was the shallop *Greenwich*, built in 1737. Shallops continued to be built in the Diving Creek vicinity as late as 1830.[12] What became known as the Delaware River shallop, which differed from the early shallop in that it had a square stern, became the common freight boat on the lower Delaware and its tributaries (e.g. the Schuylkill River) in the early nineteenth century.[13]

The sloop was another early sailing vessel that was brought to New Jersey by Europeans. In Dutch the name is spelled *sloep*. According to William A. Baker, curator of the Hart Nautical Museum at the Massachusetts Institute of Technology, seventeenth-century maritime records do not always make a clear demarcation between the sloop and the shallop. By the late seventeenth century, the sloop in North America became typed as an open boat, usually with one mast and a short gaff (a spar supporting the upper side of the quadrilateral, fore and aft, mainsail). But he cautions that until the middle of the nineteenth century sailing vessels were typed by their hull shape and use rather than by the way they were rigged, as is done nowadays. There are, for example, sloops with two masts rather than one.[14] Sloops were being built in Greenwich as early as 1735, when the *Swansey* was constructed there. Between 1738 and 1754 numerous sloops were built in the town. These "Delaware Bay" sloops were used in coastwise trade and in oystering.[15] The "Hudson River" sloops were a principal means of hauling freight on the Hudson from the seventeenth century through the beginning of the nineteenth, when they were replaced by the steamboats.[16] Hudson River sloops also navigated the Hackensack River. A view of Hackensack circa 1800 shows a rather unusual two-masted Hudson River sloop moored in the river. Normally they had one mast and a distinctive hull shape with a high sterncastle (the after cabin section of the ship) and a taffrail (the rail around a boat's stern).

According to Donald H. Rolfs, author of *Under Sail; The Dredgeboats of Delaware Bay*, "the shipwrights of the Delaware Bay reached the apex of their craft with the building of schooners."[17] A schooner is a two-masted sailing vessel with two gaff sails and a jib sail (a triangular sail carried at the bow). During the colonial period schooners were used for coastwise trade. In 1738 the schooner *Phoenix*, under Captain Ebenezer Miller, was listed as sailing out of Greenwich. In 1838 the town of Bridgeton on the Cohansey River had a shipyard where large schooners and sloops were being built, and thirty schooners and sloops listed Bridgeton as their home port.[18]

The schooners of Delaware Bay became most important as dredgeboats

Hudson River sloop

*Opposite:*
Oyster schooner

Drawings by Joseph Crilley

during the oyster boom starting in the late nineteenth century. This boom came about with the introduction of the oyster dredge and the completion of the railroad to the Maurice River in 1876. The oyster dredge was an iron rake with a mesh bag attached. It was "drudged" along the bottom of the bay and then hauled in by a mechanical winch. The oysters were dumped on the deck and culled, that is, separated into grades, and then shoveled into large piles. When the boat returned to port the oysters were either bagged in the shell or shucked (opened) in the shucking house, and then shipped by refrigerated railroad car to markets in Philadelphia. Dredging under sail continued in the Delaware Bay through the 1940s, when many of the schooners were converted to diesel power.

Shore fishing also developed along the Atlantic coast and was oriented primarily to the growing New York City market. In 1845 the fishing community of

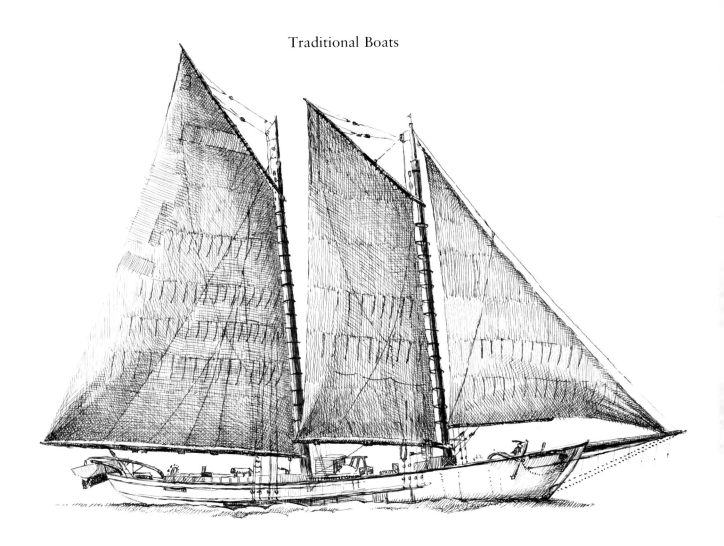

Nauvoo was established near present-day Sea Bright. It was followed by other fishing communities at Galilee (near Monmouth Beach) and Long Branch. Blue-fish, mackerel, and sea bass were caught from May to November, and some cod was caught in the winter. The type of boat that was used became known as the Sea Bright skiff. It was a light, flexible boat capable of being launched from the beach into the surf. It measured about fifteen by five feet, although later skiffs were even larger. The skiff had a square stern, a pointed bow, and a graceful sweep to the topsides. It could be rowed or sailed.

By the 1880s skiffs were being used in pound fishing along the Jersey Shore. The pound was an offshore arrangement of nets attached to poles. It consisted of three parts: the leader, the forebay, and the purse. The leader was a long net, 900 to 1,000 feet, set at right angles to the beach. The fish would hit this ob-

119

struction and swim out to sea only to be caught in the funnel-shaped forebay, which would direct them into the purse. The nets would then be hauled aboard the skiffs (or pound boats, as they were sometimes called). The boats had to be strong enough to carry the heavy load of fish and withstand the surf. Teams of horses were used to haul the loaded pound boats onto the beach. The fish were packed in ice and shipped by schooner or train to New York City or Philadelphia. Scandinavian fishermen were attracted to the Jersey Shore by this line of work. After 1907 the horses were replaced by diesel engines on the boats. But the pound fishermen could not compete with the draggers and offshore commercial fishermen, and after World War II they gradually began to disappear. By 1961 they were all gone.[19]

The garvey, one of New Jersey's indigenous boat types, is used in bays and estuaries, mainly for clamming and oystering. Garveys generally measure twelve by four feet, are made of a white oak frame with white cedar planking, have a shallow draft, and are flat bottomed.[20] Two other indigenous boat types, the Delaware ducker and the Barnegat sneakbox, are both used in duck hunting. The ducker is a double-ended skiff, usually about sixteen feet long. It is made of light cedar and has a half-deck. Although fitted with a mast, it is usually rowed to the hunting location. It accommodates two men, and is ideally suited to the exposed hunting conditions on the Delaware River.[21] According to Samuel Bonnell, the Barnegat sneakbox "is probably the best known duck hunting boat in the country."[22] It is so named because it allows the hunter to sneak up on his prey. The sneakbox is a shallow-draft boat with a curved hull. It measures ten to twelve feet in length, four feet in width, and seventeen inches in depth and weighs about 300 pounds. It draws only four to six inches of water, making it ideal for maneuvering through the shallow waters of the Barnegat Bay. On the stern it has a rack for carrying 100 to 150 duck decoys. It can be rowed or a sail can be attached to it.

We have a particularly rich description of how a sneakbox is made. Sam Hunt of Waretown has been making garveys since 1924 and sneakboxes since 1961. In April 1978 he was asked by Christopher Hoare about how one makes a sneakbox.

> SAM HUNT: Well, the first thing you do when you're starting from scratch you gotta figure out the length you want and the width you want and the curvature of the bottom and the depth you want in the middle and the depth that you want on the stern and make sure that there are no flat places. It's all a solid curve, if you look at it this way or that way. Now a garvey is flat. That's flat there where the runners go. They used to build them much flatter. When you've done that they

# Traditional Boats

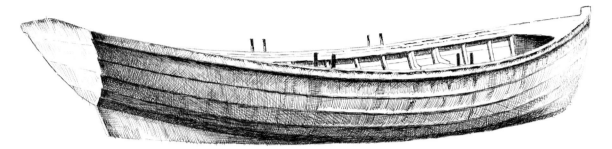

Sea Bright skiff

Garvey

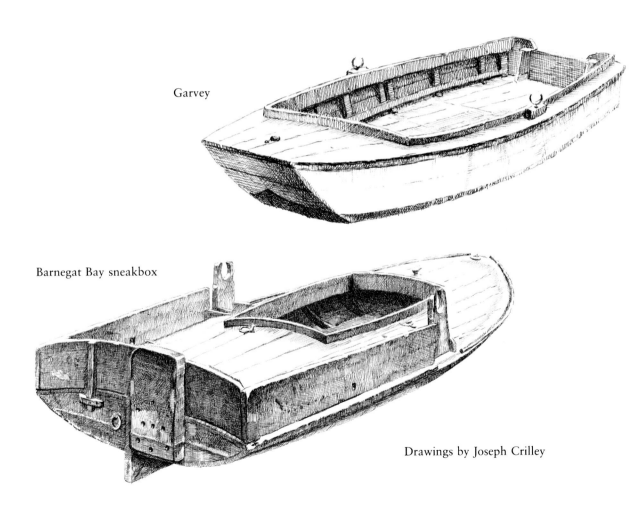

Barnegat Bay sneakbox

Drawings by Joseph Crilley

121

froze you to death in the winter time. In zero weather here's your belly up above the wind. That's why the guys wanted them deeper, so they can get down. So they could pull a hatch covering over them when the ducks ain't flying or it's cold. They used to build a sneakbox special for a man. He used to lay down on the ground and they'd draw a circle around him and build a hatch so his belly could stick out.[23]

The sneakbox is usually made of two types of wood. The frame is white oak— according to Sam Hunt, "Jersey white oak, swamp white oak that grows next to the swamp. That's tougher [and] stronger. It has more sap in it and will last ten times longer than a piece of white oak on the upland."[24] The planking is white cedar, because, according to Hunt: "Well, I never seen a piece of it really rot in a boat. Never. It's light, and it will swell. You can put it together and leave the seams that far apart and it still comes tight. It won't leak!"[25] The wood must be aged for two to three years so that it has time to dry out properly.

Sam Hunt constructs the inverted hull of his sneakboxes on a wooden form known as a "jig." Lengthwise from stem to stern on this jig he fastens furring strips, which are not actually part of the sneakbox and are later cut away. He then bends into position the "harpins," two strips of oak extending from stem to stern where the deck meets the hull. Then he bends the "timbers" across the furring strips and clamps them to the harpins. This forms the basic frame of the hull. Originally sneakbox frames were cut out of a single plank of cedar, but Hunt uses oak timbers, which he bends using a steam box. Then the "transom," a flat board forming the stern, is attached to the frame using "natural knees," elbow-shaped pieces of wood with a naturally curved grain.

He is then ready to attach the white cedar planking to the hull. The first plank is positioned down the center from stem to stern, and then the other planks are attached. This is what is known as "planking it out." According to Sam Hunt, "Every boat I build has thirteen planks on them. One in the center and six on each side. And I won't change that, because it makes the planks come out right."[26] Then the sneakbox is turned right side up, and he installs the "centerboard trunk," in which can be inserted a centerboard for sailing or a "daggerboard" for anchoring the sneakbox while decoys are put out. Hunt then attaches the "carlins," curved cedar beams running across the sneakbox on which the deck rests. Next the hatch is framed and the deck planks of white cedar attached. Finally, the accessories, such as the oarlocks, mast, and sail, are added. According to Sam Hunt, the sneakbox is the "ablest boat for the size. It's almost impossible to upset one of them. Loading the boat, I could put one in [the water] alone. The lighter the better, but they must be strong."[27]

Mary Hufford, a folklorist at the American Folklife Center of the Library of Congress, reminds us that each sneakbox maker has his own style and each sneakbox is a little different. Just as traditional tales are found in different versions, so are traditional boats. The tale type is the sum total of all the versions, and the same is true of the boat type. "The sneakbox," Hufford notes, "provides us with a classic example of a form born of, and intended for use in, a specific environment." However, the sneakbox has become a symbol. It is taken out of its context and displayed in museums and banks and on T-shirts. "What happens," Hufford asks, "when the form of the sneakbox becomes more laden with significance than with decoys? . . . What happens is that the boat joins a class of art expressive of isolation from the environment, rather than intimacy with it."[28]

Most of the boats I have discussed were originally workboats rather than pleasure craft. Today, however, sneakboxes might be considered pleasure boats, since market gunning is no longer allowed. Sloops and schooners have also become pleasure craft, especially now that fishing under sail has become obsolete. All these boats played an important role in the economic history of New Jersey, whether it was in transporting logs down the Delaware River, offshore fishing on the Atlantic coast, oystering in Delaware Bay, or hauling coal from the Lehigh Valley.

# Folk Architecture

LIKE OTHER aspects of material culture, architecture can be divided into fine, vernacular, and folk. Fine architecture refers to extraordinary structures designed by famous architects. Often this means capitols, churches, and mansions of the wealthy. Vernacular architecture, as defined by John Kouwenhoven, the author of *The Arts in Modern American Civilization*, refers to commonplace structures designed by engineers and less noted architects. It includes bridges, factories, company-town houses, tenements, suburban houses, and commercial buildings (skyscrapers, office buildings, department stores, shopping centers).[1] Folk architecture refers to buildings not designed by architects and not built from blueprints or pattern books. It is part of building traditions passed down from generation to generation of carpenters and masons, which often can be traced to European antecedents. Much of what is called colonial architecture is in fact folk architecture. Architectural historians mistakenly refer to colonial architecture as part of a medieval building tradition, despite the fact that folk architecture in Europe is not associated exclusively with the Middle Ages.[2] Some architectural historians do not distinguish between vernacular and folk architecture. There are, however, distinct differences between them in form, use, materials, and workmanship.

The dwellings of the Lenape Indians were similar to dwellings built by other Indians throughout the Eastern Woodland culture area, which extended from New England to Virginia and the Midwest. These dwellings, known as wigwams, were constructed of wooden frames made of bent saplings. The frames were then covered with bark. The floor plans were either circular or elongated. In his *A Description of the New Netherlands*, written in 1656, Adriaen van der Donck provided a detailed description of how these wigwams were constructed.

> When they build a house, they place long slender hickory saplings in the ground, having the bark stripped off, in a straight line of two rows, as far asunder as they intend the breadth of the house to be, and continuing the rows as far as it is intended the length shall be. Those sapling poles are bent over towards each other in the form of an arch, and secured together, having the appearance of a garden arbour. The sapling poles are then crossed with split poles in the form of lathing, which are well fastened to the upright work. The lathings are heaviest near the ground. A space of about a foot wide is left open in the crown of the arch. For covering they use the bark of ash, chestnut, and other trees, which they peel off in pieces of about six feet long, and as broad as they can. They cover their houses, laying the smooth side inwards, leaving an open space of about a foot wide in the crown, to let out the smoke. They lap the side edges and ends over each other, having regard to the shrinking of the bark, securing the covering with withes [tough, flexible twigs] to the lathings. A crack or rent they shut up, and in this manner they make their houses proof against wind and rain. They have one door in the centre of the house. When the bark of the ash and chestnut trees is not loose, they have recourse to the timber trees, which grow along the brooks, the bark of which can be taken off during the whole summer season.[3]

Since van der Donck lived in Rensselaerswyck at the time, his description was probably of a wigwam in the upper Hudson River Valley.

Indians of New York State and those of Pennsylvania and New Jersey seem to have constructed their wigwams in much the same way. There were, however, certain differences in their dwellings, according to Herbert C. Kraft, an archeologist at Seton Hall University, who has located the sites of several wigwams in the upper Delaware River Valley. From postmolds (soil with a slightly different coloration caused by rotting of the house posts) he reconstructed the floor plans of actual wigwams in their original locations. He has found both round-ended elongated floor plans (longhouses) with double rows of paired postmolds and an oval floor plan with a single row of postmolds. The longhouse probably was a dwelling for an extended family consisting of an older woman, her husband and children, and the families of her married daughters. The smaller oval-shaped dwelling probably housed a nuclear family. Both types of structure contained silo-shaped pits, which were used for food storage. But, Kraft notes, in the first

Reconstruction of a bark-covered longhouse of the Pahaquarra-Minisink culture.
*Archaeological Research Center, Seton Hall University*

Swedish log cabin, Hancock's Bridge, Salem County.
*Library of Congress, Historic American Building Survey*

place, there is no evidence that the New Jersey wigwams were located in forti-
fied villages surrounded by palisades. Second, unlike the New York longhouses
which had doorways on the ends, the New Jersey longhouses had their doorways on the side. Third, while birch bark was used in New York, white birch
does not grow well in New Jersey, so probably elm, linden, or chestnut bark was
used. Fourth, the New York longhouses had walkways down the center with living quarters on either side; the New Jersey longhouses had one or more parti-
tions extending three-quarters of the way across the dwelling. Finally, although
these wigwams are described as being occupied seasonally, Kraft found evidence
in the food-storage silos that those in New Jersey were occupied year-round.[4]

Log cabins have been a symbol of the American frontier, but they did not
originate in the West; nor did they originate with the English. In fact, log construction is a European tradition that was introduced to America through eastern Pennsylvania and western New Jersey. In his book *The Log Cabin Myth*,
Harold Shurtleff showed that the English did not build log cabins either in
Jamestown or in Plymouth Plantation. Shurtleff argues that they were first built
in America by the Swedes in New Sweden, which was established on both banks

German log cabin, Upper Mill, Burlington County. Photograph by Nathaniel R. Ewan.
*Library of Congress, Historic American Building Survey*

of Delaware Bay from 1638 to 1655.[5] In 1679 Jasper Danckaerts described a Swedish log house near Bordentown as being

> made according to the Swedish mode, and as they usually build their houses here, which are block-houses, being nothing else than entire trees, split through the middle, or squared out of the rough, and placed in the form of a square, one upon the other, as high as they wish to have the house; the ends of these timbers are let into each other, about a foot from the ends, half of one into half of the other. The whole structure is thus made, without a nail or a spike. The ceiling and roof do not exhibit much finer work, except among the most careful people, who have the ceiling planked and a glass window. The doors are wide enough, but very low, so that you have to stoop in entering. These houses are quite tight and warm; but the chimney is placed in a corner.[6]

A few of these Swedish log cabins are still standing in southeastern Pennsylvania

127

Early Dutch-American farmhouse, Montville vicinity, Morris County, built circa 1724. Photograph by Harry Dorer. *The Dorer Collection, Newark Public Library*

and southwestern New Jersey. The cedar plank house at Hancock's Bridge in Salem County is, however, a reconstruction of a Swedish log cabin originally located on the Salem-Hancock's Bridge road.

Henry Glassie and Fred Kniffen, a cultural geographer, argue, however, that the specific type of log construction that diffused into the American frontier was not Swedish but German. In the Swedish construction the logs were hewn square and placed one on top of another without any space between. In the German construction the logs were either hewn or left round and placed one on top of another with space between, which was filled with chinking. This type of log construction was introduced in the eighteenth century by the Pennsylvania Germans. Scotch-Irish immigrants who settled in Pennsylvania adopted it and combined it with the rectangular cabin floor plan of their thatch-roof cottages in Northern Ireland. The result, according to Glassie, was the American log cabin. The diffusion of the log cabin followed the routes of migration of the Pennsylvania Germans and Scotch-Irish. The Germans migrated into northwestern New Jersey and the mountainous region of Maryland. The Scotch-Irish migrated north into the southern tier of New York State and southwest down the Great Valley of the southern Appalachian Mountains and through the mountain passes into Kentucky, Tennessee, and the southern parts of Illinois, Indiana, and Ohio.[7] The log cabin at Upper Mill, Burlington County, reputed to have been erected in 1720 by Peter Bard, is an example of German-style log construction.

Farmstead showing Dutch barn (right), gambrel-roof Dutch-American farmhouse (left),
and "Dutch Colonial" suburban house (center rear), Closter. Photograph by R. Merritt Lacey.
*Library of Congress, Historic American Building Survey*

Dutch farmhouses delineate the Dutch culture area, not only in northern
New Jersey but also in the Hudson River Valley, on Staten Island, and on western Long Island. It has long been thought that the defining characteristic of the
Dutch farmhouse was the Dutch gambrel roof with its overhanging eaves (a
gambrel roof has two slopes on either side of the ridge). Actually, the earliest
Dutch farmhouses in New Jersey had pitched roofs with overhanging eaves. An
example of this is the Thomas Demarest house in Montville, Morris County,
built circa 1724. The gambrel roof was not introduced into Dutch architecture
in America until the middle of the eighteenth century. The framing of the Dutch
gambrel is similar to that of the English gambrel. Furthermore, there are no pro-
totypes for the gambrel roof in the Netherlands, although gambrel roofs are
common in parts of East Anglia in England. The overhanging eave appears to be
a widespread survival of thatch-roof construction which is not associated with
any one nation. There are, for example, overhanging eaves on some New England houses in Connecticut. Thus, the gambrel roof appears to be an example of
the blending of two different cultural traditions. In this case it is an English culture trait grafted onto Dutch architecture.[8]

The Dutch farmhouse type should be defined not by its gambrel roof but by
its framing and floor plan. There is a clear difference between English framing
and continental (Dutch) framing. The English built their houses with a boxlike
wooden frame. The Dutch built with a frame that consisted of a series of

Patterned brickwork farmhouse, Hancock's Bridge, Salem County.
*Library of Congress, Historic American Building Survey*

H-bents resembling goalposts. This continental frame was used in both barns and houses.[9] Some early Dutch farmhouses in the Hudson River Valley and on western Long Island have this frame. An example is the Jan Martense Schenck house in Brooklyn which was dismantled and reassembled in the Brooklyn Museum.[10] Most of the Dutch houses in New Jersey were built in the eighteenth and early nineteenth centuries. Rather than having the Dutch framing, they demonstrate a mixture of English and Dutch building traditions.

The floor plans of the Dutch farmhouses, however, demonstrate some continental survivals. Actually, there are five basic floor plans in Dutch farmhouses, three of which are clearly continental and two of which are English. The three continental floor plans are: two rooms without a hallway with one or more exterior chimneys; two rooms with two or more smaller bedrooms in the rear; and two rooms separated by a central hallway. The two English floor plans include: the Georgian floor plan, that is one or two rooms on either side of a central hallway; and the two-thirds Georgian floor plan, that is two rooms one behind the other with a hallway on the side. The fact that these last two floor plans are clearly English also demonstrates the cultural blending of English and Dutch building traditions.

The materials used in construction delineate subregions within the overall Dutch culture area. In New Jersey there are at least three such subregions, which cross the political boundaries between New York and New Jersey. In Bergen, Morris, Essex, and Passaic counties, and in Rockland County and parts of

Friends meetinghouse, Mansfield Square, Burlington County, built in 1815.
*New Jersey State Library, Archives and History, Historic American Building Survey*

Staten Island, New York, the farmhouses are constructed of red sandstone. In Monmouth County and on western Long Island the houses are of wood frame construction. And in Warren and Sussex counties they are constructed of gray fieldstone, similar to that used in the middle Hudson River Valley. Middlesex, Somerset, and Mercer counties, where the Dutch also migrated, show a mixture of traditions. These subregional differences demonstrate how folk architecture is adapted to different environments, making use of available building materials.[11]

One of the great treasures of New Jersey folk architecture is the patterned brickwork on farmhouses in Salem, Gloucester, and Burlington counties, of which a good example is the Hancock House at Hancock's Bridge in Salem County. The main part of the house has a brickwork known as "Flemish bond," in which each row of bricks has alternating "leaders" (the long side of the brick) and "headers" (the short end of the brick). This produces a modified checkered pattern. On the gable end (the short side of the house) the Flemish bond is the background for the decorative brickwork, which includes the initials "H/WS" (standing for William and Sarah Hancock), "1734" (the year in which the house was built), and a series of vertical zigzag lines, produced by glazed brick against the Flemish bond background. While the bond is called Flemish, these are not Dutch houses. Their floor plans are English Georgian with one or two rooms on either side of the central hallway. They have "pent" roofs (the elongated hoods between the first and second stories on the facade and back side of the house). Paul Love, who wrote a doctoral dissertation on patterned brickwork in Amer-

131

ica, has noted that Flemish bond can be found throughout northern Europe and eastern England.[12] According to Thomas Jefferson Wertenbaker, the historian, the pent roof has an English prototype.[13] Pent roofs are found in Philadelphia and its hinterland—Bucks and Chester counties, Pennsylvania. These South Jersey patterned brickwork houses were built by English Quakers who settled in what was then known as West New Jersey, which was a Quaker proprietary colony before the founding of Pennsylvania. These South Jersey houses place Salem, Gloucester, and Burlington counties in a Quaker culture area that includes southeastern Pennsylvania and southwestern New Jersey.

Another indicator of the Quaker culture area is the Quaker meetinghouse. Like the Puritans, the Quakers avoided the word "church" for their houses of worship. And like the Puritans, the Quakers were a plain sect who preferred a plain style in dress and in architecture. While some Quakers became wealthy merchants and departed from the plain style, the Hicksite Quakers in the nineteenth century attempted to preserve that style. The meetinghouses are simple, undecorated buildings, much like dwelling houses on the outside. Inside the "benches" (not "pews") were placed in rows facing the center on three sides of the room. The fourth side of the room had a bench for the elders or "weighty" (wise, experienced) Friends. This reflected the Quaker avoidance of preachers; silent meditation rather than sermons was emphasized. The rear row of each section of benches was called the "back bench" and was reserved for the young. Peter O. Wacker, a cultural geographer at Rutgers University, has mapped the Quaker meetinghouses built in New Jersey between 1672 and 1796.[14] His map shows the spread of the Quaker culture area from southwestern New Jersey to north central New Jersey and the Jersey Shore.

Barn types are also useful indicators of culture areas. There are three basic barn types found in New Jersey: the Dutch, the English, and the Pennsylvania German. The Dutch barn is characterized by the H-bent frame already discussed in connection with Dutch farmhouses. From the outside the Dutch barn can be recognized by the large barn door on the gable end. In 1748 Peter Kalm described Dutch barns between Trenton and New Brunswick.

> The barns had a peculiar kind of construction in this locality, of which I shall give a concise description. The main building was very large, almost the size of a small church; the roof was high, covered with wooden shingles, sloping on both sides, but not steep. The walls which supported it were not much higher than a full grown man; but on the other hand the breadth of the building was all the greater. In the middle was the threshing floor and above it, or in the loft or in the gar-

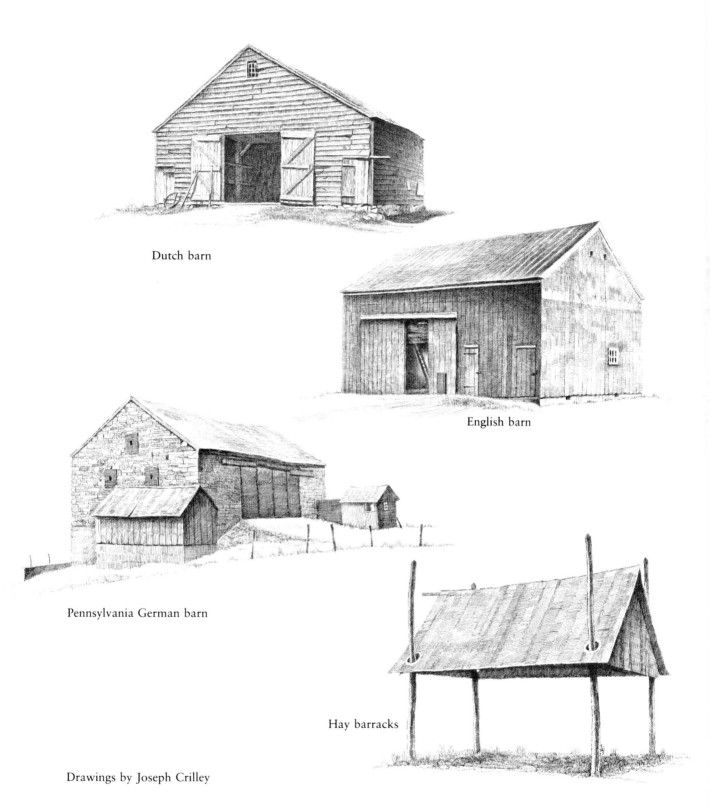

Dutch barn

English barn

Pennsylvania German barn

Hay barracks

Drawings by Joseph Crilley

ret, they put the unthreshed grain, the straw, or anything else, according to the season. On one side were stables for the horses, and on the other for the cows. The young stock had also their particular stables or stalls, and in both ends of the building were large doors, so that one could drive in with a cart and horses through one of them, and go out at the other. Here under one roof therefore were the threshing floor, the barn, the stables, the hay loft, the coach house, etc. This kind of building is used chiefly by the Dutch and Germans, for it is to be observed that the country between Trenton and New York is not inhabited by many Englishmen, but mostly by Germans or Dutch, the latter of which are especially numerous.[15]

The prototype of the Dutch barn was a combination peasant house and barn, in which the animals live at one end and the family at the other, often with no partition between them. These structures had no chimneys, and smoke from the open hearth would fill the living section, making it possible to hang smoked meats from the rafters. Such structures are found along the northern European Plain from the eastern Netherlands into northern Germany and Denmark. In the Netherlands they are known as *loeshuisen* (dirt houses). There is archeological and documentary evidence that the Dutch built this kind of peasant house in New Netherland in the early seventeenth century, including one at Achter Col in the lower Hackensack Valley.[16] But by the end of the century the Dutch in America began to build separate barns and farmhouses. Using newspaper advertisements and war damage claims for the years 1749 to 1782, Peter Wacker mapped the distribution of Dutch barns.[17] His maps shows a cluster in the Raritan and Millstone river valleys. I have located examples of Dutch barns in Bergen, Monmouth, and Sussex counties.

The English barn has a boxlike frame similar to that of the English farmhouse. From the outside it can be recognized by the location of the door on the long side of the barn. It is also taller than the squat Dutch barn. A person can just about touch the roof of some Dutch barns where it connects with the side walls. This is not possible in an English barn. English barns are found extensively in New England and are also widespread in New Jersey, where English-speaking farmers settled among the Dutch and Swedes in the late seventeenth century.

The Pennsylvania German barn is sometimes called the bank barn. It is a split-level structure, built into an embankment. A rear ramp gives access to the threshing floor and hay storage lofts on the upper level. On the lower level underneath an overhang (known as the forebay) are stables for cattle and horses.

This barn can be traced back to the combination peasant house and barn found in southern Germany, Austria, and Switzerland. In Pennsylvania the Germans built these structures solely as barns, and from there they spread to northwestern New Jersey.

A distinctive feature of rural New Jersey is the hay barracks: haystacks with four or five posts and a movable roof and base. In a letter dated 1787, Mary Capner described a hay barracks in Hunterdon County.

> Barracks are a building I have not described to you, tho I noticed them at the first coming into the country. Tommy has made one for his Bro. (It has) four poles fixed in the ground at the distance of fifteen feet in a square. The poles are squared fifteen feet or more at top and five feet at bottom unsquared. This is all above ground. In the square part of the poles there are holes bored thro at the distance of twelve inches big enough for a strong iron pin to be put thro to suport (sic) four wall plates which are tennanted at the ends, then some light spars are put upon the wall plates and thatch upon them. When it was only five feet from the ground, the room can be raised at pleasure 21 feet or any distance from the ground between that and five feet. These are to put hay or any kind of grain under and the roof is always ready to shelter it from hasty rains which is common here in summer. Those that have only two cows have the bottom part boarded at the sides and a floor laid over and the hay at top and the cow stable under.[18]

Like the Dutch barn, hay barracks can be traced back to northern Europe and indicate the Dutch culture area. Wacker mapped a large cluster present in central New Jersey during the years 1730–1782. He noted that they were adopted by other ethnic groups in New Jersey.[19] Don McTernan in 1978 located seven hay barracks in Bergen, Morris, Warren, and Hunterdon counties. He notes that while there is visual and documentary evidence of barracks having been built in New York State and Pennsylvania, none survives.[20] Perhaps the reason they survived in New Jersey is that after the opening of the Erie Canal, wheat growing shifted to western New York and the Midwest, but grain crops, especially barley and oats, continued to be raised in New Jersey throughout the nineteenth century.

Other examples of New Jersey folk architecture that define a culture area are the fisherman shanties and icehouses located along the Jersey Shore. The nineteenth-century shore fishing communites constituted a distinctive settlement pattern (see "Traditional Boats"). Communities like Nauvoo and Galilee in

Fishing village, Monmouth County.
*From* Harper's Weekly, *August 22, 1868. Courtesy, New Jersey Historical Society*

Fisherman shanties and icehouses, Monmouth County.
*From* Frank Leslie's Illustrated, *August 16, 1873. Courtesy, New Jersey Historical Society*

Interior of a fisherman's hut. *From* Frank Leslie's Illustrated, *August 16, 1873. Courtesy, New Jersey Historical Society*

Monmouth County were clusters of fisherman's shanties and icehouses. The shanties were small, one- and two-room frame buildings of batten construction. On the inside they had a wooden bunk bed, a table, and benches. Similar shanties are found throughout the maritime culture area from Nova Scotia (where they are the prototype of the Acadian house type) through New England to the Jersey Shore. The icehouses also had wooden frames and clapboard siding. They had conical roofs and measured 75 to 100 feet in circumference. They measured about 14 feet from floor to ceiling, and the floor was dug about 8 feet below ground. Sand, sawdust, and tanbark were banked along the walls as insulation. They could hold 150 to 200 tons of ice, sufficient for four two-man fishing crews. Every day the catch was brought ashore, cleaned, packed, iced, and shipped to New York by sloop or steamboat.[21] The existence of these kinds of fishing structures indicates that there was a maritime culture region along the Jersey Shore that was distinct from the Pine Barrens culture region in the interior.

Folk architecture has important uses for the historian. Since it reflects distinct building traditions, it is one index for mapping culture areas. Cultural borrowings and the blending of cultural traits can also be studied in folk architecture. New Jersey is especially interesting in this respect because so many ethnic groups came in contact with each other here.

# Folk Furniture

FOLK FURNITURE corresponds roughly with what is called country furniture.[1] But the difference between folk and fine furniture is not necessarily a distinction between the products of rural craftsmen and urban craftsmen; some fine furniture makers worked in rural places, and makers of folk furniture were found in cities as well as villages.[2] Nor is the essential difference that between the handmade object and the machine-made object.[3] Both folk and fine furniture were handmade, except for the use of lathes to make turnings. Both folk and fine craftsmen learned their craft through apprenticeship. While "fine" furniture is the accepted term, this does not mean that folk furniture is not well made. The main distinction between the two is a matter of different esthetics.

As Henry Glassie has noted about folk art generally, folk furniture reflects a particular, traditional esthetic. While there is room for individual style, creativity, and originality, these are always expressed within the prescribed boundaries of a clearly defined tradition.[4] The folk esthetic tends to be simple and functional. This accounts for its appeal even to fine art craftsmen and connoisseurs. The folk esthetic has influenced fine art craftsmen, just as the fine art esthetic influenced folk craftsmen. Glassie has noted another characteristic of material folk culture—that it tends toward regional stylistic differences, whereas the stylistic changes in fine furniture tend to occur over time.[5] Thus fine furniture fits into periods (medieval, William and Mary, Queen Anne, Chippendale, federal, empire, etc.), while folk furniture fits into regions (New England, Hudson Valley Dutch, Delaware Valley, Pennsylvania Dutch, etc.). Of course, regional differences occur within fine furniture styles, but they are not as important as the distinctions in period styles.

Estate inventories are an important source of information about the use of traditional furniture. Seventeenth- and eighteenth-century estate inventories in New Jersey contain a relatively small number of furnishings which suggest a general sparsity of material possessions. The furnishings were not generally grouped by rooms. For example, an inventory from Middletown, dated 1734, lists a shoemaker's bench, an old chest, five old chairs, an old feather-bed bolster, a feather bed and bedstead, a painted cupboard, a plain cupboard, six chairs, and a table.[6] By the late eighteenth and early nineteenth centuries, the amount of furnishings generally increased, and often the items were listed by room. For example, an inventory, dated 1821, from Franklin Township indicates that in the dwelling room there were an eight-day clock, a stand, a table, eight black chairs, six green chairs, and twelve yellow chairs; in the adjoining bedroom a bed, bedstead, and bedding (the bed was a mattresslike sack filled with straw, the bedding was the blankets and other coverings, the bedstead was the wooden frame), a chest, an old desk, a tea table, and an old stand; in the parlor a tea table; in the entry a table; in the room in back of the parlor a bed, bedstead, and bedding, and a dining table; in the back entry a Dutch cupboard (known also as a *kas*). Upstairs there were an old table, a bedstead, a chest, some trunks, and seven old Windsor chairs; and in the garret there was a cradle.[7] While this later inventory reveals a certain survival of the use of rooms for multiple purposes (the bed and the dining table together), the trend was toward a greater number of material possessions and specialization of space.

A study was done in 1959 of early nineteenth-century household furnishings in Bergen County by Frederick Banfield Hanson, then a graduate student at the Winterthur Museum. He examined 190 inventories and 113 wills dating from 1800 to 1810 and found the following major types of furniture: beds and bedding, including bedsteads, cribs, and cradles; bookcases, including secretaries and bookshelves; chairs, benches, and stools; chests, including storage chests, chests of drawers, and bureaus; clocks; cupboards, including Hackensack cupboards (the local name for *kasten* or Dutch cupboards), corner cupboards, and the like; desks; dressers; sideboards and servers; stands, including candle stands, night stands, and fireplace stands; tables, including dining tables, tea tables, breakfast tables, kitchen tables, and toilet tables; and trunks. Hanson concluded: "Some products which apparently were not produced within the county limits . . . were imported from neighboring areas . . . most furniture was either old or based on old forms, with only the addition of some new superficial details."[8]

A similar conclusion was reached by Margaret E. White, curator of an exhibition of early New Jersey furniture held at the Newark Museum in 1958–1959. White noted that because of New Jersey's position between New York City and Philadelphia, fine furniture was acquired outside the state. The furniture makers working in New Jersey were cabinetmakers and chairmakers who worked in the "old country" style for people of moderate means and Quakers with conservative tastes. She added that most of the early New Jersey furniture

makers combined this craft with other occupations, such as farming, fishing, undertaking, and broom making.[9]

One of the Old World furniture styles that continued to be made in New York and New Jersey was the Dutch *kas* (plural, *kasten*), a large wardrobe with two large paneled doors that open to shelves above a row of drawers. Usually these were large pieces of furniture with a heavy cornicelike top and bulbous ebony-colored legs. This is a traditional furniture type that can be traced to the Netherlands; there are several examples of *kasten* in the folklife museum in Arnhem. They are found extensively throughout the New World Dutch culture area, especially in the Hudson River Valley. Examples from New York can be seen at the Albany Institute for History and Art, Philipsburg Manor, the Brooklyn Museum, and the Winterthur Museum. But they also show up in inventories in New Jersey counties where the Dutch settled, variously labeled as *kasten*, Dutch cupboards, or Hackensack cupboards. The Old Barracks in Trenton has

*Opposite:* Dutch *kas.*
*Collections of the Monmouth*
*County Historical Association*

*Right:* Dutch spoon rack, marked "GL"—
Garret Longstreet, Manasquan, 1729.
*The Newark Museum Collection*

one reputed to have been made in Hightstown. Another is known to have been made by Matthew Egerton, Jr., who, like his father, was a cabinetmaker. Egerton, who kept a workshop in New Brunswick until his death in 1837, had a reputation as a fine furniture maker, but he also made traditional furniture for his Dutch clientele.[10]

Another traditional Dutch furniture form found in New Jersey is the carved spoon rack. It was made of wood and was designed to hold four to twelve spoons; some racks had a box at the bottom for knives and forks. The carving contains motifs familiar in Pennsylvania German folk art: the sunburst, the spiral, the rosette, the pentagram (five-pointed star), and the hexagram (six-pointed star). The style of carving has been described as Frisian, from the province of Friesland in the northeastern part of the Netherlands.[11] Similar spoon racks have been collected in Pennsylvania, which is not surprising, inasmuch as East Friesland is part of Germany. There are New Jersey spoon racks at the Morris-

141

town National Historic Park and in the collections of the Bergen County and the New Jersey historical societies, as well as in private collections.

It is sometimes difficult to determine whether a specific chair style demonstrates a folk style as opposed to a fine art style. That is the case with the so-called splat-back or fiddleback chair. The splat is a fiddle-shaped or urn-shaped board located between the two back posts and the cresting rail. In an article published in *Antiques* magazine in 1936, Huyler Held argued that these were Dutch chairs. They were made throughout the Hudson River Valley, on Long Island, and supposedly in New Jersey in the eighteenth century.[12] They do show up in Jersey Dutch inventories, such as that of Garret Hendrickson of Middletown, dated 1801, which mentions "six fiddle back chairs."[13] But such chairs were also made in Connecticut, Rhode Island, and Massachusetts. In his book *Colonial Furniture in America* (1951), Luke Vincent Lockwood says that the style originated in Holland but had more influence in England and America.[14] In fact, this style is probably not a Dutch folk style at all; it seems to be a survival on the folk level of the Queen Anne style common in England and America in the early eighteenth century. The fiddleback chair is probably an example of a fine furniture style that filtered down to influence a folk style.

It is often difficult to determine whether a specific piece of furniture was made in America or brought from Europe. For example, in the 1930s a Scandinavian chest was found in a Philadelphia antiques shop by Cornelius Weygandt, the author of *Down Jersey*. It had two large panels and three smaller panels, all containing inlays of traditional designs. The apron had a scalloped border and the name and date "Petr Almbaia 1668" within an inlaid rectangle. The chest was different in style and motif from Pennsylvania German painted chests and from English chests. Weygandt described it as a Finnish chest from South Jersey. There were indeed Finns as well as Swedes who settled in New Sweden. Weygandt also claimed that it was made in South Jersey, but the claim is suspect.[15]

There is a similar situation with a wainscot chair (wainscot here refers to the best oak timber, well grained and without knots) in the collection of the Monmouth County Historical Association. This kind of chair was common in English inventories during the sixteenth and seventeenth centuries, and some show up in New England and Virginia.[16] This New Jersey wainscot chair has a central panel of ornamental gouge work, a thistle, and the inscription "R / 1692 /R.I." Margaret E. White thought that the initials indicated that the chair was built by Robert Rhea of Freehold.[17] Rhea was a carpenter and joiner who came from Scotland. Leslie Byrnes, a decorative arts consultant from West Caldwell,

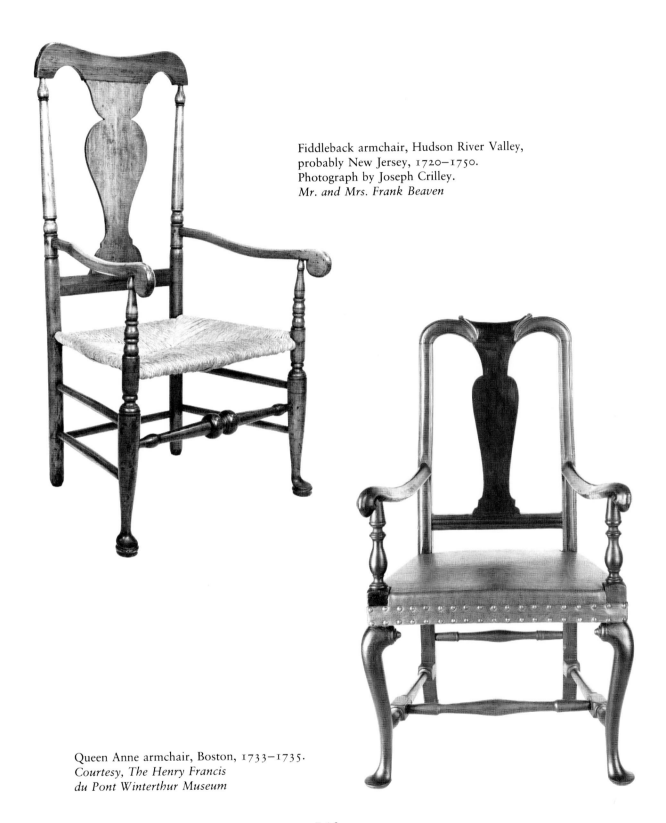

Fiddleback armchair, Hudson River Valley,
probably New Jersey, 1720–1750.
Photograph by Joseph Crilley.
*Mr. and Mrs. Frank Beaven*

Queen Anne armchair, Boston, 1733–1735.
*Courtesy, The Henry Francis
du Pont Winterthur Museum*

North Jersey ladder-back chair, marked
"C A D," believed to be Cornelius
A. Demarest. *Collections of the
Monmouth County Historical Association*

South Jersey ladder-back chair,
Roadstown, Cumberland County,
made by Maskell Ware, circa 1790.
*The Newark Museum Collection*

has suggested that the chair may not have been made in America at all and possibly was brought to New Jersey from England or Scotland.[18] The point is not whether the piece of furniture was made here or brought here, but rather that such objects represent a material culture inheritance that is associated with an ethnic background.

Another important English chair type is the Windsor chair. These are spindle-back chairs thought to have originated in the Wycombe district of Buckinghamshire and showing up in the American colonies in the early eighteenth century. Windsor chairs in New Jersey are divided into several subtypes. One is the riding seat or wagon seat, circa 1790, with spindles turned in bamboo style. This type of seat was used in the house during the week and placed in a wagon to take the family to church on Sundays. Another is a writing-arm chair made by Abraham Beach of Newark in the early nineteenth century. This chair, in the collection of the Monmouth County Historical Association, is of the comb-back type: the spindles support a top rail or comb with carved ears at the ends. A third subtype is a side chair made by W. Bowen of Cumberland County in the early nineteenth century. It is a loop-back Windsor, also known as a balloon back.[19] Here the spindles fit into a bent piece of wood shaped into a bow. While the Windsor chair was clearly an English chair style, "5 Winsor Chairs" show up in the inventory of Jacob Van Ness of Caldwell in 1820.[20] This indicates the acculturation of the Dutch settlers in New Jersey as they borrowed English artifacts.

Not all folk furniture is ethnically related. Slat-back or ladder-back chairs, the most common type of folk furniture made in New Jersey, exhibit regional rather than ethnic, stylistic differences. As with linguistic culture areas (see "Folk Speech"), so too in slat-back chair styles a major boundary extends across New Jersey. In 1933 Wilson Lynes distinguished between two types of eighteenth-century slat-back chairs: the northern and the central. The northern slat backs have four or five thin, bent slats with straight lower edges and sweeping curves on the upper edges, ring-turned posts with spherical finials (the nobs at the top of the rear posts), and well-defined separations between the post and the finial and between the front leg and the foot. In the central slat backs the rear posts have no turnings except small, simple finials, there are four to six slats that are arched at the top and bottom, the front posts are vase turned between the stretcher (the support that extends horizontally between the legs) and the seat, the feet are boldly turned in a vase, ball, or ring design, and the front stretcher is boldly turned in a ball-and-ring or vase-and-ring design. The northern or New England type can be found in New England, New York, and northern New Jersey. The central or Pennsylvania type can be found in Pennsylvania, Maryland, Delaware, and southern New Jersey.[21] What happens at the cultural boundary in New Jersey is especially interesting. "Chairs made in the intermediate territory of central New Jersey," according to Lynes, "may betray the influence of both the Northern and Central types."[22]

In 1959 William H. MacDonald made an exhaustive study of central New Jersey chairmaking in the nineteenth century. He found a variant of the northern type that was made in Monmouth, Middlesex, Mercer, and Hunterdon counties. It commonly had three slats, straight or bent rear posts, rush seats, and stenciled or hand-drawn decorations on the slats and posts. Rocking chairs tended to have four slats. There were few plank seats. Maple was used for the posts, poplar or maple for the slats, hickory for the "rounds" or "rungs" (stretchers), and ash or oak for the base of the seat. The frames of these chairs were finished with a thin coat of black paint over a primer of red, resulting in a reddish tint; the seats were usually painted yellow.[23]

Individual craftsmen had their own styles. Quite often a style can be traced from father to son or from master to journeyman and apprentice; and even among these there are individual differences which, though often minute, can be recognized. Take, for example, the Ware family of Salem and Cumberland counties, makers of the famous Ware chairs. The family was descended from Joseph Ware, a Quaker who came to America from Wales with John Fenwick in 1675. His great-grandson, Maskell Ware, was the first and most famous chairmaker in the family. He learned the craft in 1778 as an apprentice of John Lanning of Salem and then opened his own shop in Roadstown in Cumberland County.[24]

Maskell Ware used swamp maple for the frames of his chairs. He used a jig pole lathe to do the turnings. Rushes were gathered during July in the marshes of South Jersey and were cured for two weeks. There were two styles of rushing: the "straight" style, in which every strand overlapped, and the "checkered" style, in which each group of four strands overlapped the next four. The dining room chairs had five, four, or three slats, barroom chairs had two slats and no finials, ladies' sewing chairs were rockers with four or five slats, and junior rockers had three slats. Maskell Ware made some five-slat rocking chairs as well.[25]

Ware taught his seven sons how to make chairs, and five of them carried on the tradition. Each had an individual style. Maskell's chairs were characterized by globular ball turnings on the front round. His son Dan used smaller, pear-shaped turnings in his early chairs; his son Reuben used large turnings on large chairs and small turnings on small chairs; the eldest son Thomas used quarter-inch gouges arranged in groups. The finials of all the Ware chairs have a fine double line around the middle, but Maskell's have globular-shaped finials, and those of his son John are oval with a pointed top.[26] Despite these individual differences all the Ware chairs tend to have the curved slats said to be characteristic of South Jersey chairmaking.

Chairmaking in New Jersey represents an interesting intermediate position between handicraft and factory production. These chairs were certainly handmade, but machines, such as lathes, were used to make the turnings. The parts were sometimes standardized and interchangeable.[27] Yet these small shops were based on an apprenticeship system in which the craft was handed down from generation to generation, often within the same family. It makes us realize that the distinction between folk and vernacular can be blurred.

The study of chairs has importance beyond the recognition of stylistic regions or periods. As Siegfried Giedion, the historian of technology, has noted, chairs reflect changes in popular notions about physical comfort and posture. Giedion distinguishes between the oriental sitting posture, in which the body supports itself, and the European notion that a chair supports the body. This also applies to the difference between the American Indian sitting posture and the European. Giedion then shows the changes in posture and comfort from the medieval chair, which was hard and usually had no back, to the eighteenth-century chair, which had upholstered seats but straight backs, to nineteenth-century mechanical railroad chairs, which actually reclined.[28] Kenneth Ames of the Winterthur Museum has added to this framework by pointing out the distinction in the nineteenth-century American household between the fine, upholstered seats in the front parlor and the slat-back chairs and rockers in the rear kitchen. The former represents a frontal posture of formal visiting and the latter the reclining posture of informality. And so New Jersey chairs not only help us to define stylistic differences and to see cross-influences between folk and fine, they also help us to define culture areas and to understand changes in the notion of comfort.

# Quilts, Coverlets, and Samplers

MATERIAL FOLK culture does not always demonstrate significant regional differences. Quilts, samplers, and coverlets are—with the possible exception of Amish quilts—similar throughout the United States. They are important for what they tell us about changes in the production of textiles and the role of women in society.

During the colonial period, the major homespun textiles in New Jersey were linen and wool. In 1681 a writer noted about New Jersey that "the Country also produces flax and hemp which they spin and manufacture into linen. They make several stuffs and cloth of wool for apparel."[1] In 1728 Governor William Keith wrote that "every Farmer is by necessity led to employ his spare time in working up the wool of a few sheep he is obliged to keep on his Farm."[2] And in 1768, a New York newspaper made note of "Persons in Woodbridge in New-Jersey, making in their respective Families, within the Year past, both Woolen and Linen of their own raising."[3] Both men and women made homespun clothing and bedding.

Flax was planted in the spring and harvested in August. The harvesting was known as "pulling flax," because it was literally pulled up by the roots. Sometimes the pulling was done collectively in a "flax frolic." John W. Lequear, a Hunterdon County farmer born in 1823, remembered fifty or sixty people working at a flax frolic.[4] The harvested flax was dried or cured for several days and then hauled to the barn, where it was threshed. This was done by beating the grain end of the sheaf on a stone or wagon tongue. Some of the seed was saved for replanting, and the rest was sent to a mill to be crushed into linseed oil. The flax stalks were spread in the short grass in a process known as "dew retting" (rotting). Then the flax was dried in a kiln for a short time to make it ready for "braking." The "flax brake" was a heavy plank with a hinged top. The flax would be placed between the plank and the top and pounded in order to break the woody coating on the stalk. Next the stalks would be "swingled," which consisted of beating out the small pieces of bark using a long, flat wooden tool known as a "swingle."

Then the women would take over. Using a board with sharp nails protruding from it, known as a "hatchel," they would comb or hatchel the flax. In the process the flax was separated into various qualities: "tow" linen (used for sacking, filling, and wagon covers), "line" linen (for table and bed linens), and fine linen (for thread and fine linen cloth).

The fibers would be spun into linen thread or yarn on a spinning wheel. The flax wheel was a small foot-powered wheel operated from a sitting position. A "cut" of yarn consisted of 144 turns around a reel 2 yards in circumference, and eight cuts of tow or twelve of flax, that is, 3,456 yards, was considered a good day's work. Sometimes this work too was done communally in a "spinning frolic." The work was parceled out to neighboring women to be completed by a certain date at which time there was a party. The thread was called "frolic thread." In 1790 a young woman of Hunterdon County wrote, "They spin their Frollick thread very level here when they take their flax round they tell them to spin it a 3 hundred or 4 h'd thickness and they know what size that is."[5] Next the yarn was bleached by boiling it in a large kettle. Then it was dyed, using plants such as butternut, walnut, alum, or indigo. It was then ready for weaving.

In woolen production the process was somewhat different. The men sheared the sheep in the spring and washed the wool. The fleece was then sorted into different grades, the coarse wool to be used for carpets and horse blankets and the finer wool for clothing. The wool was then carded using "hand cards," which resembled hairbrushes. A small amount of wool was placed between the two cards, and it was brushed and combed to disentangle the fibers. After 1800 carding was done by machine in rural carding mills. By 1810 there was about 128 carding machines in New Jersey, and by 1815, 140.[6] When the wool fibers were long ("worsted"), the process was known as combing.

The wool was then ready for spinning into yarn on a wool spinning wheel. Unlike the flax wheel the wool wheel was worked from a standing position. The yarn was wound onto a wooden spindle and then transferred to a hand reel about six and one-half feet in circumference. Forty revolutions of the reel constituted one "knot," and ten knots equaled one "skein." A good spinner could do about four skeins in a day, about two miles of yarn. This would require about four miles of walking. John Lequear described spinning frolics in Hunterdon County: "If a neighbor wanted help they would go to the house and get the wool, take it home, spin it, and fix upon an afternoon to return the yarn, when a good supper would be provided for them. Young men could have their suppers by bringing yarn."[7]

Judging from farm inventories many farmers had their own looms. The inventories usually show these looms being located in the garrets of houses, suggesting that the weaving was done there, presumably by members of the family. This seems to have been the case in New England as well. Hector St. John de Crevecoeur in *Sketches of Eighteenth Century America* noted just prior to the Revolutionary War that in the summer women would work in the large Dutch barn so as to take advantage of the cross-breezes between the barn doors.[8] There were also journeyman weavers who would carry their own looms from house to house. One such weaver was Peter Holsart of Freehold. His account books for 1751–1758 indicate that he charged nineteen shillings for weaving thirty-nine pounds of linsey-woolsey (cloth made of a linen warp and a woolen weft), ten shillings, six pence for weaving twenty-one pounds of cotton and wool; one pound, six shillings for weaving twenty-six yards of worsted.[9] He also wove linen, coverlets, French cloth, bedticks, and rag coverlets. In 1800 Samuel Foster became his apprentice for a period of five years, during which he would receive lodging, food, wearing apparel, and six months of schooling.[10]

After the fabric was woven the next process was fulling: washing to remove the oils and allow the fabric to thicken. The woven fabric was placed in a tub with soap or soda, and someone would tread upon it with his bare feet. This process was later done at the fulling mill, using waterpower. According to Harry Weiss and Grace Ziegler, authors of *Early Fulling Mills of New Jersey*, the fulling mill "played an important part in making homespun woolens wearable. The fulling mill was also the first step in taking manufacturing out of the home."[11] The earliest fulling mill in New Jersey was established in Middletown Township in Monmouth County circa 1667 and belonged to William Lawrence. Between 1667 and 1780 at least sixty fulling mills were established in New Jersey. There were forty-one fulling mills in New Jersey in 1784, fifty-three in 1810, seventy-two in 1830, and forty-nine in 1840.[12] Fulling mills began to disappear as woolen mills took over the entire process of fabric production.

New Jersey was one of the first states to become involved in factory-made textiles, with the founding of the Society for Establishing Useful Manufactures in 1791. By 1840 Paterson had become the foremost center for manufacturing cotton duck, and at about the same time the first successful silk mill was opened in that city. The cotton and silk had to be imported from outside the state. In 1814 there were fifteen cotton mills in New Jersey: fifteen in Essex County, one in Bergen County, three in Morris County, and three in Gloucester County.[13] In the same year New Jersey had fifty-six woolen factories, with the largest number (eleven) in Sussex County.[14] Yet homespun textiles continued to be made well into the nineteenth century. As late as 1850 there were sixty-two households in rural Tewksbury Township, Hunterdon County, still reporting home manufacturing.[15] In 1910 New Jersey manufactured in homes 374,313 yards of woolen goods with a value of $360,632.[16]

Ready-made textiles did not replace homespun all at once. The journal of James Ten Eyck, Sr., a Dutch farmer on the North Branch of the Raritan River during the 1790s and early 1800s, gives us a picture of their coexistence. Although Ten Eyck bought ready-made clothing in New Brunswick, he also cultivated flax, which he, his sons, and slaves retted and swingled. He hired Peggy Van Nostrand to spin the flax into "linsey" and "toe yarn." Peter Sutphin or Abraham Voorhees did the weaving for him, and Joseph Stull or Robert Little, local tailors, made trousers, "jaccoats," great coats, summer coats, and shirts. Ten Eyck's son continued this pattern of consumption as late as 1824, although he also purchased gingham and other factory cloth from a peddler named James Jenkins. By 1853 the Ten Eyck farm no longer grew flax.[17]

The diary of Margaret Ten Eyck, the unmarried daughter of James Ten Eyck, Sr., provides insight into the growing division of labor in the production of homespun textiles in the early nineteenth century. She hired herself out to various households to do quilting, sewing, and knitting. She moved constantly from one household to another, and even had to pay room and board when she stayed with her brother James's family.

> *1 August.* The last week I was a Quilting at Peggy Cox for Ellen. I quilted 4 days. September 22, 1837. Margaret Cox Paid me 5 Dollars. She owes me 5 yet. She paid Dow 2 dollars. . . .
> *March 19, 1837.* I was at Mr. Timbrooks 3 day a Quilting and at Mrs. Farratts 3 days. . . .
> *May 1, 1838.* [?] settled with Margaret Ten Eyk all accounts to this day by me. I paid my Brother James 48 for my Board. James Ten Eyk 30 dollars interest he owed me and 10 I paid Easter and 8 Dollars he owd on our Last account 75 cents. He gave me a note of 12 Dollars and a Bank note of 7 Dollars. I was abroad 24 weaks out of the year in 1837. . . .
> I eat Breakfast at home. I spun my woll. Was at home till the 19 of June. I went to Mr. Elmondorf. I was there till the 9 of July sowing. I et dinner at Jimmeys. I was at Mr. Emmondorfs 2 weaks and 4 days. I was at Giddeon Cox's 3 days a sowing and I was a sowing at Onsh Van Pelts 3 days and the next weak I was at Onsh Van Pelts 4 days and I went to old Mrs. Stulls and was their 2 days a sowing for our Peter. The 26 of July I was at our Peters a sowing for him 1 day and this

151

weak I was there 2 days a sowing for him. I et breakfast at home. I sowed for Peter all the weak at home. . . .

*August 15.* I sowed for Easter 2 weaks and 5 days and mended stockings 2 days.

*October 22.* I nit one pare of stockings for Tunis. 6 shillings mixed ones. . . .

*Feb. 8.* I maid 2 Linnen Shirts for my Brother James. 6 Shillings.

*10.* I maid one Linsey Trouser for toney. 3 shillings.

*20.* I nit for Easter one pair for Peter Stockings better than half the day. 3 shillings.

*March* [?] I nit one pair of woolin Stockings 3 days. I was nitting them [?][18]

This diary provides a very different image of quilting, sewing, and knitting from the stereotype of the communal quilting bee and the self-sufficient household. Most quilts that are now in museums and historical society collections were made by individual women, rather than groups. The obvious exceptions to this rule are the Friendship or album quilts.

Quilts are made from three layers of already woven fabric—linen, wool, cotton, and even silk. These layers are called the "backing," the "filler," and the "top." They are sewn together by hand and then quilted into a pattern. If the top is made of small pieces of fabric that are seamed together, it is known as a "pieced quilt." But if the pattern is created by small pieces of fabric that are sewn on to a single top, it is known as an "appliqué" quilt.

The design motifs of the traditional quilts all have names. Some of the patterns in the Newark Museum collection are the "Orange Peel," also called "Robbing Peter to Pay Paul" (because pieces cut from one square are applied to the contrasting center of the adjacent square); "Delectable Mountains" (a reference to John Bunyan's *Pilgrim's Progress*: "They went till they came to the Delectable Mountains . . . behold the gardens and orchards, the vineyards and fountains of water"); and "Log Cabin" (very small strips of fabric are used as "logs"). One of the appliqué quilts in the collection is a "Masonic Quilt," which incorporates the symbols of the secret Society of Freemasons made in Newark circa 1853. Still other quilts combine the techniques of the pieced and appliqué quilts. The "Star of Bethlehem" pattern made in Perth Amboy circa 1815 consists of a large eight-pointed star made up of 100 small diamonds pieced together. Between the points of the star are appliqué representations of birds and flowers. These forms are surrounded by a rectangular band of cotton triangles in a pattern known as "Wild Goose Chase."

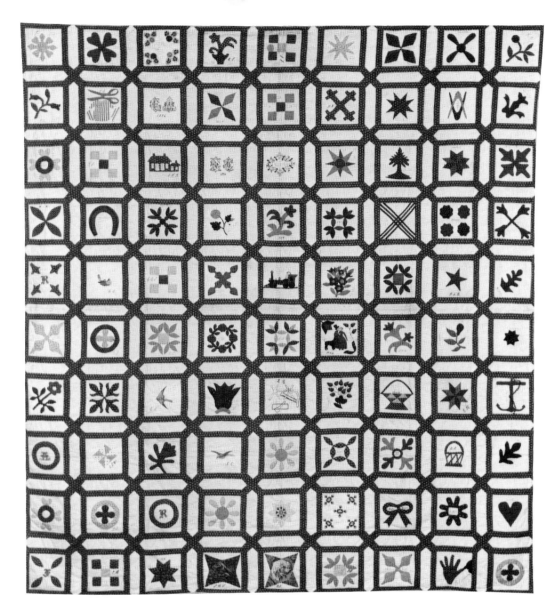

Friendship (Medley) quilt, Hackensack, circa 1876. *The Newark Museum Collection*

Two especially interesting quilts in the Newark Museum are a Friendship or Album quilt made in Hackensack circa 1876 and a Crazy quilt made in 1885. According to tradition, Friendship quilts were made at bridal showers. Each guest would bring her own block of material, and all the blocks would be pieced together at a quilting bee. The individually created blocks contain natural and domestic images, such as scissors cutting a shirt, an appliquéd house, a flower basket, and stars. Most blocks also contain an embroidered name or initials. On

Crazy quilt, circa 1885. *The Newark Museum Collection*

this particular quilt the surnames Randall and Demarest appear frequently. The Crazy quilt, so-called because it lacks the symmetry of other quilt patterns, is very unusual. The quilt maker's husband was an official of the Delaware, Lackawanna and Western Railroad, and the quilt depicts the route of the railroad from Hoboken, New Jersey, to Richfield Springs, New York. Embroidered on the quilt are the station names: Morristown, Convent, Madison, Summit, South Orange, Orange, and Newark.[19]

The State Museum in Trenton also has a quilt collection, including a Friendship quilt from Trenton, dated 1845, with a tulip and wandering foot pattern. It was made by the parishioners of the Trenton Methodist Episcopal church upon the departure of their minister, the Reverend Daniel Kidder, and his wife Harriet. A quilt from Shrewsbury, dated 1846 and dedicated "To Lucy," is an autograph patch or Album quilt based on the "Courthouse Square" pattern. It has the signatures of some fifty people from the Allen, Brown, Corlies, Parker, and Williams families among others. It also includes proverbs and biblical verses, such as "Redemption is the science and the song of all Eternity—Polish" and "May we grow up into him in all things which is the head

154

ever Christ. Eph. 4 Chapt." And a Crazy quilt from Trenton dedicated to "Kate/1885" was made by Kate Alice Stockton (1854–1918) and her friends the year before she married Monroe Berganstock Titlow.

There are two major types of handwoven coverlets made in New Jersey: the overshot weave and the double weave. The overshot weave is done on a simple four-harness loom. The pattern is made by the transverse weft threads making rather long skips over the threads of a "tabby" or plain woven fabric. The patterns have specific names. For example, in the Newark Museum's large collection of quilts and coverlets is an overshot-weave coverlet with a pattern known as "Dog Tracks" or "Dogwood Blossoms." The double weave is produced on a loom with at least eight harnesses, and is much more complicated than the weave produced by the four-harness loom. The pattern is visible on both sides of the fabric. Double-weave patterns in the Newark Museum include the "Lover's Knot" from Bergen County; the "Single Snow-Ball," thought to have been made in Hackettstown in the eighteenth century; and the "Single Snow-Ball with Pine-Tree Border," made in the 1840s in Hunterdon County.[20]

Samplers were designed to teach young girls different embroidery stitches. Some contain only alphabets, numerals, and perhaps the name of the girl who stitched it and the date she completed it. Some nineteenth-century samplers, however, contain many other design motifs, such as flowers, birds, horses, trees, human figures, and geometric shapes. Many of these samplers bear messages similar to epitaphs on tombstones. In fact, there is an interesting difference between eighteenth-century sampler messages and nineteenth-century sampler messages that parallels the differences between tombstone motifs of the two periods (see "Folk Sculpture"). A sampler done in 1786 by Mary Miller of Burlington County contains the following message:

> This Work My Friends in Hand May Have
> When I Am Dead and Laid in Grave
> The Greedy Worms My Body Eat
> Yet You May Read My Name Compleat.[21]

This sampler expresses the same morbid attitude toward death that can be seen in the death's-heads on eighteenth-century tombstones. In contrast a sampler done in 1833 by Betsy H. Fly of Vineland expresses a very different attitude.

> In eighteen hundred and thirty three
> I wrought this work that here you see
> And in the fourteenth year of age.

> Just entering on youth's giddy stage.
> O may the Lord his grace bestow
> That I may praise Him here below,
> And O may I prepared be,
> To reign with Christ eternally.[22]

This sentimental statement accords with the urns and weeping willow motifs of early nineteenth-century tombstones.

Many of the quilts and samplers made during the nineteenth century do not represent an essential handicraft tradition. That is to say, the advent of factory-made textiles and the sewing machine made these activities no longer an essential part of the domestic economy for upper- and middle-class women in the cities and even on farms except in the most isolated areas. According to the historian Ann Douglass, middle-class women by the nineteenth century had lost their essential role in feeding, clothing, and equipping the family. Ministers found themselves in a similar position, according to Douglass, as a secular, business-minded world view replaced the religious world view of the colonial period. The result was a kind of unofficial alliance between women and ministers which took the form of what Douglass has termed "the triumph of sentimentalism in the nineteenth century."[23] By the mid-nineteenth century female academies taught such "feminine" subjects as modern languages, music, sewing, literature, and history, as opposed to the "masculine" subjects of mathematics, theology, Greek, and the natural sciences.[24] In fact, many nineteenth-century samplers in museum collections were made at these academies. This preoccupation with death on the part of homebound, middle-class women in the nineteenth century expresses what Douglass has described as "the domestication of death."[25]

The making of quilts, coverlets, and samplers was revived at the turn of the twentieth century as part of the Arts and Crafts Movement. This movement originated in England with John Ruskin and William Morris as a protest against modern factory-made products and as a celebration of the handmade object. It led to a revival of dying craft traditions in places like rural New England, the southern Appalachian Mountains, and among recent immigrants in ethnic neighborhoods in the cities. Missionary schools and settlement houses were actively involved at that time in the arts and crafts revival in America. Since then there have been periodic revivals of interest in contemporary crafts as part of the same celebration of a self-reliance and individualism thought to have once existed in American life.

# Pottery, Basketry, and Glass

THE STUDY of material folk culture involves three related terms: artifact, art, and craft. These terms reflect different aspects of the same objects. Artifact puts the emphasis on use, art on esthetics, and craft on production. Henry Glassie has noted that "the bulk of folk material which is at all art is secondarily art—it is craft, that which is primarily practical and secondarily aesthetic in function."[1] Elsewhere he explained: "The artistic nature of a folk artifact is generally subordinate to its utilitarian nature so that most folk art exists within the immediate context of folk craft."[2] Certainly this is true of pottery, basketry, and glass. They were intended primarily as utensils, although their appealing designs may lead some people to put them on display as art objects.

Not all pottery, basketry, and glass qualify as folk objects. Folk objects are simple, everyday objects as opposed to decorative fine art objects. Redware and stoneware pottery are folk, but delftware and china are fine. Hand-blown bottles are folk, but crystal and cut glass are fine. Furthermore, folk objects are handmade as opposed to machine made. Thus, while hand-blown bottles are folk, flasks made in molds are vernacular. Plates handcrafted on a potter's wheel are folk, but uniform plates made from molds are vernacular.

Folk objects are what James Deetz, the archeologist, has called "small things forgotten."[3] Because they are simple and unpretentious, many people take them for granted. Today this is changing as antique collectors and others have helped us to appreciate their simple design as a form of art. Beyond that, of course, these objects can be used as important historical documents. But we must learn how to interpret folk objects, just as we must learn how to interpret other kinds of historical documents. This study is necessarily interdisciplinary, involving archeology, art history, economic history, social history, and the history of technology.

Pottery is defined as objects made of vitrified clay. This means that the clay is "fired"; that is, it is heated until it has a hard, glasslike surface that is impermeable to water. It is this quality of impermeability that makes pottery suitable

157

for liquid-bearing containers. While pottery is easily broken, the pieces (shards) do not easily decompose or discolor, which makes pottery useful to the archeologist.[4]

Pottery was made in New Jersey long before the coming of Europeans. The prehistoric ancestors of the Lenape used soapstone pots for cooking during the Transition Period (1750 B.C. to 1000 B.C.). The introduction of clay pottery marks the beginning of the Early Woodland Period (1000 B.C. to 500 B.C.).[5] This early pottery was of two types: the so-called Marcey Creek Plain type and the Ware Plain type. Both were oval or rectangular in shape with flat bottoms and sometimes with handles at the ends. Both types were constructed by pinching the clay together with the fingers. The only difference is that Marcey Creek Plain pottery was tempered with bits of crushed soapstone, and Ware Plain pottery was not. Marcey Creek Plain is named after an archeological site in Virginia, and it is found in Virginia, Maryland, Delaware, eastern Pennsylvania, New Jersey, and New York, thus grouping these places into a single culture area. Ware Plain pottery is named after a site in Salem County.[6]

From the Early Woodland Period to the Contact Period, when Europeans introduced trade articles such as iron pots, there was a development of pottery styles. Later pottery was made from coils of clay, with cone-shaped bases, and incised and impressed decorations on the interior and exterior surfaces. The collars of the vessels became successively taller.[7] Archeologists have also traced a progression in the decorative patterns from cord-impressed to cord-decorated or punctate-decorated (marked by dots) to incised or incised and punctate-decorated patterns.[8]

Geographical differences between central and southern New Jersey and northern New Jersey developed by the Late Woodland Period (700 A.D. to 1700 A.D.). The southern and central New Jersey pottery is similar to that found in Virginia, the Delmarva Peninsula, and southeastern Pennsylvania; the northern New Jersey pottery, especially that found in the upper Delaware River Valley, is similar to that found in the Mohawk Valley of New York State.[9] Thus, even in prehistory we see the cultural division between north and south that was to be repeated in historic New Jersey.

With Lenape Indian pottery there is no distinction between folk, vernacular, and fine. They had a single, folk type of pottery. But with Euro-American pottery from the colonial period through the nineteenth century these distinctions have meaning. Both folk and fine pottery were handmade. The clay was first prepared by washing (flushing it with water to remove stones, grit, and sand), kneading (manipulating it by hand to remove air bubbles), and screening (for-

Munsee incised clay pot,
Sussex County, Late Woodland Period.
Photograph by Joseph Crilley.
*New Jersey State Museum*

cing it through a sieve by means of a hand press). Then the clay was formed by turning it on a potter's wheel while shaping it by hand. Assessories such as spouts and handles were added, and the ware was decorated. Then it was fired in a kiln. Finally, if necessary, it was glazed by dipping, brushing, or pouring in order to seal it.

Euro-American pottery is classified according to the type of clay it was made of and the type of glaze used to seal it. Earthenware was made from either red clay, "redware," or yellow clay, "yellow-ware." It is soft and absorbent and consequently requires sealing. Two types of glaze were used with earthenware:

one composed of lead sulfide and the other of tin oxide added to the lead glaze. When lead sulfide was used, a white clay known as "slip" was diluted with water to the consistency of cream and applied under the glaze. The resulting pottery is termed "slipware." Sometimes the slip was painted on the surface of the object to form a design. Other times the entire object was covered with slip, and the design was scratched into the slip. In this case the object was termed "sgraffito." When tin oxide was used in the glaze, the process was known as "tin glazing," and the resulting object was an opaque, white enamel known as "majolica" or "delft." Earthenware was made in England for 1,000 years prior to American colonization. Slipware was made in England and in Europe from the early seventeenth through the late eighteenth century. Delft originated in the Netherlands and was being made in England as well by the late sixteenth century.[10]

Stoneware was made from brown or gray clay. It is hard and watertight, and therefore requires no sealing. Instead salt was shoveled into the kiln while the pottery was still hot. The vaporized salt settled on the ware; and as it cooled, the salt vapor crystallized on the surface as small drops. This process was known as "salt glazing." Stoneware was first made in Germany during the early seventeenth century, and was made in England by the 1670s.[11]

Porcelain was made from a white clay known as "kaolin." It is hard and watertight; unlike earthenware and stoneware, porcelain is translucent. It is also known as "china," because it was invented there. After the American Revolution it became a major import item in the China trade.

Pottery making in the European tradition began in New Jersey in the late seventeenth century. In 1688 Daniel Coxe, Stephen Soames, and Benjamin Bartlett formed a partnership in London for the purpose of making "white and painted earthenware and pottery vessells" in the colony of West New Jersey. John Dewilde, a "citizen and potter" of London, was hired as the manager of the pottery, and William Gill, a "potter servant" of Lambeth, Surrey, was hired as his assistant. They established their pottery in Burlington (in Burlington County). In 1692 Coxe sold most of his New Jersey property to the Society of Friends, including "a dwelling house and . . . a Pottery house newly erected by the said Daniel Coxe and used for the making of Earthenware."[12]

New Jersey decorated slipware reveals the same culture areas we have seen in other aspects of material folk culture. In an article in *Antiques*, John Ramsay noted that "in Pennsylvania, slip decoration was carried out far more elaborately than in New England."[13] He includes New Jersey in the Pennsylvania tradition of decorated slipware. There is an elaborate symbolism behind the various motifs of lilies, tulips, peacocks, doves, and the like.

Slip-decorated earthenware pie plate, probably New Jersey, nineteenth century. *Courtesy, Brooklyn Museum, Clement Collection*

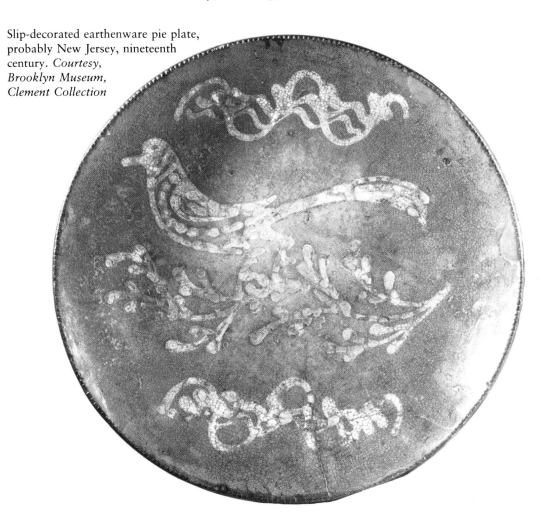

Teutonic fantasy in matters of form, and Teutonic delight in strong contrasts of bright hues led the New Jersey and Pennsylvania makers of slip-glazed wares to elaborations in the shapes and glazes of their products such as their New England contemporaries seldom thought of and still more seldom attempted.[14]

Actually there is a north-south division in slipware styles. A red earthenware bacon platter from Bergen County with the inscription "Hard Times in Jersey"—a reference to the panic of 1837—shows a spareness of design more typical of New England. A red earthenware pie plate decorated with a yellow-slip bird on a branch, thought to have been made in Matawan in the nineteenth century, is more typical of the Pennsylvania design tradition.

Stoneware was not as elaborately decorated as slipware. Some of the finest stoneware clay deposits were located on the banks of Cheesequake Creek in an area of Middlesex County that was part of South Amboy until 1869. There were three potteries there. One was founded by James Morgan, a captain and later a general in the American army during the Revolution. It was destroyed by British soldiers in 1779, according to a war damage claim filed by Morgan for "1 kiln of Stoneware not burnt."[15] In 1944 Robert J. Sim, a local historian, and Arthur W. Clement, a pottery expert, investigated the site of the Morgan pottery and found shards with deep blue and blue-gray decorations. The motifs included a coiled spring, dotted fish scales, plants, and animals. One fragment was inscribed "Liberty/1776." Another pottery at Cheesequake was operated by Thomas Warne, who married General Morgan's daughter, and Warne's son-in-law, Joshua Letts. One of their jars was signed "LIBERTY FOR EV /WARNE & LETTS 1807/S. AMBOY N JERSEY." The third pottery was operated by Noah Furman, whose mark was "N FURMAN SOUTH AMBOY."[16] There were other stoneware potteries in Hunterdon County (Ringoes and Flemington), Middlesex County (Old Bridge, South River, and New Brunswick), Bergen County (Hackensack), Essex County (Caldwell and Newark), Union County (Elizabeth), Camden County (Haddonfield), and Ocean County (Herbertsville).

Deetz notes that ceramics are related to foodways. Citing the work of the folklorist Jay Anderson, he argues that ceramics played a relatively minor role in food preparation and consumption in the early seventeenth century. Food was cooked in metal pots, kettles, and skillets, and was eaten from what were called "trenchers"—wooden trays. Ceramics played an important role only in connection with dairy foods, which were the main source of protein for the yeoman farmer. Deetz notes that the ceramics found in seventeenth-century archeological sites tend to be dairy-related articles, such as pans, jars, pitchers, colanders, and crocks. Deetz's theory is also substantiated by studies of estate inventories. In the production and storage of milk, butter, cheese, and cream there was a need for cleanliness, and lead-glazed earthenware containers could be easily cleaned.[17]

According to Deetz, while the use of pottery in the dairy continued into the eighteenth century, by the late seventeenth century new uses for ceramics had become evident. Plates, cups, bowls, and mugs—all articles related to food consumption—begin to show up in archeological sites dating from this period. Plates had apparently come to have a decorative function as well; decorated slipware plates may have been intended for display as well as for use.

In the 1760s the development of English-made creamware—described by

Salt-glazed stoneware jug, South
Amboy, Warne and Letts, 1807.
*Courtesy, Brooklyn Museum,
Clement Collection*

Deetz as "the first truly mass-produced pottery"—led to the decline of domestic
(i.e. folk) pottery making.[18] In the early nineteenth century a new method of
making pottery by pouring the clay into molds was introduced. This made it
possible to produce more elaborate shapes, such as figurines. It also transformed
the small pottery workshops into factories turning out low-priced, mass-produced ware. Redware and stoneware pottery continued to be made in New Jersey through the nineteenth century, but vernacular pottery had taken over in all
but the most remote rural areas. Around the turn of the century the Arts and
Crafts Movement revived the making of handmade pottery, but folk pottery was
never again central to people's lives.

Stamped, wood splint Indian basket, Burlington County (left);
painted, wood splint Munsee Indian basket, Sugar Loaf (right).
Photograph by Joseph Crilley. *New Jersey State Museum*

Baskets are much less durable than pottery, and so they are harder to study historically. Archeologists believe that basketry probably antedates pottery among the Indians of New Jersey. Before pottery, food was probably cooked by stone boiling, that is, dropping hot stones into tightly woven baskets containing water.[19] None of these prehistoric baskets survives, but archeologists have found on pottery impressions of the woven mats or fabric on which the pottery was made, indicating that basket-making technology existed in prehistoric times.[20] In 1908 Mark Harrington, the anthropologist, discovered among the Munsee Delaware in Canada survivals of two kinds of baskets of a type that may date back to the time the Lenape occupied New Jersey. One was a bag-shaped corn sieve made of twisted root fibers, and the other a coiled grass basket of a sort thought to have once been widespread among eastern Algonkian tribes.[21]

The Lenape Indians are known to have made splint baskets decorated either with coils or with spiral figures stamped on the basket with blocks cut out of raw vegetable sections, bone, or cork. Frank Speck notes that this latter technique was common among the Eastern Woodland Indians, but there is no evidence that it antedates the arrival of Europeans. He concluded that it was inspired by European printing technology, although the design patterns were native American.[22] Others have noted that the splint basket technique was

164

probably also borrowed from Europeans. Ives Goddard feels the Lenape probably learned it from the Swedish and Finnish settlers in New Sweden.[23] Henry Glassie notes that splint baskets were made in Britain and that they may have been an Anglo-American tradition borrowed by the Eastern Woodland Indians.[24] Indian baskets show up in some eighteenth-century inventories, such as one from Bergen County dated 1742.[25] Unfortunately it is not specified whether they were wood splint baskets or coil grass baskets. One of the last Indian basket makers in New Jersey was "Indian Ann" from Indian Mills who died in 1894.[26]

Anglo-American baskets made in New Jersey came in many shapes and sizes. Small berry baskets contained up to two quarts, larger fruit-picking baskets ranged in size from a peck to a bushel, and still larger field baskets had a capacity from half a peck to two bushels. Egg baskets were small and round. There were also household baskets or general utility farm baskets, clothes baskets, laundry baskets, medium-sized market baskets, garden baskets, cheese baskets, and grain sieves.

Along the Jersey Shore baskets were made for carrying fish and clams. An article titled "Among the Jersey Crabbers" in the *Continent*, dated 1883, shows a drawing of a clammer standing in shallow water working with a dip net attached to a long pole, and on his back is a large clam basket.[27] Another type of basket made along the Jersey Shore was the eel basket or eel pot. These were tapered cylindrical baskets similar in function but not in shape to New England wooden lobster pots. They were about twenty-eight inches long and eight inches in diameter, narrowing to four inches in diameter at the end that contained a wooden plug. Inside the basket was another funnel-shaped basket that narrowed to less than two inches in diameter at the middle of the basket. Horseshoe crabs were placed as bait in the plugged-end section of the trap; the eel was lured through the open end of the funnel and pressed open the oak strips that allowed him to enter the trap.[28]

The Museum of Early Trades and Crafts in Madison has an extensive collection of New Jersey baskets. They are made from many different materials, including ash, poplar, hickory, white oak, rush, twigs, straw, willow, and grass. According to Edgar Land, the director of the museum, most of these baskets were acquired in northern New Jersey, although it is not known whether they all were made in New Jersey. In South Jersey most of the baskets were made of white oak splints.[29] As recently as 1940 Alfred Southard from near New Egypt was making traditional baskets with a crank-operated splitting machine, a steaming box and stove, and a wooden shaving horse.[30]

In a study of an Adirondack Mountain basket maker in New York State, Henry Glassie contrasted the northern New England baskets made of relatively soft black ash in which the splints are pounded apart and the southern Appalachian baskets made from white oak in which the splints are rived apart. The former tradition is found in Maine, New Hampshire, Vermont, Rhode Island, Massachusetts, Connecticut, and the Adirondack Mountains of New York. The latter tradition is found in the southern Appalachian Mountains, the Deep South, Pennsylvania, and the Ozarks.[31] Thus basket styles are one way of defining the cultural boundary between the North and the South. South Jersey fits into the southern basketry culture area.

Glass has been made in New Jersey since the early eighteenth century. Most of this eighteenth-century glass was what we might term folk glass as opposed to fine glass. In a letter dated 1768, William Franklin, the royal governor of New Jersey, made reference to New Jersey glass.

> A Glass House was erected about Twenty Years ago in Salem County, which makes Bottles, and a very coarse Green Glass for Windows, used only in some of the Houses of the poorer Sort of People. . . . It seems probable that, notwithstanding the Duty [the tax on imported glass included in the Townshend Acts], Fine Glass can still be imported into America cheaper than it can be made there.[32]

If ever there was a statement of the difference between folk and fine glass, this is it.

Franklin was referring to the glass house at Wistarburgh along the Alloways Creek just outside the present town of Alloway in Salem County. It was founded in 1739 by Caspar Wistar, who came to Philadelphia from Hilspach, Germany in 1717. The Wistarburgh works made primarily bottles (holloware) and windows (window light). The first glassblowers—Johan Wilhelm Wentzel, Martin Halter, Caspar Halter, and Simeon Griesmeyer—were also German, and the record books of the company indicate that they were part-owners of the enterprise along with Wistar.[33] Upon the death of Caspar Wistar the business was inherited by his son Richard Wistar who continued the enterprise until his death in 1781, after which the factory stopped production. In the nineteenth century glassmaking centers were established in Glassboro, Millville, Bridgeton, Vineland, Waterford, and elsewhere in South Jersey.

*Opposite:* Piney basket maker. Photograph by Harry Dorer.
*The Dorer Collection, Newark Public Library*

According to Arlene Palmer, writing in the *Winterthur Portfolio* in 1976, "the Wistarburgh blowers were largely responsible for the dissemination of Germanic techniques and styles that characterize so much American-made glass."[34] For example, an heirloom in the Wistar family is a traditional dog-shaped drinking bottle evidently made at Wistarburgh. It is similar to the drinking bottles known as *Schnapshunden*, popular in Germany from the seventeenth through the nineteenth centuries.[35] Another example is a colorless tumbler engraved with the name of Caspar Wistar's daughter Margaret and the date 1751. The floral pattern and heart design on the tumbler were common motifs in German folk art. While it cannot be proven that this tumbler was made at Wistarburgh, it is probable that it was.[36]

Glass was made from sand, lime, and soda. In the dry state this was called the "batch." Broken glass, known as "cullet," was added to aid in the fusion of sand. These ingredients were mixed according to a "receipt" and heated in a melting furnace. Throughout the nineteenth century cord wood was used as the fuel for these furnaces. The batch was placed in baked pots known as "melting pots," in which the actual fusion took place. The fused mixture in its semi-plastic, liquid state was called the "metal." A team of men worked around a single opening ("glory hole") in the furnace.

To make a bottle, the "gatherer" would dip a hollow iron tube from two to seven feet long (the "blowpipe") into the pot of metal. He worked the metal around the head of the blowpipe until it formed a pear-shaped ball known as the "gather," "parison," or "blow." Then he rolled the gather on a polished metal or stone slab known as a "marver" to remove impurities and consolidate the gather. The gatherer then passed the blowpipe to the "blower" who would blow the bottle into the desired shape. In the eighteenth century the bottles were "free blown," that is, formed by blowing and shaping with tools. In the early nineteenth century the bottles were "moldblown," which means that the parison was placed into a mold and then blown into shape. Then the finisher or "gaffer" would attach a "pontil rod" to the base of the bottle and the blowpipe was broken off. The gaffer would shape the top and lip of the bottle. The bottle then was placed in a "leer" (from the German *lehr*) or "annealing oven" where it was gradually cooled.[37]

There were two different methods for making window lights. Under the crown method, the blower would twirl the pear-shaped parison, causing it to spread out. A helper would attach to the opposite side of the blow a small gather of metal on a punty rod. Another workman touched a cold iron to the blowpipe side, causing the blowpipe to separate. Then the glass was twirled

Tumbler made for Margaret Wistar,
reputedly made at Wistarburgh Glassworks, Salem County, or in Germany, 1751.
*Courtesy, The Henry Francis du Pont Winterthur Museum
and Elizabeth Morris Wistar*

from the punty rod side, making it basket shaped. Continued twirling resulted in the glass snapping into a disk shape about thirty-six inches in diameter. The rod was then separated from the glass disk and the latter was placed in the annealing oven. When the disk had cooled, small square or diamond panes were cut from it. The result was known as "crown glass." A twirl was evident in the translucent glass. Cast-off panes with the bull's-eye (where the rod was connected to the pane) were also sometimes used.[38]

The cylinder method, however, was the common method used in New Jersey. With repeated trips to the furnace, the gatherer would gather a large parison weighing about sixty pounds. The blower would receive the parison and insert it into an iron block and blow and swing the parison into the shape of a large cylinder about four feet long and ten inches in diameter. The cylinder was then cracked off from the blowpipe, the ends were removed, and the cylinder was split down its entire length. The curved sheet of glass was taken to the flattening ovens where heat made it flexible and flat. Then it was tempered in boiling water and cut to the desired size.[39]

Despite innovations in metals, fuels, and molds, glassmakers continued to use hand blowing throughout the nineteenth century. Not until the turn of the twentieth century was machinery for making cylinder glass and bottles introduced, and some factories continued hand blowing until the late 1930s.[40]

Pottery, basketry, and glass represent three different examples of the relationship between folk, vernacular, and fine objects. Of the three, basketry was most clearly a folk handicraft, although in the early twentieth century machines were developed to make bushel baskets. Both pottery and glass required kilns or furnaces, and so even during colonial times these crafts required greater social organization. Eighteenth-century redware and nineteenth-century stoneware were folk objects in both design and make. The introduction of poured molds by the mid-eighteenth century began a change in the pottery industry toward more standardized vernacular forms. By the mid-nineteenth century pottery was being made in factories, although certain pieces made there are today considered fine art objects. Glassworks, like the colonial iron foundries of New Jersey, required even greater organization than potteries. But unlike the iron industry, glassmaking maintained a craft tradition in the sense that most glass was hand blown throughout the nineteenth century. As with pottery, however, the introduction of molds to make flasks and bottles began the transformation to vernacular forms. That transformation was completed in the twentieth century with the development of bottle-making machines. But in the glassmaking industry, too, some fine pieces continued to be made in New Jersey during the nineteenth and twentieth centuries. These three examples show that the difference between folk, vernacular, and fine is not always the same in all areas. Often the dividing line between handicraft and industry is blurred.

# Foodways

**F**OODWAYS, as defined by Jay Anderson, include "the whole interrelated system of food conceptualization, procurement, distribution, preservation, preparation, and consumption shared by all members of a particular group."[1] Connoisseurs distinguish between provincial cooking and *haute cuisine*, which corresponds in part to the differences between folk and fine food.

Perhaps folk food would be better described as traditional home cooking, traditional recipes being passed down from generation to generation and not transmitted primarily by means of published cookbooks. Since the late nineteenth and early twentieth centuries, food production has become increasingly mechanized,[2] but while New Jersey foodways reflect changes in food preparation and consumption that occurred elsewhere in America, distinctive regional and ethnic food traditions persist.

The foodways of the Indians of New Netherland, according to Adriaen van der Donck, were very different from those of Europeans. He noted that whereas in Holland the rich lived more luxuriously than the common people, among the Indians everyone ate the same foods in the same quantities. Their food consumption was not excessive, even at their feasts. And unlike Europeans, the Indians did not eat at specified times of the day; they thought it best to eat when they were hungry. They sometimes would go for two, three, or four days with little or no food and then make up for their fasting by consuming large amounts. But van der Donck noted that there were no excessive eaters or gluttons among them. They had no special seating arrangements indicating rank, as was common among Europeans, nor did anyone serve the food to anyone else. And no ceremonies marked the beginning or ending of meals.

The Lenape Indians did not drink alcoholic beverages until the coming of Europeans. Their common drink was water, and they also drank the unfermented juice of grapes. When alcohol was introduced into their culture by European traders, the Lenape had little tolerance for it. Van der Donck noted that there was no word for drunkenness in their language. To denote a drunken man they used the word meaning "fool."[3]

Their main source of protein was fish and game. Fishing was done in the spring and summer, with seines and weirs (pounds made of upright sticks connected by nets).[4] Game meat included bears, wolves, otters, beavers, and deer. Deer were either caught with snares or killed with bow and arrows. Sometimes there were communal hunts involving as many as 100 men.[5] Fish and meat were cooked by boiling and preserved by drying and pounding, not by salt.

Agriculture was considered the province of women. The main crop was maize (corn),[6] which served as the main source of carbohydrates. It was prepared by pounding it into a meal that was called *sappaen*. Isaack de Rasieres, secretary of the province of New Netherland described how this was done.

> When they wish to make use of the grain for bread or porridge, which they call *Sappaen*, they first boil it and then beat it flat upon a stone; then they put it into a wooden mortar, which they know how to hollow out by fire, and then they have a stone pestle, which they know how to make themselves, with which they point it small, and sift it through a small basket. . . . The finest meal they mix with lukewarm water, and knead it in to dough, then they make round flat little cakes of it, of the thickness of an inch or a little more, which they bury in hot ashes, and so bake into bread; and when these are baked they have some clean fresh water by them in which they wash them while hot, one after another, and it is good bread, but heavy. The coarsest meal they boil into a porridge.[7]

*Sappaen* was eaten with all meals. Frequently it would be boiled with dried fish or meat. When they traveled long distances, the people would take a small bag of parched cornmeal. They would eat a small handful of the meal and then drink some water. Van der Donck noted that a quarter-pound of this meal was sufficient subsistence for an entire day.[8]

Their diet also contained other foods, including pumpkins, watermelons, squash, and nuts. They also ate dried beans, which they would boil with fresh meat until soft. A great feast would consist of beavers' tails, bass heads, parched cornmeal, or very fat meat stewed with shelled chestnuts.[9] An insight into their overall diet is provided by organic matter that Herbert Kraft found in food-storage pits at Indian dwelling sites in the upper Delaware River Valley. These include kernels of maize; corncobs; corn husks; beans; pumpkin and squash seeds; butternut shells and meat; shagbark or pignut hickory shells; acorns; wild plum seeds; freshwater-mussel shells; vertebrae, bone, and scales from fish; the remains of box turtles and frogs; and the remains of deer, bear, rodents, and dogs. Kraft thinks that domestic dogs were also eaten, but only in an emergency, for example in winter if starvation threatened.[10]

One of the cultural exchanges that occurred when Europeans came in contact with the Indians was a borrowing of foodways. The Dutch adopted the Indian *sappaen*, but they prepared and ate it in a European fashion, that is, as a porridge with milk. Peter Kalm has described the dish.

> In the evening they made a porridge of corn, poured it as customary into a dish, made a large hole in the center into which they poured fresh milk, but more often buttermilk. They ate it taking half a spoonful of porridge and half of milk. As they ordinarily took more milk than porridge, the milk in the dish was soon consumed. Then more milk was poured in. This was their supper nearly every evening.[11]

To make this more tasty, they would add sugar or syrup. He noted that this porridge was called by the Dutch *sappaan*.

Kalm described the typical mid-eighteenth-century meals of the Dutch in America. Breakfast consisted of tea, bread and butter, and radishes or slices of dried beef. The tea was served with sugar and without milk. They would take a bite of the sugar and sip the tea. The tea was a cultural borrowing from the English; Kalm noted that forty years earlier the Dutch colonists had only bread and butter or bread and milk for breakfast. Sometimes they also ate small round cheeses, which Kalm did not find very tasty. These they would cut into small slices and spread on the bread. They had breakfast at seven o'clock. At noon they would have another meal, but Kalm did not think there was anything distinctive about it. For supper they would usually have *sappaan* and meat or bread and butter with cheese. The cheese was grated to the consistency of coarse flour, which the Dutch thought improved its taste. If any porridge was left over, in the morning it was boiled with buttermilk until it reached the consistency of gruel. The meat was sometimes served with turnips and cabbage. With this meal they would drink water or weak beer. For dinner they would also have a large salad, with a dressing that was mostly vinegar and little or no oil. Sometimes they would have chocolate, but seldom pudding or pie, which were English. Since they were devout Calvinists, the father of the family would say grace before the meals. Kalm felt that the Dutch were more frugal in their food habits than the English. They would never put on their tables more food than they were going to consume. Nor did they drink as much as the English.[12] Yet the Dutch diet was basically similar to that of the English in New England. They both relied on dairy products as their main source of protein.

The Swedes who settled in the short-lived colony of New Sweden brought many of their foods with them. In 1749 Peter Rambo of Raccoon (Swedesboro), told Peter Kalm that his grandfather had come to New Sweden from Stockholm in 1642, bringing tree and garden seeds, including apple seeds, as well as oats and barley.[13] Nils Gustafson, a Swede who was ninety-one years old in 1749, told Kalm that the early Swedish settlers has brought their own cattle, sheep, hogs, geese, and ducks, and different kinds of grains, fruit, and herbs. The grains included wheat, rye, barley, and oats. They also cultivated white cabbage, "winter cabbage" (kale), "Swedish turnips" (rutabagas), and carrots, and they planted apple, cherry, and peach orchards.[14]

The Swedes also made buckwheat cakes which were fried in a pan or on a stone and eaten with butter in the morning.[15] As for their cheese, Kalm wrote: "The cheese made by the Swedes of Raccoon was especially good and looked very appetizing. It was molded in round, thick forms of from nine to twelve inches in diameter, and was the best made in this part of the world."[16]

Their common drink was a beer brewed from barley. They also made a "beer" from peaches. Another alcoholic drink was brewed from persimmons.

> Late in autumn after the fruit has been touched by the frost, a sufficient quantity is gathered. . . . These persimmon apples are put into a dough of wheat or other flour, formed into cakes, and put into an oven, in which they remain till they are baked and sufficiently dry, when they are taken out again. Then, in order to brew the liquor, a pot full of water is put on the fire and some of the cakes are put in. These become soft by degrees as the water grows warm, and crumble to pieces. The pot is then taken from the fire, and the water in it well stirred so that the cakes may mix with it. This is then poured into another vessel, and they continue to steep and break up as many cakes as are necessary for the brewing. Then the malt is added and one proceeds as usual with the brewing. Beer thus prepared is reckoned much preferable to other beer.[17]

A brandy was also made from persimmons.

There was an exchange of foodways between the Swedes and the Indians. The Swedes borrowed many Indian foods. Nils Gustafson told Kalm that at first the Swedes had to buy corn from the Indians for sowing and eating, but that after several years they began to sell corn to the Indians.[18] The Swedes ate the corn and fed it to their hogs. They also cultivated various kinds of pumpkins and melons, some of which were brought from Europe and others borrowed from the Indians. These were cut into slices and dried on a string, which preserved them all year long. They were eaten either boiled or stewed. Squash was a food totally borrowed from the Indians. It was boiled and eaten either with meat or by itself.[19] The Swedes also tried some of the roots that were part of the Indian diet. Among them were what the Indians called *hopniss* (a relative of the soy bean), which the Swedes ate instead of bread and the English instead of potatoes; *katniss (Sagittaria)*, which Gustafson told Kalm he ate often as a boy but which was no longer used by the Swedes; and *Taw-kee* (golden club), which some of the Swedes also ate.[20]

The Indians also borrowed some of the Swedish foods. Kalm noted that after the Swedes settled in America and planted apple and peach trees, the Indians, especially the women, stole the fruit in great quantities. The Indians also began to eat pork as a result of the fact that the Swedes allowed their hogs to wander unfenced in the woods. But the Indians taught the hogs to "follow them like dogs, and whenever they moved from one place to another their pigs always went with them."[21] The Indians also became very fond of milk, which had not been part of their diet. In fact, Kalm noted that when the Swedes gave the Indians butter or milk, they would boil or "broil" (sauté?) the seeds of the *Taw-kee* root in it.[22]

Once the Quakers began to settle in Pennsylvania and West New Jersey in great numbers the Swedes began to lose their own cultural traditions and to adopt English ones. Kalm concluded from his conversations with Gustafson that "before the English settled here they [the Swedes] followed wholly the customs of Old Sweden; but after the English had been in the country for some time, the Swedes began gradually to follow theirs."[23] For example, Kalm noted: "They celebrated Christmas with several sorts of games, and with various special dishes, as is usual in Sweden; all of which is now, for the greatest part, given up."[24] Also the Swedes began to have tea, coffee, and chocolate, which were unknown to them before the coming of the English.[25]

The foodways of a German farm family in colonial Somerset County have been described by Andrew D. Mellick, Jr., the descendant of Johannes Moelich of Bendorf, who migrated to America in 1735 and eventually settled near what is now Bedminster. In reconstructing the foodways of his ancestors, Mellick found that potatoes were a staple and that other vegetables they ate frequently were cabbages, beans, and corn. The family ate pears, apples, and a poor native variety of grapes. They ate ham, bacon, and smoked meats, which they slaughtered and cured on the farm. A traditional German dish they retained was sauerkraut, and every meal was garnished with *kohl-salat* (cabbage salad, known today as coleslaw). Their diet also included poultry, eggs, and cheese. They made buttermilk shortcakes, pies, doughnuts, and *olekokes* (literally, oil cakes), all of which were eaten at breakfast. As with the Dutch, a frequent dinner meal was *soupaan*, a cornmeal mush dish borrowed from the Indians, which the Germans ate with milk and molasses. Occasionally instead of *soupaan* they had *zweibak* (literally, "twice baked"), a raised biscuit baked in large quantities and then dried in the oven until very hard. It was eaten soaked in a bowl of milk. Another dish was a combination of chocolate and sausage links boiled in a kettle, then served in a bowl and eaten with a spoon. Beverages included hard cider, beer, and Jamaica rum. A favorite hot drink was soured beer simmered over a fire with crusts of brown bread and sweetened with molasses. Maple sugar and molasses were the common sweeteners.[26]

The agricultural historian, Hubert G. Schmidt, has described the adjustments English farm families who migrated to Hunterdon County in the colonial period had to make in their foodways. In 1787 Anne Capner, whose family had a farm west of Flemington, mentioned in her copybook such foods as pickled pork, "hung" beef, bacon, and dried fruit. She wrote: "The more we see of their ways the more we see it nessary (sic) to come into them."[27] Among these new foodways were buckwheat cakes and pie for breakfast, described by her mother, Mary Capner, in a letter in 1787.

> Buckwheat cakes are now in Season and are very good. They resemble pikelets [a kind of crumpet]. Now they can be leavened in summer tho we eat them unleavened to breakfast all summer.—Since I have had workmen I see the Utility of pye or something of that sort to Breakfast. When the cake plate is empty of Buckwheat then they will take pye to their coffee.[28]

In 1793 Mary Choyce wrote in a letter:

> Apple pye and sauce on the table three times a day constantly. They eat apple sauce to almost everything here. When the green apples are gone we shall have dried apples to serve until cherrys are ripe and then we shall have Cherry pye till we are tired of it. Apples are so plentiful here that cousin Joseph says he has eat a waggon load this winter.[29]

Another food strange to the English farmers was the German coleslaw. Mary Capner wrote: "The weomen . . . seemed fond of the Slaw. I tasted it of Curiosity. It is raw cabbage cut as thin as possible, it looks like horse radish, then there is something warm poured upon it and peper is strewed on it."[30]

Other foods were not so exotic to the English palate. For example, Mary Capner wrote: "For supper we had Boiled beef, turnips, potatoes, pickles for sauce, fowls and Ham and rice pudding and apple pye."[31] A meal served at a "raising frolic" in 1787 consisted of roast veal, beef, mutton, and potatoes served with plenty of gravy.[32] Several women awaiting the birth of a child were served tea, bread and butter, cheese, pickled cucumbers, mince pie, and pumpkin pie for breakfast; roast beef, potatoes, coleslaw, and pickles for dinner; and tea, very peppery hashed beef, cheese, honey, pickles, bread and butter, and two kinds of pie for supper.[33] In 1793 the Capner family served a visiting circuit judge a supper of tea, hot roast chicken, sliced cold beef, preserved quinces, bread, butter, and toast.[34] Other foods that were part of the diet in colonial Hunterdon County were game (rabbits, squirrels, quail, pheasants, passenger pigeons, wildfowl, turtles, and freshwater fish), wild fruit (plums, currants, mulberries, grapes, cherries, strawberries, raspberries, blackberries, huckleberries, bilberries, haws, and persimmons), and nuts (walnuts, butternuts, hickory nuts, and hazelnuts). Honey was produced from domesticated and wild bees. Local stores and peddlers sold tea, coffee, cake, chocolate, salt, rice, molasses, brown sugar, lump sugar, raisins, pepper, clams, oysters, and fish.[35]

Just as Kentucky is known for its bourbon, so New Jersey is known for its applejack. The *Columbia Encyclopedia* defines applejack as a "brandy, made from apples by partly freezing hard cider and removing the ice or by distilling hard cider or fermented apple pomace. It is popularly associated with New Jersey, and because of its potency when undiluted it is colloquially called Jersey Lightning."[36] According to Harry B. Weiss, "The early immigrants to America brought their drinking habits with them. The English drank ale and beer; the Dutch, beer, and the French and Spanish liked light wines."[37] In New England, however, the European grains did not thrive, but apple orchards did, and the English changed their drinking habits. By 1700 cider was the common drink in New England, New York, Pennsylvania, and New Jersey. In 1729 the tavern prices in Salem (Salem County) were: eight pence for a quart of cider royal (fermented cider with applejack), four pence for a quart of cider, four pence for a quart of strong beer, six pence for a gill (one-quarter pint) of brandy or cordial, three pence for a gill of rum, and one shilling for a pint of wine.[38]

Peter Kalm described how applejack was made in the eighteenth century in South Jersey.

Mr. Hesselius's daughter related how some colonists in this vicinity made a pleasant beverage of apples, as follows: some apples—which need not be the best—and apple peelings are taken and dried. Half a peck of this dried fruit is then boiled in ten gallons of water and when removed from the fire the solid part taken out. Then yeast is added to the water, which is allowed to ferment, whereupon it is poured into vessels like any other drink. One who has not tasted it before would not believe that such a palatable beverage could be prepared from apples. It was said to be better than that made from persimmons, because it retains its quality longer and does not get sour.—I forgot one thing: when the apple ale is made, some bran should be added to the water.[39]

In the nineteenth century the process was more elaborate. To make the cider the apples were "beaten" by hand with wooden pestles in a wooden or stone trough. Three or four men could beat thirty to forty bushels of apples in a day. This method was replaced by the horse mill, which consisted of a circular stone wheel stood on end and a circular stone trough in which the fruit was ground. The power was supplied by horses hitched to a lead. A later method was to use a grinder. The apples were placed in a hopper on top of the grinder. Two wheels on either side turned wooden cylinders with iron teeth which ground the ripe apples into a pomace. The pomace was then made into a "cheese" consisting of alternating layers of pomace and straw. This cheese was placed in the press, a large wooden screw that literally pressed the cider out of the cheese. The cider was then strained and kept warm in a large covered vat while it fermented. The fermenting cider was purified by percolation (racking it from vessel to vessel) or by precipitation (adding isinglass, a pure, translucent form of gelatin, derived from the air bladders of certain fish, and gently boiling it). Then the cider was put in casks or bottles.[40] Often it was allowed to continue to ferment until it became vinegar. The inventories of many New Jersey farms in the nineteenth century show kegs of cider vinegar.

The cider could be made into applejack by either of two methods. It could be frozen and the concentrated frozen liquid separated from the watery parts, thus doubling its strength. This frozen-heart product was known as "hard cider" or "applejack." The cider could also be distilled. It was placed in a vessel known as a "cucurbit" or "calabash," in which it was boiled. The distilled vapors would be conducted through a spout or tube known as the "alembic" or "worm" in which the vapor would be air-cooled, condensing the vapors back to a liquid state. The product of one distilling was known as "low wine." It was then distilled a second time in a still known as a "doubler" into high-proof alcohol. The distilled product was called "cider brandy" or "cider spirits" though these terms and hard cider or applejack were often used interchangeably. The applejack was then aged in wooden casks, after which it was bottled or sold in stoneware jugs.[41]

There is a folklore of applejack. Folk terminology, such as "Jersey Lightning" and "apple palsy," has been associated with it (see "Folk Speech"), it was prescribed as a kind of folk medicine, and it was associated with certain legendary characters. According to a Burlington County newspaper in 1891,

> In Southampton, where applejack is plenty and pine-hawkers [Pineys] numerous, it is invariably prescribed for chills and fever, grippe, coughs, colds and nervous prostration. Owley Lemon, king of the pine-hawkers, who is now 76 years of age, has been drinking applejack regularly ever since the Civil war broke out, and even now can drink a quart per day without the slightest inconvenience. . . . Despite his years, he can kick higher, dance longer and stand more exposure than any man in Southampton.[42]

By the early nineteenth century applejack had become a major industry in New Jersey. Tax returns show that in 1810 1,103,272 gallons of spirits were distilled in New Jersey, of which about three-quarters was probably applejack. By 1830 there were 388 cider distilleries in New Jersey, of which some of the principal producers were the Charles Ewan distillery in Ewansville (Burlington County), the Laird and Company distillery in Scobeyville (Monmouth County), and the D. L. Bryant distillery in Succasunna (Morris County).[43] Thus applejack was transformed from a traditional drink into a commercial product.

The nineteenth century brought about other changes in rural foodways as commercially produced food gradually replaced home preparation. These changes have been documented by Hubert Schmidt for rural Hunterdon County.[44] While most breads and pastries continued to be made at home, bakeries began to appear in the larger towns in the 1830s. Stores began to sell oranges and lemons as early as the 1820s. Crackers, usually eaten with cheese, were also sold in these stores. Ice cream and soft drinks such as root beer and birch beer, commercially produced refreshments for the summer, became common. In the mid-1850s "self-sealing" glass jars for home preservation of fruits were being advertised, and during the 1860s foods preserved in tin cans were being advertised and sold. By the late nineteenth century the springhouse—a stone structure located over a spring to keep dairy products, eggs, meats, and fruit cool—was replaced by the icebox, which used ice cut during the winter and packed in sawdust or swamp hay. All this was part of a complicated process of mechanization of food production and preservation which was occurring in America and Europe, made possible by technological innovation in agriculture, the application of assembly-line techniques to livestock slaughtering, new ways of processing and preserving foodstuffs commercially, the advent of brand names, new means of transportation such as the refrigerated railroad car, and the mechanization of the kitchen with the gas range and the electric refrigerator.[45] Gradually, uniform, commercial foodstuffs were replacing traditional foodways.

Despite the growing uniformity in foodways since the mid-nineteenth century, traditional foodways continue in New Jersey, especially in regional and ethnic cooking. Local cookbooks record the persistence of traditional recipes. Many of these cookbooks make no distinction between traditional recipes and those copied from other cookbooks or magazines, but they are useful documents nonetheless. The cookbooks from northern New Jersey contain numerous ethnic recipes, and those from South Jersey have many seafood and cranberry dishes. There is also evidence of Pennsylvania German influence in such dishes as shoo-fly pie and scrapple.

Arlene Martin Ridgway's *Chicken Foot Soup and Other Recipes from the Pine Barrens* contains examples of regional home cooking from South Jersey. Most of these recipes make use of foods available in the Pinelands and along the Jersey Shore, such as cranberries, seafood, and game. Included are recipes for clam pie, oyster pie, cranberry pie, wild rabbit pie, chicken foot soup, duck soup, clam fritters, fried snapping turtle, dandelion salad, fiddleheads (a fern that grows along the banks of streams which is prepared and served like asparagus), hot cranberry tea, and dandelion wine.[46] Cookbooks, of course, merely present recipes. They do not place food in its total cultural context, nor do we expect them to.

New Jersey foodways include not just colonial and regional traditions, but also those of more recent immigrant and ethnic groups.

Foodways, in fact, are a major way of expressing ethnic identity. The dietary laws (*kashrut*) of eastern European Jews, for example, set them apart. These are a complicated corpus of food regulations based on the Bible. The essential distinction is between kosher (permitted) foods and *treyf* (impure) foods. Kosher meat includes only four-legged animals that ruminate and have cloven hoofs, birds that do not eat carrion, and fish with scales. All other animals are *treyf*, including carnivores, rodents, shellfish, birds of prey, eaters of carrion, and reptiles. Kosher meat must be slaughtered in a special way so that the *shokhet* (slaughterer) severs the trachea and jugular vein with one stroke. There are also rules about which foods may be eaten together. *Milchik* (dairy) foods must not be eaten with *fleyshik* (meat and poultry) foods. Certain foods, however, such as flour, eggs, vegetables, fruits, salt, sugar, condiments, and fish, are *parveh* (neutral).[47] Certain foods are traditionally served on particular Jewish holidays. On Chanukah it is traditional to serve *latchas* (potato pancakes); on Purim *hamantaschen* (triangular pastries filled with poppy seeds), on Passover *matzoh brei* (unleavened bread dipped in egg batter and fried), on the Sabbath *challah* (twisted bread made with an egg dough).

Yet there are certain foods traditional among eastern European Jews that are also eaten by Poles, Russians, and Ukrainians. They may be known by the same or different names, but they are basically the same foods. For example, *borscht* (beet soup) is basically the same dish in the Russian, Ukrainian, and Yiddish culture areas. Potato dumplings are similar even though they are known as *knishes* in Yiddish, *pyrohi* in Ukrainian, and *parogie* in Polish. These similar foods are an indication of a Slavic culture area in eastern Europe. While the Jews are not a Slavic people, those who lived in eastern Europe did adopt aspects of Slavic culture. Thus Old World geographic relationships are relevant in understanding traditional immigrant culture in New Jersey.

There are equally striking differences in the foods of other ethnic groups in New Jersey. Take, for example, the different foods associated with the celebration of Christmas among Ukrainians, Italians, and Germans. On Christmas Eve the Ukrainians have a big meal consisting of twelve dishes, symbolizing the twelve apostles. Among them are borscht with *ushka* (mushroom dumplings); *holubtsi* (stuffed cabbage); *pyrohi*; fried fish, sauerkraut, and chick-peas in oil; *kutia* (boiled wheat kernels with poppy seeds, honey, and nuts); and *strutslia* (long, narrow, braided bread).[48] On Christmas Eve it is traditional among southern Italians to have a fish dinner, consisting of spaghetti *algio olio* (with a garlic and oil sauce) or spaghetti *vongole* (with mussels and oil); *buccala* (dried cod fish); *sarde* (smelts); *zeppole* (light dough balls deep fried in oil and sprinkled with sugar); and *anguilla* (eels). The eels are the most traditional part of the dinner.[49] The big German meal is on Christmas day. The traditional dish is a roast ham with baked sweet potatoes, baked potatoes, and vegetables. After dinner various kinds of traditional cakes and cookies are served including *springerle* (anise-flavored Swabian Christmas cookies), *lebkuchen* (Nuremberg gingerbread), butter cakes, and *pfeffernüsse* (ginger or spice cookies).[50]

Foodways are one measure of the degree to which ethnic traditions persist among immigrant groups in New Jersey. A study of acculturation among the Japanese-Americans who were settled after World War II at Seabrook Farms in South Jersey shows that while most members of the group are fond of traditional Japanese foods, such as *sashimi* (raw fish), *sushi* (boiled rice with vinegar stuffed with egg and vegetables and rolled into seaweed), and *mochi* (rice cakes), the first generation (*Issei*) eat mostly Japanese food and some American food, and the second generation (*Nisei*) eat mostly American food and some Japanese food.[51]

Foodways reflect the complex cultural processes that shaped the development of New Jersey cultures. Different Old World ethnic groups come into contact with a new environment and new groups. The result is cultural borrowings and adaptations. Despite the technological changes of the nineteenth century that resulted in the mass production, preservation, and distribution of foods, traditional foodways continue, especially among recent immigrants and in regional home cooking. For many people the maintenance of these traditions is an important ingredient in their cultural identity. The persistence of traditional foodways is one measure of the degree to which New Jersey and America have *not* been melting pots.

# Games and Recreation

**F**OLK GAMES and recreation are traditional leisure-time, as distinguished from commercial or professional, activities. According to the folklorists Mary and Herbert Knapp: "The distinguishing characteristic of a traditional folk game is that although it has rules, they are not written down. Nobody knows exactly what they are. The players have a tradition to guide them, but must settle among themselves the details of how to play a particular game."[1]

Brian Sutton-Smith, the folklorist, says that folk games reflect the cultures in which they are played. He distinguishes three types: games of physical skill, games of chance, and games of strategy. He argues that less complex cultures play simpler games, involving only one of these types or a combination of two of them and that more complex cultures play games that combine all three. He

notes that cultures that rely on hunting and fishing tend to play games that reflect physical skill, whereas cultures that are nomadic and face uncertain pros-
pects for survival play games of chance.[2]

Lenape Indian games seem to substantiate Sutton-Smith's theory. The Lenapes depended on hunting and fishing. Although they were sedentary for part
of the year, they dispersed into small bands during the winter. Their games reflect a combination of physical skill and chance, as predicted by Sutton-Smith.
The modern Lenape Indians play several games, only one of which can be defi-
nitely traced back to the time they occupied New Jersey. In 1655 Adriaen van
der Donck described it as "a game with pieces of reeds, resembling our card
playing."[3] Isaack de Rasieres, another Dutchman, described it in 1628.

> They are very fond of a game they call *Senneca*, played with some
> round rushes, similar to the Spanish feather-grass, which they under-
> stand how to shuffle and deal as though they were playing cards; and
> they win from each other all that they possess, even to the lappet with
> which they cover their private parts, and so they separate from each
> other quite naked.[4]

Frank Speck, the anthropologist, found the same or a similar game being played
by the Delaware Indians in Oklahoma. It was called *selá 'ta'n*, literally "scat-
tering straws." Speck noted its similarity to the European game of jackstraws.
The game is played with sixty-five straws about eight inches long. Fifty of the
straws are plain, and fifteen are marked with dots, spirals, and dashes. The plain
straws have a value of one, and the marked straws range in value from five to
seventy-five in intervals of five and fifteen. The straws are shuffled between the
palms of the player and dropped upon a blanket on the ground. They are then
removed one at a time with a quill, the thick end of which is bent to form a
hook. If the player moves any other straws in the process, he forfeits his turn.
The first player to reach a predetermined score (usually 100) wins the game.
Wagering is a big part of the game. The player with the lowest score forfeits a
blanket or must do a favor for the winner. Both men and women can play the
game, but only those who were born during the winter may play. The game is
played only during the winter, and was believed to cause storms and blizzards.[5]

From the colonial period through the early nineteenth century the boundary
between work and play was often nonexistent for European-derived cultures in
New Jersey. Work and play were combined in what were called frolics or
"bees," which were in effect work parties. This tradition enables large jobs to be
accomplished by a communal effort among neighbors and friends who work

first and then play together. Different kinds of frolics and bees were held for different kinds of work.

A "raising" was a work party to erect a barn or house. The frame would be assembled on the ground by skilled carpenters. But large numbers of men were needed to lift the assembled sides of the frame into position. Then the carpenters could enclose the frame at their leisure.[6]

A flax frolic was associated with the work of harvesting flax, usually in early August (see "Quilts, Coverlets, and Samplers"). In Hunterdon County, which was probably typical of other rural areas, a field was divided into "lands." The crews competed to see which would finish first. It was hot work, and they were supplied with plenty of water and applejack. When the sun went down there would be a supper of potpie, puddings, cakes, and fruit pies.[7]

There were also "spinning frolics" and "quilting bees." In the former the women would pick up the wool at a particular farmhouse and take it home to spin it into yarn. They would all bring the yarn back for a party at which there would be supper and games. Sometimes the spinning would be done at the party. In a "quilting bee" the women would gather together to sew a quilt. A woman from Bethlehem Township in Hunterdon County, who was ninety-seven years old in 1869, recalled that quilting and spinning frolics were common when she was a girl.[8]

Before there were many fulling mills the fulling of wool was done at a "fulling party" or "kicking frolic." Six young men and six young women would be invited. The young men would sit on chairs placed in a circle in the center of the floor. A bundle of wool moistened with warm soapsuds was placed on the floor, and the young men would kick the bundle around. When the wool was shrunk to the desired length, the young women would wring it out and hang it out to dry. This was all done in the spirit of a party.[9]

There were also "husking bees" for husking corn, "wood frolics" for cutting and hauling wood for the minister, "apple paring bees" for slicing apples and hanging the slices up to dry, "apple butter bees," and even "dung frolics" for hauling away the manure in the barnyards.[10]

Hunting is an activity that underwent a transformation from work to play. In the colonial period it was an essential activity for supplying food. But already in the mid-eighteenth century, the upper class in Philadelphia and New Jersey imitated the upper class in England by engaging in fox hunting. The Gloucester Fox Hunting Club was founded in 1766. This upper-class style of fox hunting continues to the present day in the horse country of Somerset County and in Hunterdon County.

Another kind of fox hunting is done in the South Jersey Pine Barrens. It was described in 1941 by Cornelius Weygandt in his book *Down Jersey* and more recently by Mary Hufford. The red fox, imported from England, and the gray fox, native to America, are hunted in both traditions. The upper class hunted on horseback with large packs of hounds. Fox hunting in the Pines takes place on foot with one man and two or three hounds or perhaps two men and fifteen or twenty hounds. Weygandt noted that many Piney homes had wire enclosures with doghouses for as many as seven to twenty hounds. These hounds were larger and had shorter legs than beagles, but they were not as large as the fox hounds of the hunt clubs. Weygandt maintains that since the pelt of the gray fox at that time brought only three to three and one-half dollars, many Piney fox hunters were content simply with the joy of the chase.[11] Today pickup trucks are used to transport the hounds. This kind of fox hunting is also practiced in the southern Appalachian Mountains, where it is known as "hilltopping," as well as in the Piney Woods of Georgia.

According to Hufford, the difference between the two styles of foxhunting in New Jersey is that the upper-class hunting emphasizes "social hierarchy and excellence of horsemanship," whereas fox hunting in the Pines emphasizes "intimacy with nature." There is also a difference, Hufford states, in the relationship between the hunters and the hounds. In the upper-class tradition the hunters participate in the chase and compete with each other in horsemanship. In the Piney tradition the hunters remain in their pick-up trucks and listen to the sounds of the hounds. "Competition between the hunters is carried on vicariously through hounds," Hufford writes. The hounds become "extensions of their owners," and they are described in anthropomorphic terms. Their sounds are termed "music," and the owner can pick out from the pack the "notes" of his own dogs. Thus, Hufford concludes, "For the student of culture, it follows that foxhunting is the embodiment of ideas: as significant a cultural text as a diary or house form, and every bit as prolific with its yield of insights into the world view of a people."[12]

Group games and recreation were common for both adults and children during the nineteenth century. One such activity in South Jersey was the "General Beach Party." Dr. J. F. Leaming (1822–1907) of Cape May described what one such party was like when he was a boy. It was a community event held in early September. A messenger went from house to house to invite everyone to come. Each family had an early breakfast at home and loaded the wagon. At precisely eight o'clock a cannon signaled the start of the event. Each family proceeded to the nearest boat landing where they unloaded their wagons and boarded sailboats to take them to the barrier islands, which in those days were uninhabited. Songs such as "My Old Aunt Sally" were sung. Leaming supplied a fragment of this song.

> Sally, Sally, my old Aunt Sally
> Ra, re, ri, ro,
> Round the corner Sally.

When they reached the beach, they disembarked. Three men, who had dug 600–800 clams for the occasion, took charge of the traditional "Indian" clambake. They began by placing 3 clams on end with the hinges upward and worked outward from the center until a circular bed five to six feet in diameter was formed. Then they covered this bed with some fine brush, and covered this with another layer of larger brush and sticks.

Meanwhile everyone went bathing in the surf. The north end of the beach was assigned to the men and the south end to the women. At noon the clam bed was "fired," and everyone assembled to prepare the dinner. Pots of chicken pot-pie were hung on a pole supported by two crotches above a fire. This dish was known in the restaurants of New York as "Cape May Pot Pie." Also served were roast beef or veal, fruit pies, puddings, cakes, preserves, coffee, tea, fruit, and melons. When the brush covering the clam bed was burned, the coals were swept away. The ground kept the bed warm for up to an hour. After a clergy-man said grace, one person from each table came to the clam bed. Flipping a clam on to its side with a fork opened the shell, and the clam would be trans-ferred to the plate.

After dinner, the men talked about crops and market prices, the women cleaned up and packed the leftovers, and the children played such games as "Wink'em Silly," "Lost My Glove Yesterday and Found It Today," and "Wind Tobacco Tight," the rules of which Mr. Leaming unfortunately neglected to pro-vide. At four o'clock everyone would rendezvous at the boats to return to the mainland.[13]

In Bergen County in the late nineteenth century there were "Ghost Parties" or "Sheet and Pillowcase Parties." About a dozen young men and ladies clad in white sheets and wearing pillowcases over their heads would march down the road laughing and talking, until they reached the home of a friend. Then they would knock on the door to surprise the friend, who would invite them in for a party consisting of music and games.[14] Unfortunately, we lack details about what kinds of games were played.

The nineteenth century brought the emergence of childhood. According to Philippe Ariès, in the medieval family there had been no recognition of the status of childhood. Children were dressed like little adults. They were treated as servants, especially in the apprentice system in which children were "put out" to be raised in other families as servants in order to learn a skill or trade. The games children played were the same as the games adults played. The recognition of childhood came about as the school replaced apprenticeship. This brought the child back into the home, which Ariès sees as the beginning of the modern family. For the upper classes in Europe this process began in the seventeenth century.[15] In America apprenticeship was common throughout the eighteenth century and into the early nineteenth century. It is then that we see a change in children's dress, the development of public schools, the spread of the notion of childhood innocence, and the emergence of specific children's games.

Sutton-Smith, who is a specialist in children's folklore, provides us with a useful classification of children's games, which he developed by studying children in New Zealand. It applies equally well to games played by children in New Jersey. The examples I use are all from New Jersey and were collected between 1976 and 1979 by students at Rutgers-Newark. Sutton-Smith has suggested ten major categories: singing games, dialogue games, informal games, leader games, chasing games, rhythmic games, games of chance, teasing activities, parlor games, and games of skill.[16]

In singing games the players sing a song, usually in unison, as they play the game. One such game is "Ring around the Rosey." In this game the players form a circle, hold hands, and walk in a circle as they sing in unison:

> Ring around the rosey
> Pocket full of poseys
> Ashes, ashes, all fall down.

The players then fall to the ground. Another circle game is "Motor Boat." It is done the same way, but the lyrics are:

> Motor boat, motor boat, go so slow,
> Motor boat, motor boat, go so fast,
> Motor boat, motor boat, step on the gas!

Everyone circles very fast until they all say in unison "Fast, fast, fast as you can," and everyone falls down.[17] These are what Sutton-Smith calls games of low organization.[18] They are played primarily by children four to six years old.

Dialogue games usually involve a central player, a group of players, and traditional dialogue. The game of "Pies" played in Vailsburg, an ethnic residential section of Newark, is an example. In this game one central person is called "the Mother" and another central person is called "the Wolf." The rest of the children are the pies, each having an identity as a type of pie (e.g. Apple, Peach, Strawberry) which is kept secret. The dialogue goes as follows:

> WOLF (knocking on the door): Do you have any pies?
> MOTHER: No, I don't have any pies.
> (Children on steps clap their hands)
> WOLF: I can hear them baking in the oven.
> MOTHER: O.K. What kind do you want?

The wolf has to guess the identity of a pie. If he guesses the secret identity of a "pie" on the steps, that child gets up and runs around the house. The wolf has to pay the mother by tapping her hand five times, thus giving the "pie" a headstart. If the wolf catches the "pie" before it gets around the house, that child either becomes the wolf or is put in the "pickle jar" to wait until the next wolf takes over.

A variant of this game is called "Fruits." It is played the same way, but the personae are "Ma-Ma," "the But," and various kinds of fruit. According to Sutton-Smith, the girls who play these games act out their feelings about the relationships between children and adults by impersonating good and bad mothers and good and bad children.

Examples of informal games are make-believe, imitative activities, playing with toys, and pack games such as "Cowboys and Indians." Imitative games include playing house or store. A contemporary informal game using a homemade toy is playing with a "Dewey," a string tied around a rock or stone which is tossed into a tree or onto telephone wires.[19] People who grew up at the turn of the century on canal boats along the Morris Canal were interviewed by James Lee about their games and toys. They remember such things as homemade slingshots, whistles made of willows, whistles made of chestnuts tied together with a string, and dolls made of clothes pegs and corn husks with apple-heads.[20] Homemade go-carts were popular in the 1950s when I was a boy in northern New Jersey, although even then the more organized, business-sponsored Soap Box Derby had replaced this activity for some boys. While commercial toys have been around since the nineteenth century, in recent years there have been fewer and fewer homemade toys, as commercial manufacturers using television advertisements have made a big business of children's games.

In leader games one player is a central person who directs the activity of the other players.[21] In "Red Light" the central person turns his back on the rest of the players while they try to sneak up on him. He can control the game by saying, "one, two, three, red light" and turning around to face them. Any player caught moving when the central person turns around must go back to the beginning. If a player is able to approach the central person and tag him, that player becomes the central person.[22]

Sutton-Smith divides chasing games into two categories: central-person chasing games in which the central person competes against all the other players; and team-chasing games in which two teams compete against each other.[23] In the first category is "Hide and Seek" in which the central person is called "It." He closes his eyes and counts to 100 while the other players all hide within a designated area. When "It" finishes counting, he yells

Apple, peaches, pumpkin pie
Who's not ready?
Holler "I."

If no one says "I," the central person goes looking for the other players. When the central person finds another player, he has to run to "home base" and tap it, saying

Tap, Tap
I see (name of person)
(location of person).

The caught person has to remain at home base until all the others are caught unless another player can outrun the central person to home base and yell, "Home, free all," in which case everyone at home base is free.

In the second category is "Ringalareo" ("Ringaleveo"), which is played by preadolescent children in fifth and sixth grades. The teams consist of the boys against the girls. The boys run after the girls, and when a boy catches a girl, she has to do whatever he wants. Usually this means making her sit in the corner or making her kiss another boy.[24] This game falls into the specific subcategory of the "chasing-kiss game," according to Sutton-Smith.[25]

Rhythmic games are divided into skipping or jumping, hand-clapping, and ball-bouncing games. They are usually accompanied by rhymes.[26] Of these jump-rope rhymes are the most universal. Some span the generations with certain variations. For example, two versions of "Teddy Bear" were collected from two generations.

| Version A | Version B |
|---|---|
| Teddy Bear, Teddy Bear, | Teddy Bear, Teddy Bear, |
| touch the ground, | touch the ground, |
| Teddy Bear, Teddy Bear, | Teddy Bear, Teddy Bear, |
| touch your shoe, | turn around, |
| Teddy Bear, Teddy Bear, | Teddy Bear, Teddy Bear, |
| twenty-three skiddoo.[27] | say your prayers, |
| | Teddy Bear, Teddy Bear, |
| | go to bed.[28] |

The first version was collected from a woman who grew up in the 1920s, which is reflected in the slang expression "twenty-three skiddoo." The second is more recent and less dated. Many jump-rope rhymes express psychologically suggestive attitudes. For example, this version of "Cinderella" shows an attitude of young girls toward the physical attributes of adult women.

> Cinderella dressed in yella,
> Went downtown to meet her fella,
> On her way her girdle busted,
> How many people were disgusted.
> 1, 2, 3, 4, . . .[29]

The following rhyme shows a concern with grown-up decisions about marriage and courtship.

> Who shall I marry? Who shall I marry?
> Rich man, poor man, beggar man, thief,
> Doctor, lawyer, Indian chief.[30]

The next category is games of chance. They include counting-out rhymes, which are used to choose sides or to determine who will be the central person. One way is for everyone to yell "Not it"; the last person to yell "Not it" is "It." Another way is to play "Odds and Evens" in which each player choses either odds or evens and holds out one or two fingers. If the fingers are the same, then evens wins; if they are different, odds wins. This was called "duking it out" in the Vailsburg section of Newark in the 1960s, presumably because the matter is settled by using one's fists ("dukes").[31] One of the most popular ways to count out is for everyone to make a fist; the counter recites the following rhyme while tapping each fist in succession.

> One potato, two potato, three potato, four;
> Five potato, six potato, seven potato, more.

Each person on whom the word "more" lands is "out" until everyone has been eliminated. As the folklorist Kenneth Goldstein has shown, this is not always completely left to chance, because some children figure out in advance where the word "more" will fall and predetermine the outcome by beginning with the right person.[32]

The category of teasing activities includes taunts and jeers such as

> I see China.
> I see France.
> I see (name of person)'s underpants.

Often there are traditional comebacks, such as

> Sticks and stones will break my bones,
> But names will never hurt me.

Taunts and jeers are carried to an extreme degree of verbal competition among Afro-American teenage boys in what is known as "signifying" or "playing the dozens." In this they compete in trying to put down the other person's family and relatives in sexual terms. This is especially common among urban youths. Similar put-downs are common in other cultural traditions.

Parlor games are those intended for special indoor occasions, such as play parties. Perhaps most common are the kissing games played by adolescents. Sutton-Smith groups these in a subcategory of "forfeit games," in which the losers are penalized. "Spin the Bottle" is one in which the person who spins the bottle has to kiss whomever the bottle points to when it stops spinning. In "Post Office" the names of all the persons of the opposite sex are put in a box, and the person who picks a name has to go into the back room and kiss the partner he picked for a specified period of time. There are variations on this game. Sutton-Smith suggests that kissing games remain popular because "one may enjoy a kissing relationship, but be protected from a more total and intimate commitment."[33]

The final category covers games of skill. An example from the turn of the century is a game known as "caddy." The caddy was a stick that was sharpened at one end. It was placed on the ground, and its pointed end was hit with another stick so that it would bounce off the ground, whereupon it would be hit again. The person who batted the caddy furthest was the winner. This game was played in the streets of Irvington as well as by youngsters who grew up on the Morris Canal.[34]

Jacks was another game of skill popular at about the same time. Although today jacks is almost exclusively a girls' game, it was popular then among boys as well. The game was played with eight (or ten) jacks and a ball. The ball was thrown in the air, and the player had to pick up one jack and catch the ball without touching any other jacks. He continued picking up the jacks one at a time until he had picked up all eight. He then picked them all up two at a time, then three at a time, and so on until he had picked all eight on a single throw. Anyone who missed a catch or touched another jack forfeited his turn.[35] There are many variations on this pattern, some of them involving considerable manual dexterity.

Another perennially favorite game of skill, especially for boys, was marbles or agates. In one of the variations a big circle called "the pot" was drawn. Everyone's marbles were put into the pot, and the players took turns trying to "shoot" the marbles outside the circle. Any marble you knocked outside the circle was yours.[36] I remember this game being banned in my grade school, because the principal considered it a form of gambling.

Sutton-Smith describes the evolution that occurs in the games children play as they grow older. The kissing games, of course, are played by older preadolescent and adolescent children. In the six- to nine-year age group, games that involve all players in carrying out the same actions are most popular. Furthermore the majority of the games played by children up to eleven years old are central-person games involving the central person in a limelight role, a dominating maternal or paternal role, or a fearsome role. After the age of ten their central-person games change to a more competitive mode of attacking the central person or making the central person into a scapegoat. This coincides with the rise of more individual skill games. A similar transition occurs in team games. Those played by children younger than ten tend to be more dramatic enactments than the simple competition that characterizes team games played at ages ten and eleven. Sutton-Smith concludes that "games would not have their meaningfulness to children if they were not thus intrinsically related to the fabric of human development."[37]

Games also evolve over time. In a study of the changes in game preferences of American children in Worcester, Massachusetts in 1896, South Carolina in 1898, San Francisco in 1921, and northwestern Ohio in 1959, Sutton-Smith and B. G. Rosenberg found a decline in singing games, dialogue games, team guessing and acting games, cooperative parlor games, and couple games. The game preferences of girls have tended to become more like those of the boys, while the boys are becoming more limited in their choices. This is a result in part of the changing role of women in American society and in part of the decline of formality, causing spontaneous play to replace more formal games.[38]

The study of games also provides insights into the immigration experience. For example, among the Italians of Newark the game of *morra* was played a generation or two ago. It was similar to "Odds and Evens," except that it was played by men. Two or more men would face each other and throw out any number of fingers. The object was to guess the sum of the combined fingers thrown out and call it out before your opponent.[39] The folklorist Elizabeth Mathias found that first-generation Italian-American men tended to play this game more as a game of strategy, but second-generation men tried aggressively to intimidate their opponent.[40] Today it is rarely played in New Jersey.

Koji Shimada reports a similar disappearance of traditional games among Japanese-Americans in Seabrook. Such games as *go* (a territorial game similar to checkers) and *shogi* (similar to chess) were played in the 1940s by the first generation, but later generations no longer play them. Another disappearing game is *karuta*. This is a card game involving 100 cards each containing the last verse of a Japanese poem. The cards are laid out on the floor, and the caller recites the first part of the poem. The players compete by saying the correct concluding verse, in which case they can pick up the card. The game involves good hearing and fast reflexes.[41]

As we have seen in other aspects of folklife, in the late nineteenth and early twentieth centuries there developed an increased professionalization and commercialization of leisure-time activity. Entertainment that formerly was initiated by the individual, the family, the peer group, or the community was being handled more and more by specialized and commercial institutions. The movies, the phonograph, radio, television, professional sports, the amusement park, and the summer and winter resorts in the mountains and at the seashore have gradually replaced folk games and recreation. Despite this trend, folk games and traditional recreational activities do persist.

# Festivals, Ceremonies, and Rituals

FESTIVALS, CEREMONIES, and rituals are three types of traditional symbolic behavior, representing a decreasing order of complexity. Festivals involve large groups, such as communities, nations, and religions, and complex aggregates of activities. Ceremonies and rituals involve smaller groups and less complex aggregates of activities. Festivals consist of several ceremonies; ceremonies consist of several rituals. Rituals and ceremonies are performed either by groups or by individuals, but essentially they are group behavior patterns, because they are traditional, which means they are passed from generation to generation. Festivals, ceremonies, and rituals celebrate important occasions in the yearly cycle and the life cycle, such as rites of passage (birth, puberty, marriage, and death), the changing seasons (the winter and summer solstices and the spring and fall equinoxes), and the agricultural work cycle (plowing, planting, harvesting).

The term "rites of passage" was coined in 1908 by Arnold Van Gennep, the anthropologist. He noted that the life cycle consists of a series of stages: birth, puberty, marriage, parenthood, and death. He defined rites of passage as ceremonies that celebrate the passage of the individual from one stage to the next, and he described three kinds: rites of separation (e.g. funerals), transition rites (e.g. pregnancy, betrothal, initiation), and rites of incorporation (e.g. marriage).[1]

One of the cross-cultural themes in these rites of passage is the seclusion of women during childbirth and menstruation. In 1656 Adriaen van der Donck described the birth customs of the Indians of New Netherland. The pregnant woman, he wrote, went off alone to a secluded place near a source of water, where she prepared a shelter. She gave birth to the child without any aid.[2] Indian women were also secluded when they first began to menstruate. In 1636 David Pietersz. de Vries described the following puberty custom among the Lenape Indians.

The girls consider themselves to have arrived at womanhood when they begin to have their monthly terms, and as soon as they have them, they

194

go and disguise themselves with a garment, which they throw over their body, drawing it over the head so that they can hardly see with their eyes, and run off for two or three months, lamenting that they must lose their virginity; and they therefore do not engage in any diversion by night, or other unseasonable time.[3]

Such seclusion is common not only in tribal cultures. In the Orthodox Jewish tradition a woman is separated from society for seven days after the birth of a boy and fourteen days after the birth of a girl. Complete purification requires, respectively, thirty-three and sixty-six more days, during which she is not allowed to touch any holy thing or come into any holy place (Lev. 12:1–5). In the Orthodox tradition there is no rite of passage when a girl reaches puberty. But a tradition existed among eastern European Jewish women that when the daughter informed her mother about her first menstruation the mother slapped her daughter on both cheeks, which would give her a rosy complexion for the rest of her life.[4] Once a woman is married the biblical rules pertaining to menstruation apply. When menstruation begins she is segregated for seven days, during which she may not touch or hand anything to a man, not even her husband (Lev. 15:19–28). After seven days she goes to the *mikva* (the community ritual bath), and that night she is obliged to have sexual intercourse with her husband. These rituals continue to be observed by some Orthodox Jews in New Jersey, and several suburban communities have *mikvot.*

These customs are related to an ambiguity in the symbolic meaning of blood. Menstrual blood is thought to be unclean; the Bible makes explicit reference to the women being "cleansed from the issue of her blood" (Lev. 12:7). The *mikva* is used for purification, not for physical cleanliness. While men also use the *mikva* once a week to purify themselves for the Sabbath, women use it monthly specifically in connection with menstruation.

The association of menstrual blood with impurity has led some feminist writers to criticize these traditions as the product of male anxieties about these female bodily processes.[5] As with most symbols, however, the meaning of these rituals is subject to several interpretations. Van Gennep argued that these pregnancy and childbirth rituals must be viewed as a whole, combining aspects of rites of separation, transition, and incorporation. He explained that first the woman is separated from society, and then passes through a transition followed by her reintegration into society with her new status as mother.[6]

Blood is also part of another rite of passage: circumcision. While many hospitals perform this operation for hygienic reasons, in the Jewish tradition it is part of a traditional religious ceremony, known as a *bris,* which is based on the biblical injunction, "And in the eighth day the flesh of his foreskin shall be circumcised" (Lev. 12:3). The ceremony is performed at home by a man known as a *mohel*, who is experienced in these operations. Margaret Mead, terming circumcision "synthetic male menstruation," explained it as a form of "bloodletting for males in which they also can rid themselves of their 'bad blood' and so be healthy as females."[7] In the eastern European Jewish tradition there is a ritual known as the *metsutsa*, in which a pious old man sucks the first drop of blood.[8] One of the prayers said at the *bris* contains the following biblical verse: "And . . . I passed by thee, and . . . I said unto thee . . . in thy blood, Live" (Ezek. 16:6). Thus there is the symbolic meaning of blood as a life-sustaining substance.

Van Gennep viewed circumcision as a rite of separation and incorporation. He held that the idea behind cutting is to remove the individual from the rest of humanity and incorporate him into a defined group. "The Jewish circumcision is in no way extraordinary; it is clearly a 'sign of union' with a particular deity, and a mark of membership in a single community of the faithful."[9] He further noted that since the operation results in an ineradicable change in the body of the boy, the incorporation into the group is permanent. This interpretation is plausible. The prayer said by the father immediately after the circumcision is "Blessed art thou, O Lord Our God, King of the Universe, who has hallowed us by thy commandments, and hast commanded us to make our sons enter into the covenant of Abraham our father." Rabbi Julian Morgenstern made a comparative study of circumcision customs among various Semitic peoples (e.g. the ancient Hebrews, the Bedouin) and concluded that circumcision was originally performed on all the boys and possibly all the men at an ancient desert festival held in early spring. This festival at which circumcision takes place is still held by the Bedouin. Among the ancient Hebrews circumcision became associated with the festival of Passover. According to Morgenstern, the blood of circumcision is analogous to the blood of the paschal lamb with which the children of Israel marked their doors to avoid the sacrifice of the firstborn. Thus, he argues, circumcision blood is a substitute for the human sacrifice of the firstborn son.[10]

Water, too, is a symbol with multiple meanings. In many cultures it is thought to have properties of spiritual purification, as we have seen with the Jewish ritual bath. Among the Lenape Indians water was associated with spiritual purification. Adriaen van der Donck found the following custom among the Indians of New Netherland: "After their children were born, and if they are males, although the weather be ever so cold and freezing, they immerse them some time in the water, which, they say, makes them strong brave men and hardy hunters."[11] De Vries's report of the Lenape use of sweat lodges and cold water to purify themselves has already been mentioned (see "Folk Medicine"). The notion that water can be used for spiritual purification is involved also in Christian baptism, another rite of passage. In some Christian denominations infants are baptized forty days after birth. Other denominations practice adult baptism. In either case the baptismal water is associated with spiritual redemption. In the New Testament, John the Baptist says: "I indeed baptize you with water unto repentance: but he that cometh after me is mightier than I, whose shoes I am not worthy to bear: he shall baptize you with the Holy Ghost, and with fire" (Matt. 3:11). Morgenstern sees a close relationship between Christian baptism and Jewish circumcision. Both were common among ancient Semitic peoples. He notes that in the early Christian church, infant baptism was performed at Easter, that is, about the same time of the year as the early Israelite circumcision festival of Passover. In both cases, it was a rite of passage marking initiation into the group.[12]

Courtship and wedding customs represent another kind of rite of passage. According to de Vries, when young Indian women were ready to marry they would

> deck themselves with a quantity of *Zeewan* [wampum] upon the body, head and neck; they then go and sit in some place, in company with some squaws, showing that they are up for a bargain. Whoever gives the most *Zeewan* is the successful suitor. They go home with him, and remain sometimes one, three, or four months with him, and then go with another; sometimes remaining with him, according as they are inclined to each other.[13]

While marriages were probably not quite as casual as de Vries indicates, they were less binding than the European marriages of that day. Van der Donck partly confirms de Vries's description: "Marriages with them are not so binding but that either party may altogether dissolve the union, which they frequently do. I have known an Indian who changed his wife every year, although he had little or no reason for it."[14] Polygamy was practiced only by chiefs. Van der Donck noted that "the natives generally marry but one wife, and no more, unless it be [a] chief, who is great and powerful."[15] He confirmed the courtship customs described by de Vries.

> When one of their young women is *rijp* (for that is the native term),[16] and wishes to be married, it is customary on such occasions that they

veil their faces completely, and sit covered as an indication of their desire; whereupon propositions are made to such persons, and the practice is common with young women who have suitors, whereby they give publicity of their indication of their desire. . . . The men, according to their condition, must always present their intended and betrothed bride with a marriage gift, as a confirmation of their agreement and of his intention, being similar to the marriage pledge of the ancients.[17]

Weddings usually involve an exchange of property, which is expressed symbolically in ritual. Writing in the mid-eighteenth century Peter Kalm described a "curious" marriage custom in New Sweden.

A woman went, with no other dress than her nightgown, out of the house of her deceased husband to that of her bridegroom, who met her half way with fine new clothes, and said, before all who were present, that he lent them to his bride, and put them on her with his own hands.[18]

Kalm explained that the meaning of this custom was that an impoverished widow must leave behind all her possessions, including her clothing, or else her new husband would be liable for her late husband's debts.

Later immigrant groups brought their wedding customs with them to New Jersey. The wedding of Ike Merochnick and Dora Weiss in the first decade of this century at Carmel was described by Louis Mounier (see "Folk Music, Folk Song, and Folk Dance"). The guests gathered at the bride's home on the evening of the wedding. They were given lighted candles and formed a procession four abreast behind the bride and bridegroom. Two musicians led the procession through the streets from the bride's home to the synagogue. After the ceremony the procession continued to a nearby hall for the reception; the newlyweds sat at the head table until one or two o'clock in the morning. Mounier noted: "This was not the first Jewish wedding at which we had been present, but it was the first of its kind, that is, one such as were celebrated in the Pale Settlement in the Lithuanian part of Russia."[19]

Funerals Van Gennep termed rites of separation, in that they observe the ultimate separation of the individual from the group. The Lenape Indians buried their dead, but they would later exhume the body. According to Peter Lindestrom, a Swedish engineer who resided in New Sweden from 1653 to 1655, the death was announced by a person who went around the countryside crying and lamenting. After a few days the deceased was buried in a sitting position with his wealth. In his mouth was placed a pipe filled with tobacco, believed to be his food for the journey after death. The grave pit was filled, and a scaffold consisting of four poles with three fringed shelves was built over it. The relatives and friends mourned at the grave site for a month, after which they dug up the body, placed the gifts in a box on the lowest shelf of the scaffold, and stripped the flesh from the body, wrapped it in bark, and placed it on the upper shelf. Then they would bury the intestines. They mourned for another fourteen days, after which they divided the wealth and departed, leaving the scaffold to fall apart.[20] Herbert Kraft has excavated Indian grave sites in New Jersey showing the skeletons in a flexed rather than sitting position. He also found confirmation of the practice of exhuming the body and wrapping parts in bark bundles.[21] But we do not know the reason for this custom.

Funerals serve important psychological functions. In Italian-American homes, for example, all the clocks in the house are stopped at the moment of death, mirrors are covered with sheets, and shades are drawn. Thus the activities of ordinary life are suspended during the first phase of the mourning period. In the days before professional undertakers, the family would lay out the body at home, and embalming was generally not practiced. The deceased is dressed in his or her best clothing—if young, in a communion outfit; if a woman, in her bridal gown. A cherished item is placed in the coffin. The family sits with the body for one or two days while visitors pay their respects. Visitors do not ring the doorbell. Often they bring minestrone soup for the grieving family, because it is believed to replace the body fluids lost in crying. It is traditional to touch or kiss the body before leaving the room. And it is considered bad luck to go out by the same door you came in.

The funeral is celebrated in church with a mass. When the family returns from the cemetery the house is made cheerful again, except for the death room, which is closed for forty-eight hours and purified by sulphur candles. After the funeral the family sits down to the "dinner of consolement," an elaborate meal including veal, which symbolizes new life. This marks the end of the first phase of mourning. Psychologically this clear demarcation makes the mourning ceremonies function somewhat like the Irish wake; that is, they establish symbolically for the mourners the idea that life must go on.

Mourning continues after the funeral, but now in a context in which normal activities are gradually resumed. The family avoids music, dancing, and entertainment for a year after the death. The length of the mourning period depends on the closeness of the relative; also, it is short for a child, longer for a parent or spouse. Women wear black as a sign of mourning; in large families older women wear black almost all the time. It is customary to visit the grave yearly. Masses, followed by a family dinner, celebrate the anniversary of the death. These family or communal rituals function to reassert the solidarity of the group after the loss of one of its members.

While many of the functions of funerals are the same in all cultures, specific customs differ of course. For example, in his study of the Japanese-American community in Seabrook in 1974, Koji Shimada reported that while some of the traditional Japanese funeral customs have become Americanized, "the funeral service is probably the one ceremony which has undergone the least change among the various functions of the Buddhist Church."[22] The bathing, dressing, and placing of the deceased in the coffin are now done by funeral parlors. The funeral customs have been simplified; for example, the *O-tsuya* or vigil now lasts only a few hours instead of all night. Two traditions that persist are the incense offerings and name giving. A ceremonial Buddhist name, given to the deceased by the priest at the funeral, is considered indispensable in the afterlife.

Among the Hungarians in New Brunswick until the 1950s it was the custom to deliver a formal funeral oration known as *búcsúztatás* (literally, "farewell"). These orations listed the names of friends and family of the deceased in order of importance. The custom began to decline because it was thought to be morbid and potentially insulting to people whose names were omitted or incorrectly placed. A poll of seventy men in 1953 showed that only 23 per cent of them intended to have a *búcsúztatás* read at their funerals.[23]

Festivals, ceremonies, and rituals celebrate the yearly cycle on the folk calendar. New Year's Day among the Dutch in the seventeenth century was ostensibly a religious holiday to be observed by church attendance and thanksgiving. But the actual experience was otherwise. It was traditional to drink excessively and to fire guns on this holiday, as is evident from a law enacted in 1655.

> Whereas experience has manifested and shown us, that irregularities are committed besides other sorrowful accidents such as woundings frequently arising therefrom, by Firing, Mayplanting and Carousing, in addition to the unnecessary waste of powder, to prevent which for the future, the Director General and Council expressly forbid that from now henceforward there shall be, within this Province of New Netherland, on New Years or May Days, any Firing of Guns, or any Planting of May Poles, or any beating of Drums, or any treating with Brandy, wine or Beer.[24]

The folk festivities associated with Shrove Tuesday (the day before Ash Wednesday, the beginning of Lent) were disapproved of by the Dutch Reformed church in New Netherland, but they continued nonetheless. The principal activity on this folk holiday was "riding the goose," in which a greased goose was suspended by a rope while riders on horseback tried to pull off its head. This custom, common among the farmers' servants and other country people, was repeatedly banned by the government to no avail. In 1655, Cornelis van Tienhoven, the secretary of New Netherland, stated "that he had been informed that the country people intended Riding the Goose again as they did last year, and enquired, therefore, if their worships of the Court would do anything to oppose it."[25] The court again decided to ban it.

Pentecost or Whitsunday was known as *Pinkster* among the Dutch in New Netherland. Its religious significance was to commemorate the appearance of the Holy Ghost to the apostles after Christ's crucifixion. In its folk manifestation *Pinkster* was a springtime "festival of flowers." Its celebration was common throughout the Dutch culture area in New York and New Jersey among both the Dutch farmers and their slaves. In 1797 a British traveler through the Dutch settlements along the Passaic River found that on *Pinkster* "every public house is crowded with merry makers and waggon's full of rustic beaux and bells met us at every mile. The blacks as well as their masters were frolicking."[26] *Pinkster* survived among the blacks after it had disappeared among the Dutch. In 1874 Gabriel Furman, a local historian, noted that on Long Island, "poor *Pinckster* has lost its rank among the festivals, and is only kept by the negroes; with them, however, especially on the west end of this island, it is still much of a holiday."[27] While I have found no New Jersey example, it is probable that it survived among blacks in this state as well.

Harvest festivals also mark the yearly cycle. The relationship between the present-day celebration of Thanksgiving and the folk festivals from which it derives is evident in the following entry, dating from 1761, in the diary of a New Jersey farmer named Jan Vorstrang: "There was much rejoicing and some merriment today when the family came together for the Feast of the Harvest. The children with their own [children] traveled many miles as there had been snow and good riding."[28]

When peasant folk traditions were brought to America by immigrants they rarely survived in their original form. An example of this is seen in the harvest festivals in Bohemia, Moravia, and Slovakia, which in the Old Country had remained basically unchanged for centuries. Special harvesting songs were sung that dealt mainly with mating themes. The last handfuls of standing grain were called "wolf," "goat," and "hare," and these names were transferred to the reapers who cut them. The expression was that the reapers "ride" on the wolf or goat or hare. If the "rider" was a girl, songs were sung about her "riding on the tail." The last sheaf was called the "old woman" or the "old man," and it was dressed in clothing and placed on a decorated wagon. A large wreath was made of various kinds of grain, and there was a procession to the home of the man of authority in the village. His wife sprinkled one of the peasant girls with water, and the girl in turn placed a wreath on the head of the authority figure. Then the peasants danced inside the big wreath and mocked and eventually destroyed the "old woman."

A few Slovaks and Moravians who had settled in the small farming community of Hightstown during World War II attempted to revive this festival. But there were certain differences. They used two rented trucks; on one there were people dressed as European peasants and on the other people dressed as American farmers. Sheaves and wreaths had to be purchased in Trenton, because in America only the ears were cut, and the straw was left standing in the field. There was no "old woman," and the "peasants" and the "farmers" sang Slovak folk songs instead of the harvest songs. Instead of the ritual killing of the "old woman" there was a party at the house of someone impersonating the "land-owner." According to Svatana Pirkova-Jakobson, who studied the Old World and New World manifestations of this harvest festival,

> imitating the model, the Heightstown [sic] Slovaks transformed it; and all their unintentional modifications converged towards the same end: the agricultural constituents and symbols of the ritual were weakened in favor of the socially communal manifestations. . . . The participants experienced a collective identification with the ancestral society, and the celebration planned as a mock-performance ended in giving them an actual belief by enhancing their ethnic cohesion.[29]

Some ethnic festivals are revivals of Old World folk festivals that either did not survive the migration to America or were subsequently stamped out by communal authorities in America. The Feast of Lights in the Chambersburg section of Trenton was an Italian-American saint's festival (*festa*) honoring the Madonna di Casadrino (the Blessed Mother of Casadrino, a small town near Naples). The festival, sponsored by the local Neapolitan Society, started in Trenton in 1906 among the first-generation immigrants who settled in the working-class neighborhood near the Roebling wire factory. It was celebrated on the second Sunday in September. It began with a high mass in the morning, followed

Saint Gerard festival, Newark, 1924. Photograph by Harry Dorer.
*The Dorer Collection, Newark Public Library*

203

by a procession through the neighborhood in the afternoon led by the priests and choir boys. The members of the Holy Name Society carried a huge set of rosary beads that spread across the width of the street. A band played traditional Italian marching tunes. The statue of the saint was carried on the shoulders of the members of the Neapolitan Society, and people pinned money to the cape of the Blessed Mother. At the conclusion of the procession there was a street carnival where Italian food and trinkets were sold.

Church authorities were uneasy about this manifestation of folk religion, considering it too much like a carnival and devoid of religious significance. In 1967 the pastor of Saint Joachim's Church, supported by the bishop of the Trenton archidiocese, succeeded in stopping the festival. At the insistence of the community, it was revived in 1977, but with some changes. The Virgin Mary was substituted for the local saint of Casadrino, and money was no longer pinned to the statue.[30] The history of this festival illustrates the differences between revivals and traditional folk festivals; it also shows us something about the relationship between organized religion and folk religion.

A comparison of some of the folk customs associated with the yearly cycle of holidays reveals the diversity of ethnic traditions in New Jersey. Among the Scots there is a traditional New Year's Eve custom called "First Footing." The first person to cross the threshold after midnight is called the "first foot." If this person has dark hair it is considered good luck. The first foot carries a bottle of liquor ("to refresh you and to signify that you would always have liquid refreshment for the coming year"), a piece of cake or shortbread or currant bun ("to hope that you would have food for the coming year"), and a piece of coal ("to bring warmth to your home and to your family"). This is according to Thomas MacFarlane, who was born in Glasgow and was interviewed in 1978 by Thomas K. Daly.

> MacFarlane: I was dark-haired and my own brother was red-haired, but if the both of us came to the house—we'll say the lady next door, who was a good friend—she would never allow my red-haired brother to cross the threshold first. I would have to go in first. And she was emphatic about it. She would say (to my brother): "Would you allow Tom to come in first—to be my first foot?" . . . Whereas in my family, my father was always the first foot.
>
> Daly: And what about now with your family?
>
> MacFarlane: Two minutes before—three minutes before 12:00, my father would leave the house and he would go outside with his piece of

cake, his bottle of whiskey, his piece of coal, and as soon as he would
hear the church bells, he would knock on the door and my mother
would greet him and my brother and I and he would kiss my mother
and say "Happy New Year" and my brother and I would shake hands
and say "Happy New Year" and we would proceed to have a little refreshment.[31]

Some Scots in New Jersey make a point of keeping this tradition alive, but
among others it has died out. An Englishman from Lancaster who has lived for
years in Philadelphia told me that he had made an effort to keep a similar tradition alive, but without reinforcement from others he has given it up.

Many ethnic festivals exist only in memory. Zoriana Tkacz of Maplewood
discussed the traditional Christmas celebration in the Ukraine with her grandmother, Anastasia Kysilewska, who was eighty-seven in 1978, when the interview was recorded. Mrs. Kysilewska said that before Christmas Eve dinner the
master of the house (i.e. the father) went out to the stable with the food that was
to be placed on the family table that evening and fed some of it to the cattle and
other animals. It was believed that on Christmas night the animals had the ability to speak. "Yes, well, we didn't believe it strongly, but the villagers did and
they even claimed that they heard how the animals licked the hands of the master of the house, as he threw the traditional foods into the stable." While the father was in the stable the children appeared. The father returned to the house
carrying the *diduch* (literally the "old man"), a figure made from a large sheaf of
rye hay. The *diduch* was placed in the corner, and hay was also placed under the
table. The mother threw nuts into the hay for the children to look for as they
played under the table. The meal consisted of twelve courses, symbolizing the
twelve disciples of Christ. It was the custom for the father to take a spoonful of
*kutia* and throw it up at the ceiling. If it stuck the harvest would be good that
year, and if it fell back down there would be a poor harvest. While the agricultural aspects of this observance have been abandoned in suburban and urban
New Jersey, the foodways and other elements of the tradition persist (see
"Foodways").[32]

Some folk traditions are shared by several ethnic groups. For example, decorated Easter eggs are traditional among Ukrainians, Poles, Russians, Hungarians, and Slovaks. The Easter baskets are taken to the church on Holy Saturday
to be blessed by the priest. Andrew Szproch was born in 1957 in the Slovak
town of Krempachy in the Carpathian Mountains of southern Poland. In 1968
his family moved to New Jersey. He described the blessing of the decorated eggs
to Kevin Guta in 1978.

The blessing of the food is called *świenconka*. The food is blessed the Saturday before Easter in the church. Our family puts the food in the basket—the meat, the bread, the cake,—and it's blessed in front of the altar. [It is] brought up in a line of people, and the priest stands there [and] blesses it. There is also in the food a *baranka*. This is a little lamb made of either sugar or cake. This stands like a symbol of Jesus. In the *baranka*—the lamb—there's a flag with a cross on it which stands for Jesus being risen.[33]

Szproch also described another folk tradition associated with Easter.

On Easter night there's a party. It's a weird type of party, because it's where the men or the boys they sprinkle water or perfume on the girls. The girls are waiting for it expectantly. They could be home, lights out, and people sneak in, and the men sneak in and they spray them with either water or perfume. It's called *smigus*. It's an old tradition still being done even in places like Wallington—Polish people's homes—Passaic. On Easter it was done. My father went there.[34]

A similar tradition was practiced by the Hungarians in New Brunswick, but on Easter Monday. The boys chased the girls and sprinkled them with water. In return the girls kissed the boys. The Hungarians called this tradition the *locsokodas*. People recalled it as having been quite rowdy, with girls throwing buckets of water out of windows on the men in retaliation. By the 1920s, however, the custom had been replaced by an Easter Monday dance.[35] The similarity of the folk traditions of these particular ethnic groups reflects the Slavic culture area of eastern Europe, in which, despite national differences, certain culture trait complexes are shared.

One might ask what these diverse folk customs have to do with New Jersey. Few, if any, of them are unique to the state. But that is the point. The study of folklore and folklife involves some aspects that are very particular and some that are universal. If a custom is practiced by a group of people living in New Jersey, whether they be early settlers or later immigrants, it is part of the folklife of the state. These festivals, ceremonies, and rituals reflect the ethnic diversity of New Jersey. Besides showing the persistence of ethnic traditions, they provide some insight into the relationship between history and psychology, specifically the social psychology of the past. These are the traditions to which people turn at the most important times of their lives. They express their innermost feelings toward birth, puberty, marriage, and death.

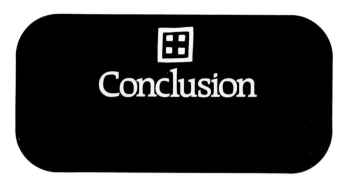

# Conclusion

SEVERAL YEARS ago there was a debate among folklorists that focused on the titles of two books and what they suggested about the relation between America's folklore and its national character. Richard Dorson in *American Folklore* took the position that there is something characteristic or unique about this country's folklore.[1] Tristram P. Coffin and Hennig Cohen, on the other hand, argued in *Folklore in America* that while there is indeed folklore in America, much of it is not necessarily characteristic or unique.[2] The same issue might be raised about New Jersey folklore versus folklore in New Jersey. Is there a New Jersey "character" that is reflected in its folklore?

We have seen that New Jersey is divided into several folk cultural regions. There is a major linguistic boundary in folk speech between the Northern and the Midland dialect areas that cuts across New Jersey, roughly paralleling the old political boundary between East and West Jersey. The North Jersey ladder-back chairs are similar to those from New England, and the South Jersey chairs are similar to those from Pennsylvania. The South Jersey baskets are like those from the southern Appalachian Mountains, while North Jersey baskets reflect a mixture of traditions. Even among the Lenape Indians there were cultural differences in dialect and pottery between the Munsee in the north and the Unami in the south.

The folk cultural boundaries in New Jersey reflect not just this north-south division. Overlapping this division are the culture areas created by the various colonial settlers in New Jersey. Dutch farmhouses, barns, and hay barracks remind us that New Jersey was once part of New Netherland. All that remains of New Sweden, however, are some place names and a few Swedish log cabins. The Puritan influence in New Jersey is seen in central-chimney farmhouses, English barns, and tombstone carvings. Plain style meetinghouses and patterned brick-work farmhouses tell us where in New Jersey the Quakers settled. The Pennsylvania German culture area extends into northwestern New Jersey, as evidenced by bank barns, German log cabins, and illuminated manuscripts (*fraktur*).

Clearly, New Jersey's folk cultural boundaries extend beyond the political boundaries of the state.

New Jersey's folk culture also reflects the various immigrant and ethnic groups that migrated and immigrated more recently than the first effective settlement. New Jersey has a large number of ethnic groups, only a few of which have had their folklore collected. These include Cubans, Germans, Hungarians, Irish, Italians, Japanese, eastern European Jews, Poles, Portuguese, Puerto Ricans, Scots, and Ukrainians. Many of these ethnic groups have clustered in certain neighborhoods thereby creating ethnic culture areas. Each group has its own language, music, dance, customs, games, rituals, and ceremonies. In fact, the diversity of the ethnic population of New Jersey makes it an especially interesting place to collect folklore.

Afro-American folklore has also shaped New Jersey's folk heritage. There are few examples of the folklore and folklife of the slave and free black population: the cigar-store Indian carved by Job, the folk medicine of Dr. James Still, descriptions and fragments of folk music. Thanks to the work of Herbert Halpert we have some examples of the folklore of southern blacks who migrated to New Jersey during and after World War I. Little or nothing has been collected from the Caribbean blacks who immigrated to New Jersey after World War II.

There are also two enclave groups that became isolated socially and geographically from the rest of New Jersey. These are the Ramapo Mountain People in the north and the Pineys in the south. Both were known by derogatory names; both have had legends told about their origins; both have been the victims of stereotypes. All of this is reflected in folklore.

Then, too, there is a diversity in traditional occupations and activities in New Jersey. Fisherman shanties, traditional boats, and duck decoys indicate that the Jersey Shore should be grouped with the Atlantic maritime culture area. The ghost towns of South Jersey attest to the once thriving bog-iron and glass industries of the Pine Barrens. The boatmen on the Morris Canal and the rivermen on the Delaware River each had their own folklore. Women also have their folk traditions, as we saw with quilts, embroidery, traditional recipes, and midwifery. Children too have folk traditions, especially in their games and rhymes.

Not all the folklore and folklife of New Jersey fits into regional patterns. Quilts, samplers, coverlets, and pottery made in New Jersey are not distinctly different from those made elsewhere in America. Legends, myths, and folk songs collected in New Jersey are often localized versions of those found elsewhere. The games children play, the festivals and rituals observed by various ethnic groups, and the tools used in traditional occupations are not unique to New Jersey.

Does this mean that New Jersey does not have a distinct character? The answer is no. The character of New Jersey, like that of America as a whole, is diverse, complex, and not easily reduced to a single image. Such simple images are stereotypes. New Jersey's character is the sum total of the people and places found within its borders. That combination is found only in New Jersey. New Jersey is not a microcosm of America, nor is it a case study of other states. The fact that so many cultural boundaries cut across the state is not a problem—quite the contrary. It is at the cultural boundaries that the truly interesting cultural processes occur. New Jersey is not just a location between New York and Philadelphia; it is a unique place with its own identity.

# Notes

## Introduction

1. David Steven Cohen, *The Ramapo Mountain People*, pp. 3–42.
2. Gary B. Mills, *The Forgotten People.*
3. John Kouwenhoven, *The Arts in Modern American Civilization*, pp. 13–14.
4. Henry Glassie, *Pattern in the Material Folk Culture of the Eastern United States*, p. 6.
5. Kenneth L. Ames, *Beyond Necessity*, p. 14.
6. E. McClung Fleming, "Early American Decorative Arts as Social Documents," p. 276.
7. Henry Glassie, *Folk Housing in Middle Virginia*, p. 11.

## The Jersey Joke

1. "The Jokes Don't Matter in Hoboken."
2. Michael Aaron Rockland, "What's So Funny about New Jersey?" p. 49.
3. William Cullen Bryant, *Picturesque America*, p. 47.
4. Charles M. Skinner, *American Myths and Legends*, 2: 239–240.
5. Ibid., p. 240.
6. Rockland, "What's So Funny," p. 49.
7. Federal Writers' Project, *The Swedes and Finns in New Jersey*, p. 151.
8. Quoted in ibid.
9. [Peter Kalm], *The America of 1750*, 1: 76–77.
10. Rockland, "What's So Funny," pp. 49, 50, 52.

## A Lenape Indian Myth

1. Daniel Garrison Brinton, *The Lenape and Their Legends*, p. 158.
2. William W. Newcomb, Jr., "The Walam Olum of the Delaware Indians in Perspective," p. 62.
3. [Jasper Danckaerts], *Journal of Jasper Danckaerts, 1679–1680*, pp. 76–78.
4. Ibid., p. 175.
5. Ibid., p. 174.

# Names

1. Henry Charlton Beck, *The Roads of Home*, pp. 242, 249.
2. William Augustine, "Egg Harbor's Scrambled Names," sec. 2: 9.
3. A. R. Dunlap, "Barnegat," pp. 232–233; Cornelius C. Vermuele, "Some Early New Jersey Place-Names," p. 246.
4. Earl Schenck Miers, *Where the Raritan Flows*, p. 13.
5. Henry Charlton Beck, *Forgotten Towns of Southern New Jersey*, pp. 19–20.
6. Ibid., pp. 267–268.
7. Mary B. Dolan, "Folklore in New Jersey," p. 31.
8. Henry Charlton Beck, *The Jersey Midlands*, pp. 228–229.
9. Frances A. Westervelt, ed., *History of Bergen County, New Jersey*, 1: 93–96.
10. David Steven Cohen, "The Origin of the 'Jackson Whites,'" pp. 263–264.
11. Elizabeth Kite, "Report on Social Conditions in the Pine Belt," pp. 8, 16.
12. Henry Herbert Goddard, *The Kallikak Family*.
13. Francis B. Lee, "Jerseyisms," p. 332.
14. Quoted in Harry B. Weiss, *The History of Applejack*, p. 122.
15. W. F. Mayer, "In the Pines," pp. 566–567.

# Folk Speech

1. Ives Goddard, "The Delaware Language, Past and Present," p. 103.
2. Lois M. Feister, "Linguistic Communication between the Dutch and Indians in New Netherland."
3. Goddard, "Delaware Language," p. 105.
4. John Dyneley Prince, "An Ancient New Jersey Indian Jargon."
5. Goddard, "Delaware Language," p. 105.
6. John Dyneley Prince, "The Jersey Dutch Dialect," p. 459.
7. Ives Goddard, "Dutch Loanwords in Delaware," pp. 158–159.
8. Ibid., pp. 154, 156, 155.
9. Ibid., pp. 154, 155.
10. William Strickland, *Journal of a Tour in the United States of America, 1794–1795*, p. 74.
11. Prince, "Jersey Dutch," p. 460.
12. James B. H. Storms, *A Jersey Dutch Vocabulary*, n.p.
13. Anna Gausmann Noyes, *Three Petticoats*, pp. 70–71.
14. [Peter Kalm], *The America of 1750*, 1: 683.
15. Ibid., p. 687.
16. Goddard, "Dutch Loanwords," p. 159.
17. Hans Kurath, *A Word Geography of the Eastern United States*, fig. 3.
18. Ibid., pp. 13–14.
19. Ibid., p. 21.
20. Ibid.
21. Ibid., pp. 26, 63, 64.
22. Ibid., pp. 26, 79.
23. Francis B. Lee, "Jerseyisms," pp. 327, 330, 331.
24. Ibid., pp. 329, 334.
25. Ibid., pp. 328, 329, 332, 334.
26. Ibid., pp. 335–336.
27. Ibid., pp. 329–330.
28. Ibid., pp. 336–337.

# Legend

1. See Robert A. Georges, "The General Concept of Legend," in Wayland D. Hand, ed., *American Folk Legend*.

2. For differing points of view on this subject see ibid.; Linda Degh, "The 'Belief Legend' in Modern Society," in Hand, ed., *American Folk Legend*; Herbert Halpert, "Definition and Variation in Folk Legend," in ibid.; and Linda Degh and Andrew Vazsonyi, "Legend and Belief."

3. John Witthoft, "The Grasshopper War Folktale," p. 295.

4. Ibid., p. 296.

5. Ibid.

6. Ibid., p. 301.

7. Quoted in C. G. Hine, *The Old Mine Road*, p. 7.

8. Ibid., pp. 7–8.

9. Ibid., p. 8.

10. Herbert C. Kraft, *The Minisink Settlements*, pp. 25, 28, 30.

11. Don McTernan, "The Esopus-Minisink Way," pp. 103, 115, 117.

12. David Steven Cohen, "The Origin of the 'Jackson Whites'"; *The Ramapo Mountain People*, pp. 3–24.

13. Nathaniel R. Ewan, "New Jersey's Pineys."

14. Herbert Halpert, "Folk Tales and Legends from the New Jersey Pines," 1: 163–164.

15. Ibid., p. 264.

16. Cohen, *The Ramapo Mountain People*, pp. 156–157.

17. Ibid., p. 157.

18. Richard Dorson, *American Folklore*, pp. 124–128.

19. Ibid., pp. 202–243.

20. Frederick W. Crumb, *Tom Quick*, p. iv.

21. W. F. Mayer, "In the Pines," p. 567.

# Folk Belief

1. Don Yoder, "Official Religion versus Folk Religion," p. 38.

2. [David Brainerd], *Memoirs of the Rev. David Brainerd*, pp. 344–345.

3. Ibid., p. 345.

4. Ibid., p. 346.

5. Ibid., pp. 347–348.

6. Ibid., pp. 348–349.

7. *Proceedings of the New Jersey Historical Society*, 2nd ser. 8–9.

8. Motif D 1318.5.2, "Corpse Bleeds When Murderer Touches It," in Stith Thompson, *Motif-Index of Folk Literature*.

9. Richard M. Dorson, *American Folklore*, pp. 31–33.

10. Robert A. Georges, "The General Concept of Legend," in Wayland D. Hand, ed., *American Folk Legend*; Linda Degh, "The 'Belief Legend' in Modern Society," in ibid.; Herbert Halpert, "Definition and Variation in Folk Legend," in ibid.

11. John W. Barber and Henry Howe, *Historical Collections of the State of New Jersey*, pp. 92–93.

12. Theodore Sedgwick, Jr., *A Memoir of the Life of William Livingston*, pp. 353–354.

13. Quoted in Daniel G. Hoffman, "Stephen Crane's New Jersey Ghosts."

14. Anne H. Sidwa, "The Topielce of Żywiec: 1. The Sirens of the Soła."
15. Anne H. Sidwa, "The Topielce of Żywiec: 2. The Vengeance of the Soła."
16. George Lyman Kittredge, *Witchcraft in Old and New England*; M. A. Murray, *The Witch-Cult in Western Europe*.
17. *Archives of the State of New Jersey*, vol. 11, *Newspaper Extracts*, vol. 1, *1704–1739*, p. 220.
18. Quoted in Francis B. Lee, "Some Legal Allusions to Witchcraft in New Jersey," p. 170.
19. Quoted in ibid., pp. 170–171.
20. *An Account of the Beginnings, Transactions, and Discovery of Ransford Rogers*, pp. 7–8.
21. Barber and Howe, *Historical Collections*, pp. 148–149.
22. *Landscape*, November 1889, p. 2; see also David Steven Cohen, "Alfred P. Smith," p. 31.
23. Herbert Halpert, "Folk Tales and Legends from the New Jersey Pines," 1: 277–278.
24. David Steven Cohen, *The Ramapo Mountain People*, pp. 183–184, 187.
25. Interview with Mary Rozman.
26. [Peter Kalm], *The America of 1750*, 1: 263.
27. "Weather Notions."
28. *Polish Folklore* 3 (1958): 27.
29. Anne H. Sidwa, "Eyes . . . Devil Eyes and Talking Eyes."
30. See Clarence Maloney, ed., *The Evil Eye*, pp. 1–15, 42–61, 175–222, 286–328.

## Folk Medicine

1. Don Yoder, "Folk Medicine," pp. 191–194.
2. Ibid., p. 192.
3. John Heckewelder, *History, Manners, and Customs of the Indian Nations Who Once Inhabited Pennsylvania and the Neighboring States*, pp. 228–229.
4. Ibid., p. 229.
5. David Pietersz. de Vries, "Voyages from Holland to America, A.D. 1632 to 1644," p. 106.
6. [David Brainerd], *Memoirs of the Rev. David Brainerd*, p. 348.
7. Ibid., p. 350.
8. Adriaen van der Donck, *A Description of the New Netherlands*, p. 28.
9. [Peter Kalm], *The America of 1750*, 1: 312.
10. David L. Cowen, *Medicine in Revolutionary New Jersey*, p. 6.
11. Ibid., p. 5.
12. Peter Smith, *The Indian Doctor's Dispensatory*, p. x.
13. Ibid., pp. x–xi.
14. Ibid., pp. 74–75.
15. [James Still], *Early Recollections and Life of Dr. James Still, 1812–1885*, pp. 178–179.
16. Ibid., p. 194.
17. Ibid., pp. 114–123.
18. [Martha Reeves], "Martha Reeves, Midwife of Cumberland County, N.J. and Her Record Book of Births, 1820–1831," 24: 247–248.
19. David Steven Cohen, *The Ramapo Mountain People*, pp. 177–178.
20. Interview with Anna Vaccaro.
21. "Folk Medicine in a Homogeneous Puerto Rican Community," pp. 7, 17, 20–23.
22. Phyllis H. Williams, *South Italian Folkways in Europe and America*.
23. Ellen J. Stekert, "Focus for Conflict."

# Folk Music, Folk Song, and Folk Dance

1. Adriaen van der Donck, *A Description of the New Netherlands*, p. 88.
2. John Heckewelder, *History, Manners, and Customs of the Indian Nations Who Once Inhabited Pennsylvania and the Neighboring States*, pp. 208–209.
3. Ibid., p. 209.
4. Ibid., p. 211.
5. Charles H. Kaufman, "Music in New Jersey, 1665–1860," p. xxv.
6. Quoted in ibid., p. xxvi.
7. Quoted in ibid.
8. Quoted in ibid.
9. Quoted in ibid., pp. xxvi–xxvii.
10. [Peter Kalm], *The America of 1750*, 2: 649–650.
11. Anna Gausmann Noyes, *Three Petticoats*, p. 60.
12. Ibid.
13. Ibid., pp. 20–21, 62, 65–70, 82.
14. Charles H. Kaufman, *The Music of Eighteenth Century New Jersey*, p. 6.
15. Quoted in David Steven Cohen, "Alfred P. Smith," p. 27.
16. Noyes, *Three Petticoats*, p. 72.
17. John Hosey Osborn, *Life in the Old Dutch Homesteads*, p. 157.
18. Lydia Parrish, *Slave Songs of the Georgia Sea Islands*, p. ix.
19. Ibid., p. x.
20. David Steven Cohen, *The Ramapo Mountain People*, pp. 137–141.
21. Charles H. Kaufman, "An Ethnomusicological Survey among the People of the Ramapo Mountains," pp. 124–126.
22. Cornelius Weygandt, *Down Jersey*, pp. 279–280.
23. Ibid., p. 281.
24. Herbert Halpert, "The Piney Folk-Singers," p. 5.
25. Ibid., p. 6.
26. Ibid., p. 15; idem, "Some Ballads and Folk Songs from New Jersey."
27. James Lee, *Tales the Boatmen Told*, pp. 9–10.
28. Ibid., p. 276.
29. Ibid., p. 244.
30. Donald H. Rolfs, *Under Sail*, p. 42.
31. Leslie C. Wood, *Rafting on the Delaware River*, p. 207.
32. Ibid., p. 208.
33. Charles W. Churchill, *The Italians of Newark*, pp. 145–147.
34. Louis Mounier, "Glimpses of Jewish Life in the Colonies of Southern New Jersey," p. 512.
35. Ibid.
36. Ibid., p. 513.
37. Anne Lutz, "The Ballad of the Butcher Boy in the Ramapo Mountains."
38. Ibid.
39. Halpert, "Some Ballads and Folk Songs," pp. 67–68.
40. Angus K. Gillespie and Tom Ayres, "Folklore in the Pine Barrens."
41. Bruno Nettl, *Folk Music in the United States*, p. 14.

# Folk Painting

1. John Michael Vlach, "Quaker Tradition and the Paintings of Edward Hicks."
2. *American Naive Paintings from the Eighteenth and Nineteenth Centuries*; *American Primitives*, pp. 8, 13, 14; Elinor Robinson Bradshaw, "American

Folk Art in the Collection of the Newark Museum"; Kenneth L. Ames, *Beyond Necessity*, pp. 95–97.

3. Bradshaw, "American Folk Art."

4. Henry Glassie, "Folk Art," p. 263.

5. Alice Winchester, "Introduction," in Jean Lipman and Alice Winchester, *The Flowering of American Folk Art*, p. 13.

6. Bradshaw, "American Folk Art."

7. Winchester, "Introduction," in Lipman and Winchester, *Flowering of American Folk Art*.

8. *American Primitives*.

9. Quoted in Mrs. Irwin F. Cortelyou, "Micah Williams," pp. 8–9.

10. Colleen Cowles Heslip, *Mrs. Susan C. Waters*; idem, "Susan C. Waters."

11. Quoted in *Henry Thomas Gulick*, n.p.

12. Ibid.

13. Alice Morse Earle, *Two Centuries of Costume in America*, 2: 511–520.

14. Ibid., pp. 527–531, 783–793.

15. Ibid., p. 770.

16. Philippe Ariès, *Centuries of Childhood*, pp. 339–364.

17. Arthur W. Calhoun, *A Social History of the American Family*, 2: 51–77.

18. Earle, *Costume in America*, 2: 763–780.

19. Ibid., pp. 550–554.

20. Interview with Ed Morgan.

21. John Joseph Stoudt, *Early Pennsylvania Arts and Crafts*, p. 310.

22. Ibid., pp. 310–312.

23. David McGrail, "New Jersey Fractur."

# Folk Sculpture

1. *American Folk Sculpture*.

2. Myrna Kaye, *Yankee Weathervanes*, pp. 1–3.

3. Ibid., p. 16.

4. Homer Eaton Keyes, quoted in Elinor Robinson Bradshaw, "American Folk Art in the Collection of the Newark Museum," p. 54.

5. Kaye, *Yankee Weathervanes*, pp. 145, 150–151.

6. Cecil A. Meadows, *Trade Signs and Their Origin*, p. 1.

7. Mason L. Weems, *The Life of Washington*.

8. John W. Barber and Henry Howe, *Historical Collections of the State of New Jersey*.

9. Charles S. Boyer, *Old Inns and Taverns in West New Jersey*, p. 141.

10. Jacob Larwood and John Camden Hotten, *The History of Signboards from the Earliest Times to the Present Day*, p. 199.

11. Boyer, *Old Inns and Taverns*, facing p. 152.

12. Ibid.; Elise Lathrop, *Early American Inns and Taverns*, pp. 125–141.

13. Louis Winkler, "Some Unique Involvements with Seven Stars in the Delaware Valley Area."

14. Meadows, *Trade Signs*, pp. 13, 77, 131–132.

15. Joseph C. Robert, *The Story of Tobacco in America*, pp. 95–105; Jean Lipman, *American Folk Art in Wood, Metal, and Stone*, p. 73.

16. Lipman, *American Folk Art in Wood*.

17. Quoted in Jean Lipman and Alice Winchester, *The Flowering of American Folk Art*, p. 153.

18. Ibid., p. 157.

19. E. McClung Fleming, "From Indian Princess to Greek Goddess."
20. Albert E. Wier, ed., *The Book of a Thousand Songs*, p. 73.
21. Allan I. Ludwig, *Graven Images*, p. 67.
22. Quoted in Emily Wasserman, *Gravestone Designs*, p. 23.
23. Quoted in ibid., p. 25.
24. Quoted in ibid., p. iii.
25. Ibid., p. 30; Ludwig, *Graven Images*, p. 225.
26. August C. Mahr, "Origin and Significance of Pennsylvania Dutch Barn Symbols," pp. 380–381.
27. Ludwig, *Graven Images*, p. 424.
28. Wasserman, *Gravestone Designs*, pp. 26–27.
29. Quoted in ibid., p. 20.
30. Ibid., p. viii.
31. Ibid., pp. 16–18.
32. Ibid., p. v.
33. Joel Barber, *Wild Fowl Decoys*, pp. 23–32.
34. William T. Mackey, Jr., *American Bird Decoys*, p. 12.
35. Ibid., p. 13.
36. Barber, *Wild Fowl Decoys*, pp. 33–38.
37. David S. Webster and William Kehoe, *Decoys at Shelburne Museum*, p. 10.
38. Mackey, *American Bird Decoys*, p. 16.
39. Ibid., pp. 63, 112.
40. Ibid., pp. 112–134, 137.
41. Bernard Herman and David Orr, "Decoys and Their Use," pp. 4–7.
42. Barber, *Wild Fowl Decoys*, p. 20.
43. Richard H. Moeller, "On Barnegat Bay with George Harvey," in Webster and Kehoe, *Decoys at Shelburne*, pp. 81–82.
44. Webster and Kehoe, *Decoys at Shelburne*, p. 48.
45. Ibid., p. 6.
46. Ibid.; Mackey, *American Bird Decoys*, p. 125.
47. William T. Mackey, "Harry Shourdes [sic], Decoy Maker," in Webster and Kehoe, *Decoys at Shelburne*, p. 86.
48. Interview with Harry V. Shourds.

## Traditional Boats

1. Quoted in "From the 'New World,' by Johan De Laet, 1625, 1630, 1633, 1640," in J. Franklin Jameson, ed., *Narratives of New Netherland, 1609–1664*, p. 48.
2. "From 'The Third Voyage of Master Henry Hudson,' by Robert Juet, 1610," in Jameson, *Narratives of New Netherland*, p. 19.
3. De Laet, "From the 'New World'," in Jameson, *Narratives of New Netherland*, p. 57.
4. Dorothy Cross, *New Jersey's Indians*, p. 43.
5. Harry B. Weiss and Grace M. Weiss, *Rafting on the Delaware*, pp. 8, 10.
6. Ibid., pp. 14–18; Charles T. Curtis, *Rafting on the Delaware*, pp. 24–25.
7. Weiss and Weiss, *Rafting on the Delaware*, p. 21.
8. Ibid., pp. 35–37; William M. E. Hess, "The Durham Boat," in *On History's Trail*, vol. 2.
9. Richard F. Veit, *The Old Canals of*

*New Jersey*, pp. 23, 45–46, 55–56, 65, 75, 78, 82–84; James Lee, *The Morris Canal*, pp. 12, 14, 19, 23; idem, *Tales the Boatmen Told*, pp. 7, 117–118, 120–121, 152, 196, 278, 280.

10. William A. Baker, *Sloops and Shallops*, pp. 11, 18, 20, 156.

11. Barbara Lipton, "Whaling Days in New Jersey," pp. 4–5.

12. Donald H. Rolfs, *Under Sail*, pp. 9–10.

13. Baker, *Sloops and Shallops*, p. 129.

14. Ibid., p. 157.

15. Rolfs, *Under Sail*, p. 10.

16. *Hudson River Sloops*, pp. 4–12.

17. Rolfs, *Under Sail*, p. 10.

18. Ibid., p. 11.

19. Peter J. Guthorn, *The Sea Bright Skiff and Other Jersey Shore Boats*, pp. 3–18; Hess, "The Fishing Industry," in *On History's Trail*, vol. 2.

20. Guthorn, *The Sea Bright Skiff*, pp. 212–213.

21. Bernard Herman and David Orr, "Decoys and Their Use," p. 4.

22. Samuel Bonnell, "Barnegat Bay," p. 107.

23. Interview with Sam Hunt.

24. Ibid.

25. Ibid.

26. Ibid.

27. Ibid.

28. Mary Hufford, "One Reason God Made Trees," pp. 1, 8–9.

## Folk Architecture

1. John Kouwenhoven, *The Arts in Modern American Civilization*, pp. 13–42.

2. Alan Gowans, *Architecture in New Jersey*, pp. 23–29.

3. Adriaen van der Donck, *A Description of the New Netherlands*, pp. 79–80.

4. Herbert C. Kraft, "Prehistoric Indian House Patterns in New Jersey"; idem, *The Minisink Settlements*, pp. 11–13; idem, *The Archaeology of the Tocks Island Area*, pp. 73–86.

5. Harold R. Shurtleff, *The Log Cabin Myth*, pp. 51–56, 209–215.

6. [Jasper Danckaerts], *Journal of Jasper Danckaerts, 1679–1680*, p. 98.

7. Fred Kniffen and Henry Glassie, "Building in Wood in the Eastern United States"; Henry Glassie, "The Types of the Southern Mountain Cabin."

8. David Steven Cohen, "Defining the Dutch-American Farmhouse Types."

9. John Frederick Kelly, *The Early Domestic Architecture of Connecticut*, pp. 59–60; Theodore H. M. Prudon, "The Dutch Barn in America," pp. 125–130; John Fitchen, *The New World Dutch Barn*.

10. Marvin D. Schwartz, *The Jan Martense Schenck House*.

11. Cohen, "Dutch-American Farmhouse Types."

12. Paul Love, "Patterned Brickwork in Southern New Jersey."

13. Thomas Jefferson Wertenbaker, *The Founding of American Civilization*, pp. 233–236.

14. Peter O. Wacker, *Land and People*, p. 179.

15. [Peter Kalm], *The America of 1750*, 2: 118–119.

16. Reginald McMahon, "The Achter Col Colony on the Hackensack."

17. Peter O. Wacker, "Folk Architecture as an Indicator of Culture Areas and Culture Diffusion," p. 40.

18. Quoted in Hubert G. Schmidt, *Rural Hunterdon*, p. 95.
19. Wacker, "Folk Architecture," p. 41.

20. Don McTernan, "The Barrack."
21. Peter J. Guthorn, *The Sea Bright Skiff and Other Jersey Shore Boats*, p. 4.

# Folk Furniture

1. John D. Morse, ed., *Country Cabinetwork and Simple City Furniture*; Ralph Kovel and Terry Kovel, *American Country Furniture, 1780–1875*.
2. Charles S. Parsons, "The Dunlaps of New Hampshire and Their Furniture," in Morse, *Country Cabinetwork*; Bruce Buckley, "A Folklorist Looks at the Traditional Craftsman," in ibid.
3. Michael Owen Jones, *The Hand Made Object and Its Maker*, p. 20.
4. Henry Glassie, "Folk Art."
5. Henry Glassie, *Pattern in the Material Folk Culture of the Eastern United States*, p. 33.
6. Estate inventory of Henricus Kipp.
7. Estate inventory of Abraham Staats.
8. Frederick Banfield Hanson, "The Interior Architecture and Household Furnishings of Bergen County, New Jersey, 1800–1810," p. 128.
9. Margaret E. White, *Early Furniture Made in New Jersey, 1690–1870*, p. 1.
10. Walter Hamilton Van Hoesen, *Crafts and Craftsmen of New Jersey*, pp. 39–45; W. M. Horner, Jr., "Three Generations of Cabinetmakers."
11. Wallace Nutting, "Carved Spoon Racks."
12. Huyler Held, "Long Island Dutch Slat Backs," p. 168; Charles F. Hummel, "The Dominys of East Hampton, Long Island, and Their Furniture," in Morse,

*Country Cabinetwork*, pp. 35–67.
13. Estate inventory of Garret Hendrickson.
14. Luke Vincent Lockwood, *Colonial Furniture in America*, 2: 56.
15. Cornelius Weygandt, *Down Jersey*, pp. 173–176.
16. Lockwood, *Colonial Furniture*, 2: 20–27.
17. White, *Early Furniture*, p. 5.
18. Leslie Byrnes, "An Aspect of New Jersey Furniture."
19. White, *Early Furniture*, pp. 20–21.
20. Estate inventory of Jacob Van Ness.
21. Wilson Lynes, "Slat-Back Chairs of New England and the Middle Atlantic States," vol. 24.
22. Ibid., 24: 210.
23. William H. MacDonald, "Central New Jersey Chairmaking of the Nineteenth Century," pp. 128–129.
24. Sara Carlisle Watson and Richard Joslin King, *American Craftsmen*, pp. 2–3.
25. Mabel Crispin Powers, "The Ware Chairs of South Jersey," p. 307.
26. Ibid., pp. 308–309.
27. Benno M. Forman, "Delaware Valley 'Crookt Foot' and Slat-Back Chairs," pp. 42, 45–46.
28. Siegfried Giedion, *Mechanization Takes Command*, pp. 258–468.

# Quilts, Coverlets, and Samplers

1. Quoted in Harry B. Weiss and Grace M. Ziegler, *The Early Woolen Industry of New Jersey*, p. 19.
2. Ibid.
3. Ibid.
4. Hubert G. Schmidt, *Flax Culture in Hunterdon County, New Jersey*, p. 6.
5. Quoted in ibid., p. 9.
6. Weiss and Ziegler, *Early Woolen Industry*, p. 38.
7. Quoted in ibid., p. 54.
8. Ibid.
9. Ibid., p. 22.
10. Ibid., p. 23.
11. Harry B. Weiss and Grace M. Ziegler, *The Early Fulling Mills of New Jersey*, p. 5.
12. Ibid., p. 21.
13. *New Jersey Assembly Minutes, 1814–1816*, p. 233.
14. Ibid.
15. Hubert G. Schmidt, *Rural Hunterdon*, p. 232.
16. Weiss and Ziegler, *Early Woolen Industry*, p. 30.
17. Hubert G. Schmidt, *Agriculture in New Jersey*, p. 176.
18. Diary of Margaret Ten Eyck.
19. Phillip H. Curtis, "American Quilts in the Newark Museum."
20. Margaret E. White, *American Handwoven Coverlets in the Newark Museum*.
21. Elisabeth Donaghy Garrett, "The Theodore H. Kapnek Collection of American Samplers," p. 547.
22. E. T. Darling, "Vineland Samplers."
23. Ann Douglass, *The Feminization of American Culture*, p. 255.
24. Ibid., p. 58.
25. Ibid., p. 200.

# Pottery, Basketry, and Glass

1. Henry Glassie, *Pattern in the Material Folk Culture of the Eastern United States*, p. 30.
2. Henry Glassie, "Folk Art," p. 253.
3. James Deetz, *In Small Things Forgotten*.
4. Ibid., p. 46.
5. Herbert C. Kraft, "Indian Prehistory of New Jersey," p. 23.
6. Herbert C. Kraft, *The Miller Field Site, Warren County, N.J.*, pp. 113–114, 116–119.
7. Kraft, "Indian Prehistory," pp. 23–46.
8. Ibid.; idem, *The Minisink Site*, p. 83.
9. Kraft, "Indian Prehistory," p. 30; idem, *The Minisink Site*, pp. 82–89.
10. Deetz, *In Small Things Forgotten*, pp. 47–48.
11. Ibid., pp. 48–49.
12. Arthur W. Clement, *Notes on American Ceramics*, pp. 5–7; idem, *The Pottery and Porcelain of New Jersey, 1688–1900*, p. 7.
13. John Ramsay, "Early American Pottery," p. 227.
14. Ibid., p. 226.
15. Robert J. Sim and Arthur W. Clement, "The Cheesequake Potteries," p. 123.
16. Ibid., pp. 123–125.
17. Deetz, *In Small Things Forgotten*, pp. 50, 52–53.
18. Ibid., pp. 55–58.
19. Kraft, "Indian Prehistory," p. 19.
20. Kraft, *The Miller Field Site*, p. 137.
21. M. R. Harrington, "Vestiges of Ma-

terial Culture among the Canadian Delaware," pp. 410–411.
22. Frank G. Speck, *Eastern Algonkian Block-Stamp Decoration*, pp. 17–19, 30–32.
23. Ives Goddard, "Delaware," p. 227.
24. Henry Glassie, "William Houck," pp. 42–44.
25. Estate inventory of Isaac van Giesen.
26. C. A. Weslager, *The Delaware Indians*, p. 277.
27. William Willard Howard, "Among the Jersey Crabbers," p. 740.
28. Cornelius Weygandt, *Down Jersey*, pp. 182–183; Robert J. Sim, *Pages from the Past of Rural New Jersey*, pp. 83–86.
29. Ibid., p. 85; Robert J. Sim, *Some Vanishing Phases of Rural Life in New Jersey*, p. 25.

30. Sim, *Some Vanishing Phases*, p. 26.
31. Glassie, "William Houck," pp. 40–42.
32. Quoted in Arlene Palmer, "Glass Production in Eighteenth-Century America," p. 98.
33. Ibid., pp. 77–78, 77n.
34. Ibid., p. 78.
35. Ibid., pp. 88–89.
36. Ibid., pp. 96–97.
37. Budd Wilson, "The Pine Barrens Glass Industry," pp. 219–222; Adeline Pepper, *The Glass Gaffers of New Jersey*, pp. 313–315.
38. Pepper, *Glass Gaffers*, pp. 60–61.
39. Ibid., pp. 63–64; Wilson, "Pine Barrens Glass Industry," pp. 222–223.
40. Pepper, *Glass Gaffers*, pp. 65, 246, 247.

# Foodways

1. Jay Anderson, "A Solid Sufficiency," p. 2.
2. Siegfried Giedion, *Mechanization Takes Command*, pp. 6–7.
3. Adriaen van der Donck, *A Description of the New Netherlands*, pp. 74, 76.
4. "From the 'Korte Historiael ende Journaels Aenteyckeninge,' by David Pietersz. de Vries, 1633–1643 (1655)," in J. Franklin Jameson, ed., *Narratives of New Netherland, 1609–1664*, pp. 222–223.
5. Ibid., p. 220.
6. "Letter of Isaack de Rasieres to Samuel Blommaert, 1628 (?)," in Jameson, *Narratives of New Netherland*, p. 107.
7. Ibid.
8. Van der Donck, *Description of the New Netherlands*, pp. 76–77.
9. Ibid., p. 76.
10. Herbert C. Kraft, *The Archaeology of the Tocks Island Area*, p. 85.

11. [Peter Kalm], *The America of 1750*, 2: 602.
12. Ibid., 1: 346–347; 2: 602–603, 614–615, 628–629.
13. Kalm, *America of 1750*, 2: 712.
14. Ibid., 1: 266–268.
15. Ibid., p. 184.
16. Ibid., 2: 647.
17. Ibid., 1: 181–182.
18. Ibid., p. 267.
19. Ibid., p. 183.
20. Ibid., pp. 259–262.
21. Ibid., p. 269.
22. Ibid., p. 262.
23. Ibid., p. 273.
24. Ibid.
25. Ibid., p. 272.
26. Andrew D. Mellick, Jr., *The Old Farm*, pp. 116–118.
27. Quoted in Hubert G. Schmidt, *Rural Hunterdon*, p. 277.
28. Ibid.

29. Ibid., p. 278.
30. Ibid., p. 277.
31. Ibid.
32. Ibid.
33. Ibid.
34. Ibid.
35. Ibid., pp. 278–279.
36. *Columbia Encyclopedia*, 2d. ed. s.v. "applejack."
37. Harry B. Weiss, *The History of Applejack or Apple Brandy in New Jersey from Colonial Times to the Present*, p. 9.
38. Ibid., p. 12.
39. Kalm, *America of 1750*, 2: 643.
40. Ibid., pp. 19–25, 29–31.
41. Ibid., pp. 35–36, 51, 53, 72–73.
42. Ibid., pp. 122–123.
43. Ibid., pp. 75–76.

44. Schmidt, *Rural Hunterdon*, pp. 280–281.
45. Giedion, *Mechanization Takes Command*, pp. 130–256, 512–547, 596–606, 612–627.
46. Arlene Martin Ridgway, ed., *Chicken Foot Soup and Other Recipes from the Pine Barrens*.
47. Mark Zborowski and Elizabeth Herzog, *Life Is with People*, pp. 362–380.
48. Interview with Anastasia Kysilewska.
49. Interview with Modestino Magliacane.
50. Interview with Lillian Dieter.
51. Koji Shimada, "Education, Assimilation, and Acculturation: A Case Study of a Japanese-American Community in New Jersey," pp. 115–117.

## Games and Recreation

1. Mary Knapp and Herbert Knapp, *One Potato, Two Potato*, p. 17.
2. Brian Sutton-Smith, ed., *The Folkgames of Children*, pp. 297–298.
3. Adriaen van der Donck, *A Description of the New Netherlands*, p. 94.
4. "Letter of Isaack De Rasieres to Samuel Blommaert, 1628 (?)," in J. Franklin Jameson, ed., *Narratives of New Netherland*, p. 106.
5. Frank G. Speck, *Oklahoma Delaware Ceremonies, Feasts, and Dances*, pp. 104–106.
6. Harry B. Weiss and Grace M. Weiss, *Early Sports and Pastimes in New Jersey*, pp. 1–2.
7. Ibid., pp. 2–3.
8. Ibid., p. 3.
9. Ibid., pp. 4–5.
10. Ibid.
11. Cornelius Weygandt, *Down Jersey*, pp. 62–64.

12. Mary Hufford, "Foxhunting in the Pine Barrens," pp. 222–224, 229.
13. J. F. Leaming, "The General Beach Party."
14. "Local Folklore," p. 3.
15. Philippe Ariès, *Centuries of Childhood*, pp. 50–99, 365–371.
16. Sutton-Smith, ed., *Folkgames of Children*, pp. 18–214.
17. Interview with Nona, Patricia, Billie, and Theresa Schuesssler.
18. Sutton-Smith, ed., *Folkgames of Children*, p. 18.
19. Interview with Mark A. Spelker.
20. James Lee, *Tales the Boatmen Told*, pp. 14, 111–112, 208.
21. Sutton-Smith, ed., *Folkgames of Children*, p. 66.
22. Schuessler interview.
23. Sutton-Smith, ed., *Folkgames of Children*, p. 75.
24. Schuessler interview.

25. Sutton-Smith, ed., *Folkgames of Children*, p. 490.
26. Ibid., pp. 99–100.
27. Interview with Alice Wallenstein Nirmaier.
28. Schuessler interview.
29. Ibid.
30. Ibid.
31. Ibid.
32. Kenneth A. Goldstein, "Strategy in Counting Out: An Ethnographic Folklore Field Study."
33. Brian Sutton-Smith, "The Kissing Games of Adolescents in Ohio," in Brian Sutton-Smith, ed., *The Folkgames of Children*, p. 489.

34. Interview with Earle A. Nirmaier, Sr.; Lee, *Tales the Boatmen Told*, p. 209.
35. Alice Nirmaier interview; Lee, *Tales the Boatmen Told*, p. 112.
36. Earle A. Nirmaier interview.
37. Sutton-Smith, ed., *Folkgames of Children*, p. 214.
38. Ibid., pp. 258–281.
39. Charles W. Churchill, *The Italians of Newark*, p. 143.
40. Elizabeth Lay Mathias, "From Folklore to Mass Culture."
41. Koji Shimada, "Education, Assimilation, and Acculturation," pp. 125–126.

## Festivals, Ceremonies, and Rituals

1. Arnold Van Gennep, *The Rites of Passage*, pp. 3, 10–11.
2. Adriaen van der Donck, *A Description of the New Netherlands*, pp. 84–85.
3. David Pietersz. de Vries, "Voyages from Holland to America, A.D. 1632 to 1644," p. 106.
4. Mark Zborowski and Elizabeth Herzog, *Life Is with People*, pp. 347–348.
5. H. R. Hays, *The Dangerous Sex*, pp. 39–41.
6. Van Gennep, *Rites of Passage*, p. 41.
7. Margaret Mead, *Male and Female*, p. 181.
8. Zborowski and Herzog, *Life Is with People*, p. 319.
9. Van Gennep, *Rites of Passage*, p. 72.
10. Julian Morgenstern, *Rites of Birth, Marriage, Death and Kindred Occasions among the Semites*, pp. 77–80.
11. Van der Donck, *Description of the New Netherlands*, p. 85.
12. Morgenstern, *Rites of Birth, Marriage, Death*, pp. 81–83.

13. De Vries, "Voyages from Holland to America," p. 106.
14. Van der Donck, *Description of the New Netherlands*, p. 83.
15. Ibid., p. 82.
16. This is not an Indian word. Either van der Donck was wrong or the Indians had borrowed a Dutch word.
17. Van der Donck, *Description of the New Netherlands*, pp. 84, 83.
18. [Peter Kalm], *The America of 1750*, 2: 225.
19. Louis Mounier, "Glimpses of Jewish Life in the Colonies of Southern New Jersey," p. 512.
20. Peter Lindestrom, *Geographia America, with an Account of the Delaware Indians*, pp. 249–250.
21. Herbert C. Kraft, "Indian Prehistory of New Jersey," p. 45.
22. Koji Shimada, "Education, Assimilation, and Acculturation," p. 188.
23. Jeanne T. Reock, "The Hungarian Community of New Brunswick," p. 24.

24. Berthold Fernow, ed., *The Records of New Amsterdam from 1653 to 1674*, 1: 420.

25. Ibid., p. 286.

26. [William Dunlap], *Diary of William Dunlap*, 1: 65.

27. Gabriel Furman, *Antiquities of Long Island*, pp. 265–266.

28. Quoted in Mary Dolan, "Folklore in New Jersey," pp. 7–8.

29. Svatana Pirkova-Jakobson, "Harvest Festivals among Czechs and Slovaks in America," p. 75.

30. Peter A. Peroni II, *The Burg*, pp. 36–37.

31. Interview with Thomas MacFarlane.

32. Interview with Anastasia Kysilewska.

33. Interview with Andrew Szproch.

34. Ibid.

35. Reock, "Hungarian Community of New Brunswick," p. 25.

# Conclusion

1. Richard Dorson, *American Folklore*.

2. Tristram P. Coffin and Hennig Cohen, eds., *Folklore in America*.

# Works Cited

Readers interested in pursuing the study of American folklore and folklife more generally should consult the following works: Jan Harold Brunvand, *The Study of American Folklore: An Introduction* (New York: W.W. Norton, 1968), a good introductory textbook; Richard M. Dorson, ed., *Folklore and Folklife: An Introduction* (Chicago and London: University of Chicago Press, 1972), a collection of general essays introducing the various folklore and folklife genres; Kenneth S. Goldstein, *A Guide for Fieldworkers in Folklore* (Hatboro, Pa.: Folklore Associates, 1964), a manual on collecting and documenting folklore and folklife; Charles Haywood, ed., *A Bibliography of North American Folklore and Folksong* (New York: Greenberg, 1951), a good, albeit out-of-date, bibliography of folklore research.

*An Account of the Beginnings, Transactions, and Discovery of Ransford Rogers* . . . Newark: Printed by John Woods, 1792.

*American Folk Sculpture: The Work of Eighteenth and Nineteenth Century Craftsmen.* October 20, 1931–January 31, 1932. Newark: Newark Museum, 1931.

*American Naive Paintings from the Eighteenth and Nineteenth Centuries; 111 Masterpieces from the Collection of Edgar William and Bernice Chrysler Garbisch.* New York: American Federation of Arts, 1969.

*American Primitives: An Exhibit of the Paintings of Nineteenth Century Folk Artists.* November 4, 1930–February 1, 1931. Newark: Newark Museum, 1930.

Ames, Kenneth L. *Beyond Necessity: Art in the Folk Tradition.* Winterthur: Winterthur Museum, 1977.

Anderson, Jay. "A Solid Sufficiency: An Ethnography of Yeomen Foodways in Stuart England." Ph.D. dissertation, University of Pennsylvania, 1971.

# Works Cited

*Archives of the State of New Jersey*, edited by William Nelson. Vol. 11, *Newspaper Extracts*. Vol. 1, *1704–1739*. Paterson: Press Printing and Publishing Co., 1894.

Ariès, Philippe. *Centuries of Childhood: A Social History of Family Life*. 1967. Reprint. New York: Vintage Books, 1965.

Augustine, William. "Egg Harbor's Scrambled Names." *Newark Star-Ledger*, June 4, 1967, 2: 9.

Baker, William A. *Sloops and Shallops*. Barre, Mass.: Barre Publishing Co., 1966.

Barber, Joel. *Wild Fowl Decoys*. New York: Dover Publications, 1954.

Barber, John W. and Henry Howe. *Historical Collections of the State of New Jersey*. New York: S. Tuttle, 1844.

Beck, Henry Charlton. *Forgotten Towns of Southern New Jersey*. New Brunswick: Rutgers University Press, 1961.

———. *The Jersey Midlands*. New Brunswick: Rutgers University Press, 1961.

———. *The Roads of Home*. New Brunswick: Rutgers University Press, 1962.

Bonnell, Samuel. "Barnegat Bay." In *Duck Shooting along the Atlantic Tidewater*, edited by Eugene V. Connett. New York: William Morrow, 1947.

Boyer, Charles S. *Old Inns and Taverns in West New Jersey*. Camden: Camden County Historical Society, 1962.

Bradshaw, Elinor Robinson. "American Folk Art in the Collection of the Newark Museum." *Museum*, n.s. 19 (1967): 1–57.

[Brainerd, David.] *Memoirs of the Rev. David Brainerd: Missionary to the Indians on the Borders of New York, New Jersey, and Pennsylvania*. 1822. Reprint. New York: Scholarly Press, 1970.

Brinton, Daniel Garrison. *The Lenape and Their Legends*. Philadelphia: D. G. Brinton, 1885.

Bryant, William Cullen. *Picturesque America* . . . New York: D. Appleton & Co., 1874.

Byrnes, Leslie. "An Aspect of New Jersey Furniture." Talk delivered at the Research Roundtable on New Jersey Decorative and Fine Arts. Trenton, April 12, 1980.

Calhoun, Arthur W. *A Social History of the American Family*. 1817. Reprint. 2 vols. New York: Barnes and Noble, 1945.

Churchill, Charles W. *The Italians of Newark: A Community Study*. 1942. Reprint. New York: Arno Press, 1975.

Clement, Arthur W. *Notes on American Ceramics*. Brooklyn: Brooklyn Museum, 1944.

———. *The Pottery and Porcelain of New Jersey, 1688–1900.* Newark: Newark Museum, 1947.

Coffin, Tristram P. and Hennig Cohen, eds. *Folklore in America.* Garden City, N.Y.: Doubleday & Co., 1966.

Cohen, David Steven. "Alfred P. Smith: Bergen County's Latter-Day Ben Franklin." *Journal of the Rutgers University Libraries* 38 (1976): 23–33.

———. "Defining the Dutch-American Farmhouse Types." In *Patterns from the Past: New Jersey's Architectural Heritage.* Trenton: New Jersey Historical Commission, forthcoming.

———. *Folklife in New Jersey: An Annotated Bibliography.* Trenton: New Jersey Historical Commission, 1982.

———. "The Origin of the 'Jackson Whites': History and Legend among the Ramapo Mountain People." *Journal of American Folklore* 85 (1972): 260–266.

———. *The Ramapo Mountain People.* New Brunswick: Rutgers University Press, 1974.

*Columbia Encyclopedia.* 2d ed. New York: Columbia University Press, 1950.

Cortelyou, Mrs. Irwin F. "Micah Williams: New Jersey Primitive Portrait Artist." *Monmouth Historian* 2 (1974): 4–15.

Cowen, David L. *Medicine in Revolutionary New Jersey.* New Jersey's Revolutionary Experience. Trenton: New Jersey Historical Commission, 1975.

Cross, Dorothy. *New Jersey's Indians.* Report no. 1. Trenton: New Jersey State Museum, 1965.

Crumb, Fredrick W. *Tom Quick: Early American.* Narrowsburg, N.Y.: Delaware Valley Press, 1936.

Curtis, Charles T. *Rafting on the Delaware.* Ithaca: De Witt Historical Society of Tompkins County, 1921.

Curtis, Philip H. "American Quilts in the Newark Museum." *Museum* n.s. 25 (1973): 2–68.

[Danckaerts, Jasper.] *Journal of Jasper Danckaerts, 1679–1680,* edited by Bartlett Burleigh James and J. Franklin Jameson. New York: Charles Scribner's Sons, 1913.

Darling, E. T. "Vineland Samplers." *Vineland Historical Magazine* 2 (1925): 241.

Deetz, James. *In Small Things Forgotten: The Archeology of Early American Life.* Garden City, N.Y.: Anchor Books, 1977.

Degh, Linda and Andrew Vazsonyi. "Legend and Belief." In *Folklore Genres,* edited by Dan Ben-Amos. Austin and London: University of Texas Press, 1976.

de Vries, David Pietersz. "Voyages from Holland to America, A.D. 1632 to 1644." Translated by Henry C. Murphy. In *Historic Chronicles of New Amsterdam, Colonial New York, and Early Long Island*, 1st ser., edited by Cornell Jaray. Port Washington, N.Y.: Ira J. Friedman, 1968.

Dieter, Lillian. Interviewed by Patricia Slattery. March 19, 1978.

Dolan, Mary B. "Folklore in New Jersey." Master's thesis, Rutgers University, 1934.

Donck, Adriaen van der. *A Description of the New Netherlands*. 1656. Edited by Thomas F. O'Donnell. Syracuse: Syracuse University Press, 1968.

Dorson, Richard M. *American Folklore*. Chicago: University of Chicago Press, 1959.

Douglass, Ann. *The Feminization of American Culture*. New York: Alfred A. Knopf, 1977.

Dunlap, A. R. "Barnegat." *American Speech* 13 (1938): 232–233.

[Dunlap, William.] *Diary of William Dunlap*. 3 vols. New York Historical Society Collections. New York: New York Historical Society, 1929–1931.

Earle, Alice Morse. *Two Centuries of Costume in America*. 2 vols. New York and London: Macmillan, 1903.

Ewan, Nathaniel R. "New Jersey's Pineys: The Truth about a Much Maligned and Misunderstood Section of Our Population." *New Jersey Compass* 1 (1947): 10–12.

Federal Writers' Project. *The Swedes and Finns in New Jersey*. Bayonne: New Jersey Commission to Commemorate the 300th Anniversary of the Settlement of the Swedes and Finns on the Delaware, 1938.

Feister, Lois M. "Linguistic Communication between the Dutch and Indians in New Netherland, 1609–1664." *Ethnohistory* 20 (1973): 25–38.

Fernow, Berthold, ed. *The Records of New Amsterdam from 1653 to 1674*. Vol. 1, *Court Minutes of New Amsterdam*. New York: Knickerbocker Press, 1897.

Fitchen, John. *The New World Dutch Barn*. Syracuse: Syracuse University Press, 1968.

Fleming, E. McClung. "Early American Decorative Arts as Social Documents." *Mississippi Valley Historical Review* 45 (1958): 276–284.

———. "From Indian Princess to Greek Goddess: The American Image, 1783–1815." *Winterthur Portfolio* 2 (1967): 37–66.

"Folk Medicine in a Homogeneous Puerto Rican Community: Vineland's Transplanted Village of Utuadeños." Report of the Puerto Rican Congress of New Jersey, 1977.

Forman, Benno M. "Delaware Valley 'Crookt Foot' and Slat-Back Chairs: The Fussell-Savery Connection." *Winterthur Portfolio* 15 (1980): 41–64.

Furman, Gabriel. *Antiquities of Long Island*. New York: J. W. Bouton, 1874.

Garrett, Elisabeth Donaghy. "The Theodore H. Kapnek Collection of American Samplers." *Antiques* 114 (1978): 540–559.

Giedion, Siegfried. *Mechanization Takes Command: A Contribution to Anonymous History*. 1948. Reprint. New York: W. W. Norton, 1969.

Giesen, Isaac van. Estate inventory. August 24, 1742. Archives and History, State Library, Trenton.

Gillespie, Angus K. and Tom Ayres. "Folklore in the Pine Barrens: The Pinelands Cultural Society," *New Jersey History* 97 (1979): 221–243.

Glassie, Henry. "Folk Art." In *Folklore and Folklife: An Introduction*, edited by Richard M. Dorson. Chicago and London: University of Chicago Press, 1972.

———. *Folk Housing in Middle Virginia*. Knoxville: University of Tennessee Press, 1975.

———. *Pattern in the Material Folk Culture of the Eastern United States*. Philadelphia: University of Pennsylvania Press, 1968.

———. "The Types of the Southern Mountain Cabin." In *The Study of American Folklore: An Introduction*, by Jan Harold Brunvand. New York: W. W. Norton, 1968.

———. "William Houck: Maker of Pounded Ash Adirondack Pack-Baskets." *Keystone Folklore Quarterly* 12 (1967): 23–54.

Goddard, Henry Herbert. *The Kallikak Family: A Study in the Heredity of Feeble-Mindedness*. New York: Macmillan, 1912.

Goddard, Ives. "Delaware." In *Handbook of North American Indians*, edited by William C. Sturtevant. Vol. 15, *Northeast*, edited by Bruce G. Trigger. Washington, D.C.: Smithsonian Institution, 1978.

———. "The Delaware Language, Past and Present." In *A Delaware Indian Symposium*, edited by Herbert C. Kraft. Harrisburg: Pennsylvania Historical and Museum Commission, 1974.

———. "Dutch Loanwords in Delaware." In *A Delaware Indian Symposium*, edited by Herbert C. Kraft. Harrisburg: Pennsylvania Historical and Museum Commission, 1974.

Goldstein, Kenneth A. "Strategy in Counting Out: An Ethnographic Folklore

Field Study." In *The Study of Games*, edited by Elliott M. Avedon and Brian Sutton-Smith. New York: John Wiley and Sons, 1971.

Gowans, Alan. *Architecture in New Jersey*. Princeton: D. Van Nostrand, 1964.

Guthorn, Peter J. *The Sea Bright Skiff and Other Jersey Shore Boats*. New Brunswick: Rutgers University Press, 1971.

Halpert, Herbert. "Folk Tales and Legends from the New Jersey Pines: A Collection and a Study." 2 vols. Ph.D. dissertation, Indiana University, 1947.

———. "The Piney Folk-Singers." *Direction* 2 (1939): 4–6, 15.

———. "Some Ballads and Folk Songs from New Jersey." *Journal of American Folklore* 52 (1939): 52–69.

Hand, Wayland D., ed. *American Folk Legend: A Symposium*. Los Angeles and Berkeley: University of California Press, 1971.

Hanson, Frederick Banfield. "The Interior Architecture and Household Furnishings of Bergen County, New Jersey, 1800–1810." Master's thesis, University of Delaware, 1959.

Harrington, M. R. "Vestiges of Material Culture among the Canadian Delaware." *American Anthropologist* 10 (1908): 408–418.

Hays, H. R. *The Dangerous Sex: The Myth of Feminine Evil*. New York: G. P. Putnam, 1964.

Heckewelder, John. *History, Manners, and Customs of the Indian Nations Who Once Inhabited Pennsylvania and the Neighboring States*. 1876. Reprint. New York: Arno Press, 1971.

Held, Huyler. "Long Island Dutch Slat Backs." *Antiques* 20 (1936): 168–170.

Hendrickson, Garret. Estate inventory. December 9, 1801. Archives and History, State Library, Trenton.

*Henry Thomas Gulick: New Jersey's Native Painter*. Montclair: Montclair Art Museum, 1974.

Herman, Bernard and David Orr. "Decoys and Their Use: A Cultural Interpretation." In *Philadelphia Wildfowl Exposition*. Philadelphia: Academy of National Sciences of Philadelphia, 1979.

Heslip, Colleen Cowles. *Mrs. Susan C. Waters: 19th-Century Itinerant Painter*. Farmville, Va.: Longwood Fine Arts Center, 1979.

———. "Susan C. Waters." *Antiques* 126 (1979): 769–777.

Hess, William M. E. *On History's Trail*. 2 vols. Point Pleasant: Barnegat Products, 1976.

Hine, C. G. *The Old Mine Road*. 1909. Reprint. New Brunswick: Rutgers University Press, 1963.

Hoffman, Daniel G. "Stephen Crane's New Jersey Ghosts." *Proceedings of the New Jersey Historical Society* 71 (1953): 239–253.

Horner, W. M., Jr. "Three Generations of Cabinetmakers." In *Collecting New Jersey Antiques*. Union City: Books about New Jersey, 1978.

Howard, William Willard. "Among the Jersey Crabbers." *Continent*, June 13, 1883, pp. 737–746.

*Hudson River Sloops*. Hastings-on-Hudson: Hudson River Sloop Restoration, 1970.

Hufford, Mary. "Foxhunting in the Pine Barrens." In *History, Culture and Archeology of the New Jersey Pine Barrens*, edited by John W. Sinton. Pomona: Center for Environmental Research, Stockton State College, 1982.

———. "One Reason God Made Trees: The Form and Ecology of the Barnegat Sneakbox." Paper delivered at the American Folklore Society annual meeting, Pittsburgh, October 1980.

Hunt, Sam. Interviewed by Christopher Hoare. April 28, 1978.

Jameson, J. Franklin, ed. *Narratives of New Netherland, 1609–1664*. New York: Charles Scribner's Sons, 1909.

"The Jokes Don't Matter in Hoboken." *New York Times*, December 6, 1979, B1.

Jones, Michael Owen. *The Hand Made Object and Its Maker*. Berkeley, Los Angeles, and London: University of California Press, 1975.

[Kalm, Peter.] *The America of 1750: Peter Kalm's Travels in North America . . .*, edited by Adolph B. Benson. 2 vols. New York: Wilson-Erickson, 1937.

Kaufman, Charles H. "An Ethnomusicological Survey among the People of the Ramapo Mountains." *New York Folklore Quarterly* 23 (1967): 3–43, 109–131.

———. "Music in New Jersey, 1665–1860: A Study of Musical Activity and Musicians in New Jersey from Its First Settlement to the Civil War." Ph.D. dissertation, New York University, 1974.

———. *The Music of Eighteenth Century New Jersey*. New Jersey's Revolutionary Experience Series. No. 11. Trenton: New Jersey Historical Commission, 1975.

Kaye, Myrna. *Yankee Weathervanes*. New York: E. P. Dutton, 1975.

Kelly, John Frederick. *The Early Domestic Architecture of Connecticut*. New Haven: Yale University Press, 1924.

Kipp, Henricus. Estate inventory, April 20, 1734. Archives and History, State Library, Trenton.

Kite, Elizabeth. "Report on Social Conditions in the Pine Belt." In *Research Work in New Jersey*. Rahway: Department of Charities and Corrections, 1913.

Kittredge, George Lyman. *Witchcraft in Old and New England*. 1929. Reprint. New York: Atheneum, 1972.

Knapp, Mary and Herbert Knapp. *One Potato, Two Potato: The Secret Education of American Children*. New York: W. W. Norton, 1976.

Kniffen, Fred and Henry Glassie. "Building in Wood in the Eastern United States: A Time-Place Perspective." *Geographical Review* 56 (1966): 40–66.

Kouwenhoven, John. *The Arts in Modern American Civilization*. New York: W. W. Norton, 1948.

Kovel, Ralph and Terry Kovel. *American Country Furniture, 1780–1875*. New York: Crown, 1965.

Kraft, Herbert C. *The Archaeology of the Tocks Island Area*. South Orange: Archaeological Research Center, Seton Hall University Museum, 1975.

———, ed. *A Delaware Indian Symposium*. Harrisburg: Pennsylvania Historical and Museum Commission, 1974.

———. "Indian Prehistory of New Jersey." In *A Delaware Indian Symposium*, edited by Herbert C. Kraft. Harrisburg: Pennsylvania Historical and Museum Commission, 1974.

———. *The Miller Field Site, Warren County, N.J.: A Study in Prehistoric Archaeology*. South Orange: Seton Hall University Press, 1970.

———. *The Minisink Settlements: An Investigation into a Prehistoric and Early Historic Site in Sussex County, New Jersey*. South Orange: Archaeological Research Center, Seton Hall University Museum, 1977.

———. *The Minisink Site: A Reevaluation of a Late Prehistoric and Early Historic Contact Site in Sussex County, New Jersey*. South Orange: Archaeological Research Center, Seton Hall University Museum, 1978.

———. "Prehistoric Indian House Patterns in New Jersey." *Bulletin of the Archaeological Society of New Jersey* 26 (1970): 1–11.

Kurath, Hans. *A Word Geography of the Eastern United States*. Ann Arbor: University of Michigan Press, 1949.

Kysilewska, Anastasia. Interviewed by Zoriana Tkacz. December 4, 1978.

*Landscape* (Saddle River). 1888–1889.

Larwood, Jacob and John Camden Hotten. *The History of Signboards from the Earliest Times to the Present Day*. London: John Camden Hotten, 1868.

Lathrop, Elise. *Early American Inns and Taverns*. 1926. Reprint. New York: Arno Press, 1977.

Leaming, J. F. "The General Beach Party." *Cape May County Magazine of History and Genealogy* 5 (1962): 342–353.

Lee, Francis B. "Jerseyisms." *Dialect Notes* 1 (1893): 327–337.

———. "Some Legal Allusions to Witchcraft in New Jersey." *New Jersey Law Journal* 17 (1894): 169–172.

Lee, James. *The Morris Canal: A Photographic History.* Easton, Pa.: Delaware Press, 1979.

———. *Tales the Boatmen Told.* Exton, Pa.: Canal Press, 1977.

Lindestrom, Peter. *Geographia America, with an Account of the Delaware Indians.* Philadelphia: Swedish Colonial Society, 1925.

Lipman, Jean. *American Folk Art in Wood, Metal, and Stone.* New York: Dover Publications, 1948.

Lipman, Jean and Alice Winchester. *The Flowering of American Folk Art.* New York: Whitney Museum of American Art, 1974.

Lipton, Barbara. "Whaling Days in New Jersey." *Newark Museum Quarterly* 26 (1975): 1–72.

"Local Folklore." *Relics* 2 (1957): [2–3].

Lockwood, Luke Vincent. *Colonial Furniture in America.* 2 vols. New York: Charles Scribner's Sons, 1951.

Love, Paul. "Patterned Brickwork in Southern New Jersey." *Proceedings of the New Jersey Historical Society* 73 (1955): 182–208.

Ludwig, Allan I. *Graven Images: New England Stonecarving and Its Symbols 1650–1815.* Middletown: Wesleyan University Press, 1966.

Lutz, Anne. "The Ballad of the Butcher Boy in the Ramapo Mountains." *New York Folklore Quarterly* 3 (1947): 28–35.

Lynes, Wilson. "Slat-Back Chairs of New England and the Middle-Atlantic States: A Consideration of Their Derivation and Development." *Antiques* 24 (1933): 208–210; 25 (1934): 104–107, 116.

MacDonald, William H. "Central New Jersey Chairmaking of the Nineteenth Century." *Proceedings of the New Jersey Historical Society* 77 (1959): 128–138, 185–207.

MacFarlane, Thomas. Interviewed by Thomas K. Daly. December 20, 1978.

McGrail, David. "New Jersey Fractur." Talk delivered at the Research Roundtable on New Jersey Decorative and Fine Arts. Trenton, April 12, 1980.

Mackey, William T., Jr. *American Bird Decoys.* New York: E. P. Dutton, 1965.

McMahon, Reginald. "The Achter Col Colony on the Hackensack." *New Jersey History* 89 (1971): 221–240.

Works Cited

McTernan, Don. "The Barrack: A Relic Feature on the North American Cultural Landscape." *Transactions of the Pioneer American Society* (1978): 57–69.

———. "The Esopus-Minisink Way: A Short History . . . with an Examination of the 'Old Mine Road.'" Master's thesis, Cooper Union College, 1969.

Magliacane, Modestino. Interviewed by Valerie Ruscitto. December 10, 1978.

Mahr, August C. "Origin and Significance of Pennsylvania Dutch Barn Symbols." In *The Study of Folklore*, edited by Alan Dundes. Englewood Cliffs: Prentice-Hall, 1976.

Maloney, Clarence, ed. *The Evil Eye*. New York: Columbia University Press, 1976.

Mathias, Elizabeth Lay. "From Folklore to Mass Culture: Dynamics of Acculturation in the Games of Italian-American Men." Ph.D. dissertation, University of Pennsylvania, 1974.

Mayer, W. F. "In the Pines." *Atlantic Monthly* 3 (1859): 560–569.

Mead, Margaret. *Male and Female: A Study of the Sexes in a Changing World*. New York: William Morrow, 1949.

Meadows, Cecil A. *Trade Signs and Their Origin*. London: Routledge and Kegan Paul, 1957.

Mellick, Andrew D., Jr. *The Old Farm*, edited by Hubert G. Schmidt. New Brunswick: Rutgers University Press, 1948.

Miers, Earl Schenck. *Where the Raritan Flows*. New Brunswick: Rutgers University Press, 1964.

Mills, Gary B. *The Forgotten People: Cane River's Creoles of Color*. Baton Rouge: Louisiana State University Press, 1977.

Morgan, Ed. Interviewed by David S. Cohen. March 21, 1971.

Morgenstern, Julian. *Rites of Birth, Marriage, Death and Kindred Occasions among the Semites*. Cincinnati and Chicago: Hebrew Union College Press and Quadrangle Books, 1966.

Morse, John D., ed. *Country Cabinetwork and Simple City Furniture*. Winterthur Conference Report. Charlottesville: University Press of Virginia, 1970.

Mounier, Louis. "Glimpses of Jewish Life in the Colonies of Southern New Jersey: Ike Merochnick's Wedding in Carmel." *Vineland Historical Magazine* 44 (1965): 512–513.

Murray, M. A. *The Witch-Cult in Western Europe*. 1921. Reprint. Oxford: Oxford University Press, 1962.

Nettl, Bruno. *Folk Music in the United States: An Introduction.* Detroit: Wayne State University Press, 1976.

Newcomb, William W., Jr. "The Walam Olum of the Delaware Indians in Perspective." *Bulletin of the Archaeological Society of New Jersey* 30 (1974): 57–63.

*New Jersey Assembly Minutes, 1814–1816.* Trenton: James J. Wilson, 1814.

Nirmaier, Alice Wallenstein. Interviewed by Audrey N. Spelker. December 5, 1978.

Nirmaier, Earle A., Sr. Interviewed by Audrey N. Spelker. December 5, 1978.

Noyes, Anna Gausmann. *Three Petticoats.* Leonia: n.p., 1955.

Nutting, Wallace. "Carved Spoon Racks." *Antiques* 7 (1925): 312–315.

Osborn, John Hosey. *Life in the Old Dutch Homesteads: Saddle River, New Jersey, from 1708.* Paramus: Highway Printing Co., 1967.

Palmer, Arlene. "Glass Production in Eighteenth-Century America: The Wistarburgh Enterprise." *Winterthur Portfolio* 11 (1976): 75–101.

Parrish, Lydia. *Slave Songs of the Georgia Sea Islands.* 1942. Reprint. Hatboro, Pa.: Folklore Associates, 1965.

Pepper, Adeline. *The Glass Gaffers of New Jersey.* New York: Charles Scribner's Sons, 1971.

Peroni, Peter A. II. *The Burg: An Italian American Community at Bay in Trenton.* Washington, D.C.: University Press of America, 1979.

Pirkova-Jakobson, Svatana. "Harvest Festivals among Czechs and Slovaks in America." In *Slavic Folklore: A Symposium,* edited by Albert Bates Lord. Bibliographical and Special Series, vol. 6. Philadelphia: American Folklore Society, 1956.

*Polish Folklore* 3 (1958): 27.

Powers, Mabel Crispin. "The Ware Chairs of South Jersey." *Antiques* 9 (1926): 307–311.

Prince, John Dyneley. "An Ancient New Jersey Indian Jargon." *American Anthropologist* 14 (1912): 508–524.

———. "The Jersey Dutch Dialect." *Dialect Notes* 3 (1910): 459–484.

*Proceedings of the New Jersey Historical Society,* 2d ser. 7 (1882–1883): 9.

Prudon, Theodore H. M. "The Dutch Barn in America: Survival of a Medieval Structural Frame." *New York Folklore* 2 (1976): 123–142.

Ramsay, John. "Early American Pottery: A Résumé." *Antiques* 20 (1931): 224–229.

[Reeves, Martha.] "Martha Reeves, Midwife of Cumberland County, N.J. and Her Record Book of Births, 1820–1931." *Vineland Historical Magazine* 24 (1939): 247–252, 264–267; 25 (1940): 27–35, 57–63, 90–104.

# Works Cited

Reock, Jeanne T. "The Hungarian Community of New Brunswick." New Jersey College for Women, 1953.

Ridgway, Arlene Martin, ed. *Chicken Foot Soup and Other Recipes from the Pine Barrens*. New Brunswick: Rutgers University Press, 1980.

Robert, Joseph C. *The Story of Tobacco in America*. Chapel Hill: University of North Carolina Press, 1949.

Rockland, Michael Aaron. "What's So Funny About New Jersey?" *New Jersey Monthly* (April 1979): 49–105.

Rolfs, Donald H. *Under Sail: The Dredgeboats of Delaware Bay*. Millville: Wheaton Historical Association, 1971.

Rozman, Mary. Interviewed by Cynthia Joy Skibo. 1975.

Schmidt, Hubert G. *Agriculture in New Jersey: A Three-Hundred-Year History*. New Brunswick: Rutgers University Press, 1973.

———. *Flax Culture in Hunterdon County, New Jersey*. Flemington: Hunterdon County Historical Society, 1939.

———. *Rural Hunterdon: An Agricultural History*. New Brunswick: Rutgers University Press, 1947.

Schuessler, Billie; Nona Schuessler; Patricia Schuessler; and Theresa Schuessler. Interview by Sharon Schuessler. Spring 1978.

Schwartz, Marvin D. *The Jan Martense Schenck House*. Brooklyn: Brooklyn Museum, 1964.

Sedgwick, Theodore, Jr. *A Memoir of the Life of William Livingston*. New York: J. & J. Harper, 1833.

Shimada, Koji. "Education, Assimilation, and Acculturation: A Case Study of a Japanese-American Community in New Jersey." Ph.D. dissertation, Temple University, 1974.

Shourds, Harry V. Interviewed by David S. Cohen. April 16, 1981.

Shurtleff, Harold R. *The Log Cabin Myth*. 1939. Reprint. Gloucester, Mass.: Peter Smith, 1967.

Sidwa, Anne H. "Eyes . . . Devil Eyes and Talking Eyes." *Polish Folklore* 5 (1960): 23.

———. "The Topielce of Żywiec: 1. The Sirens of the Soła." *Polish Folklore* 3 (1958): 38–40.

———. "The Topielce of Żywiec: 2. The Vengeance of the Soła." *Polish Folklore* 4 (1959): 27–28.

Sim, Robert J. *Pages from the Past of Rural New Jersey*. 1949. Reprint. Trenton: New Jersey Agricultural Society, 1975.

———. *Some Vanishing Phases of Rural Life in New Jersey*. Trenton: New Jersey Department of Agriculture, 1941.

# Works Cited

Sim, Robert J. and Arthur W. Clement. "The Cheesequake Potteries." *Antiques* 45 (1944): 122–125.

Skinner, Charles M. *American Myths and Legends.* Philadelphia: J. B. Lippincott, 1903.

Smith, Peter. *The Indian Doctor's Dispensatory.* Cincinnati: Brown and Looker, 1812.

Speck, Frank G. *Eastern Algonkian Block-Stamp Decoration: A New World Original or an Acculturated Art.* Trenton: Archaeological Society of New Jersey, 1947.

———. *Oklahoma Delaware Ceremonies, Feasts, and Dances.* Philadelphia: American Philosophical Society, 1937.

Spelker, Mark A. Interviewed by Audrey Spelker. December 5, 1978.

Staats, Abraham. Estate inventory. May 10, 1821. Archives and History, State Library, Trenton.

Stekert, Ellen J. "Focus for Conflict: Southern Mountain Medical Beliefs in Detroit." In *The Urban Experience and Folk Tradition,* edited by Americo Paredes and Ellen J. Stekert. Austin and London: University of Texas Press, 1971.

[Still, James.] *Early Recollections and Life of Dr. James Still, 1812–1885.* 1877. Facsimile ed. Medford: Medford Historical Society, 1971.

Storms, James B. H. *A Jersey Dutch Vocabulary.* Park Ridge: Pascack Historical Society, 1964.

Stoudt, John Joseph. *Early Pennsylvania Arts and Crafts.* New York and London: A. S. Barnes & Co. and Thomas Yoseloff, 1964.

Strickland, William. *Journal of a Tour in the United States of America, 1794–1795,* edited by J. E. Strickland. New York: New York Historical Society, 1971.

Sutton-Smith, Brian, ed. *The Folkgames of Children.* Publications of the American Folklore Society. Austin and London: University of Texas Press, 1972.

Szproch, Andrew. Interviewed by Kevin Guta. April 1, 1978.

Ten Eyck, Margaret. Diary, 1834, 1837–1844. Special Collections, Rutgers University Library, New Brunswick.

Thompson, Stith. *Motif-Index of Folk Literature.* Bloomington: Indiana University Press, 1955–1958.

Vaccaro, Anna. Interviewed by Barbara Schulz. November 10, 1977.

Van Gennep, Arnold. *The Rites of Passage.* Translated by Monika B. Vizedom and Gabrielle L. Caffee. 1908. Reprint. London: Routledge and Kegan Paul, 1960.

# Works Cited

Van Hoesen, Walter Hamilton. *Crafts and Craftsmen of New Jersey*. Rutherford, Madison, and Teaneck: Fairleigh Dickinson University Press, 1973.

Van Ness, Jacob. Estate inventory. May 15, 1821. Archives and History, State Library, Trenton.

Veit, Richard F. *The Old Canals of New Jersey: A Historical Geography*. Little Falls: New Jersey Geographical Press, 1963.

Vermuele, Cornelius C. "Some Early New Jersey Place-Names." *Proceedings of the New Jersey Historical Society* 10 (1925): 243–256.

Vlach, John Michael. "Quaker Tradition and the Paintings of Edward Hicks: A Strategy for the Study of Folk Art." *Journal of American Folklore* 94 (1981): 145–165.

Wacker, Peter O. "Folk Architecture as an Indicator of Culture Areas and Culture Diffusion: Dutch Barns and Barracks in New Jersey." *Pioneer America* 5 (1973): 36–47.

———. *Land and People: A Cultural Geography of Preindustrial New Jersey*. New Brunswick: Rutgers University Press, 1975.

Wasserman, Emily. *Gravestone Designs: Rubbings and Photographs from Early New York and New Jersey*. New York: Dover Publications, 1972.

Watson, Sara Carlisle and Richard Joslin King. *American Craftsmen: The Ware Chairmakers*. Bridgeton: n.p., n.d.

"Weather Notions." *Polish Folklore* 4 (1959): 39.

Webster, David S. and William Kehoe. *Decoys at Shelburne Museum*. Shelburne, Vt.: Shelburne Museum, 1961.

Weems, Mason L. *The Life of Washington*. 1800. Reprint, edited by Marcus Cunliffe. Cambridge: Harvard University Press, 1962.

Weiss, Harry B. *The History of Applejack or Apple Brandy in New Jersey from Colonial Times to the Present*. Trenton: New Jersey Agricultural Society, 1954.

Weiss, Harry B. and Grace M. Weiss. *Early Sports and Pastimes in New Jersey*. Trenton: Past Times Press, 1960.

———. *Rafting on the Delaware*. Trenton: New Jersey Agricultural Society, 1967.

Weiss, Harry B. and Grace M. Ziegler. *The Early Fulling Mills of New Jersey*. Trenton: New Jersey Agricultural Society, 1957.

———. *The Early Woolen Industry of New Jersey*. Trenton: New Jersey Agricultural Society, 1958.

Wertenbaker, Thomas Jefferson. *The Founding of American Civilization: The Middle Colonies*. 1938. Reprint. New York: Cooper Square, 1963.

# Works Cited

Weslager, C. A. *The Delaware Indians: A History*. New Brunswick: Rutgers University Press, 1972.

Westervelt, Frances A., ed. *History of Bergen County, New Jersey*. 3 vols. New York and Chicago: Lewis Historical Publishing Co., 1913.

Weygandt, Cornelius. *Down Jersey: Folks and Their Jobs, Pine Barrens, Salt Marsh and Sea Islands*. New York and London: D. Appleton-Century, 1940.

White, Margaret E. *American Hand-Woven Coverlets in the Newark Museum*. Newark: Newark Museum, 1947.

———. *Early Furniture Made in New Jersey, 1690–1870*. Exhibition catalogue. Newark Museum. October 10, 1958–January 11, 1959. Newark: Newark Museum Association, 1958.

Wier, Albert E., ed. *The Book of a Thousand Songs*. New York: Mumil, 1918.

Williams, Phyllis H. *South Italian Folkways in Europe and America*. 1938. Reprint. New York: Russell and Russell, 1969.

Wilson, Budd. "The Pine Barrens Glass Industry." In *Natural and Cultural Resources of New Jersey Pine Barrens*, edited by John W. Sinton. Pomona: Stockton State College, 1979.

Winkler, Louis. "Some Unique Involvements with Seven Stars in the Delaware Valley Area." *Keystone Folklore Quarterly* 15 (1970): 115–127.

Witthoft, John. "The Grasshopper War Folktale." *Journal of American Folklore* 66 (1953): 295–301.

Wood, Leslie C. *Rafting on the Delaware River*. Livingston Manor, N.Y.: Livingston Manor Times, 1934.

Yoder, Don. "Folk Medicine." In *Folklore and Folklife: An Introduction*, edited by Richard M. Dorson. Chicago and London: University of Chicago Press, 1972.

———. "Official Religion versus Folk Religion." *Pennsylvania Folklife* 15 (1965–1966): 36–52.

Zborowski, Mark and Elizabeth Herzog. *Life Is with People: The Culture of the Shtetl*. 1952. Reprint. New York: Schocken Books, 1962.

# Index

*Page numbers in italics indicate illustrations*